Hank Greenwald

This Copyrighted Broadcast

Woodford Press • San Francisco • 1999

Second printing, May, 1999.
Printed in the United States.

Book and cover design:
Jim Santore, Woodford Press
Dust-jacket photograph by Martha Jane Stanton.

Library of Congress Catalog number 99-61548.
ISBN: 0-942627-45-8

Distributed in the United States, Canada and Europe by
Andrews McMeel Universal
4500 Main Street
Kansas City, MO 64111-7701

Woodford Press / Woodford Publishing Inc.
660 Market Street
San Francisco, CA 94104
www.woodfordpub.com

Daniel C. Ross, CEO and Publisher
C. David Burgin, Editor and Publisher

Associates: Franklin M. Dumm, William F. Duane, Esq.,
William W. Scott, Esq., William B. McGuire, Esq., Laurence Hyman

Please note . . .
A percentage of the proceeds from the sale of this book will be donated to the Marin Association for Retarded Citizens, in San Rafael, California, and to Support for Families of Children with Disabilities, in San Francisco.

Dedication

This book is dedicated to the memory of Eric Faigle, former Dean of the School of Speech and Dramatic Arts at Syracuse University. His spirit lives in the successes of those he refused to let fail.

Acknowledgments

Shortly after my decision to leave the daily grind of broadcasting major league baseball, David Burgin, Editor and Publisher of Woodford Publishing, asked if I would like to write a book. I told him I would need at least a year to gain some perspective. I was surprised and flattered when, a year later, he said he still wanted to publish my story. Without his encouragement I wouldn't have done this. I kept thinking about something James Michener once said: "You can't write a book unless you have something to say." By the time I finished this project I decided I'd said enough. As well as you think you know your own life, it takes the help of others to confirm that you are still capable of remembering things and correcting half of what you thought you remembered.

When I was taking broadcasting classes at Syracuse University, we were taught to write short sentences. Announcers, after all, have to breathe. Now that I was writing for the printed page, I tried too often to compensate for those days by writing long sentences such as this one. If this book is at all readable, it's because of the dedication and patience of my editor, Ted Brock. Ted's calming influence and his perspectives made me realize there were other, and better, ways to put things. He was the navigator on my maiden voyage into writing and enabled me to reach my destination safely.

The only person who worked harder on this book than I did was my wife. Each day Carla spent more time correcting the pages I handed her than it took me to write them. I was a broadcaster. I didn't have to know how to spell or punctuate. There was no greater example of her dedication to this venture than the times she gave up Stone Phillips on NBC's *Dateline*.

Most parents know the torch has been passed when they realize their kids are smarter than they are. I came to this conclusion when my son, Doug, was 5. His contribution to this book was his astonishing recall. He saved me hours searching for baseball-related facts.

My thanks to Pat Gallagher, who was especially helpful regarding the San Francisco Giants' new ballpark.

Zelda Spoelstra of the National Basketball Association and Hall of Fame writer Leonard Koppett assisted me with respect to the early days of the league.

Al Attles and Nate Thurmond helped to recapture the mood of the wonderful days I spent with the San Francisco Warriors.

Bill King's recollections of games played more than 30 years ago were of incalculable help. The story of his walk from San Francisco to Sausalito in 1967 could not have come from a better source.

Much of my support throughout this experience came from Jerry Hoffman. His picture can be found in any dictionary under the word "friend." I would not submit the chapter on my days in Syracuse without his reading it first.

My thanks to Colonel Lyman Hammond, Jr. for all he's done for me over the years. Colonel Hammond recently retired as Director of the Douglas MacArthur Memorial Foundation, and was most helpful in my research.

I was within reach of the finish line in the writing of this book when my computer died. Fellow San Franciscans Ann and Hunt Bennett rescued me. The Bennetts are now my neighbors at Eagle Creek Country Club in Naples, Florida, and I practically moved in with them so that I could use their computer. In the process I even got to like their dog Charlie.

Hank Greenwald

CONTENTS

Foreword

Bob Costas

One night in the late 1960s, when I was 16 and should have been studying, I was instead searching for enlightenment in the pages of a New York Knicks yearbook. This proved a wise move, as it was then I discovered that Knicks broadcaster Marv Albert and his predecessor Marty Glickman both had gone to Syracuse University. This sparked my interest, and my guidance counselor (without whose guidance I was no doubt bent for ruin) subsequently informed me that Syracuse had a fine journalism school.

These facts, coupled with a rejection slip from Princeton, led me to upstate New York in pursuit of higher education and broadcasting adventure.

Later, I learned that Dick Stockton, Andy Musser, Dick Clark and Ted Koppel were also Syracuse alums. It was only long after my days at Syracuse that I learned Hank Greenwald had also matriculated there. This information came to me too late to change my mind.

At any rate, it's standard procedure, at this stage of a book, for the person writing the foreword to entertain the reader with tales of personal encounters with the author, anecdotes from their shared personal history. Stuff like this: "I'll never forget the time Hank Greenwald and I happened to bump into each other at the All-Star Game in Seattle. We began talking baseball, quaffed a couple of beers, climbed the Space Needle, and before we knew it we'd both missed our early morning flights."

The problem here is that nothing like that happened — at least not when I was with Hank. Make no mistake, I do enjoy the redoubtable Mr. G's company, and in fact we have spent time together talking baseball and broadcasting.

We even worked a game together in the summer of 1993, when Hank's Giants found themselves in the heat of that season's National League West pennant race — the last true pennant race that will ever be, by the way, but before I digress further, I'll just say you can read more about that in my upcoming treatise, *Wild Cards and the Decline of American Culture*.

Now back to the subject at hand, which was? Oh, yes, Hank Greenwald. The truth is I've spent most of my time with Hank the way most of you have — listening to him on the radio.

He's always struck me as a genial and reasonable man. As baseball has become more crass and more unreasonable, Hank's style may have seemed to some out of step with the prevailing *zeitgeist*. (That's a word I've never used on the air and one that, with the passing of Howard Cosell, is unlikely to be heard on any sports broadcast in our lifetime.)

Hank is really a radio guy, as opposed to somebody on the radio just hoping to get on network television. In that sense, he's an appealing throwback. Amid all the schlock and hype, the literate, sane voices — those with a sense of proportion, those with a gentler approach — should be appreciated all the more.

Through the years, whenever I'd visit the San Francisco Bay Area, it was always a pleasure to tune in Hank and listen to the ease with which he'd blend his wry wit with the narrative of a Giants game. The Giants of the early '80s were laughable in a different way, and I noted Hank's ability to turn fans' misery to cheer, if only for a moment, between mediocre, or worse, performances on the field.

During a game in Montreal, Hank and his broadcast partner were bantering between pitches in the game's middle innings, reflecting on the city's cultural oddities. "Everyone seems to smoke in restaurants here in Montreal," Hank said. "When you ask for the non-smoking section, they send you to Toronto."

In a game with the Phillies from The Vet, Hank noted, "This is such a rabid baseball town, even the trucks were named for Connie Mack."

When Ken Caminiti, playing third base for Houston at the time, left a game with what was described as "stomach problems," Hank commented, "It seems only right that the guy with all the hits and RBIs should also have the runs."

Hank's delivery was always understated, always in keeping with the game's conversational pace. It made his well-measured crescendo to a moment of drama all the more effective. You knew the same outlook complemented both the relaxation and the excitement. The mixture was baseball itself.

Hank's style was not as immediately distinctive as that of Vin Scully, Harry Caray or his Bay Area colleague Bill King. But he had an abundance of an important quality for a baseball announcer — he was good company. He sounded like someone you'd like to sit and watch a game with, someone who could add to your enjoyment of the afternoon without getting on your nerves or forcing himself on you.

These days, it seems almost every broadcaster out there, and every one coming into the business, has a shtick. There seems to be an unwritten rule that unless you can put together a signature song and dance, you're not going to get noticed. Well, Hank had a style, not a shtick. There was respect in his voice and in his storytelling that invited his audience in, rather than putting him on stage. Hank narrowed the distance between the fan and the game.

For years Hank's audience tuned in knowing there was a good chance they'd come away from his broadcast with at least one or two reasons to ask a friend, "Did you hear what Hank Greenwald said today?" I know this because broadcasting colleagues and fans have shared some of Hank's "greatest hits" with me.

For instance, I can identify more than a little with Hank's moment of frustration before a telecast from Pittsburgh's Three Rivers Stadium. As the story goes, he was taping the opening segment, beginning with the usual, "Good evening, everybody, I'm Hank Greenwald, along with Duane Kuiper. We're here at Three Rivers Stadium. . . and we'll be back in just a moment with the starting lineups for tonight's game."

His producer said, "That was good, but could you shorten it a bit?" Hank tried again, and the producer still wasn't quite satisfied. Could he do one more take, just a little shorter this time?

Hank waited for the countdown, faced the camera and said, deadpan, "Good evening, everybody. I'm Hank Greenwald, along with Duane Kuiper. We're here at Two Rivers Stadium. . ."

Of all the Hank Greenwald stories out there, though, the one I hear repeated most took place when the Giants were playing in the Houston Astrodome. During a broadcast, Hank took a look at the pitching match-ups for the following night, and the night after that, when the Giants would be playing in Atlanta.

He noted a coincidence. In those two games, they'd be facing the knuckleball-throwing Niekro brothers back-to-back. Mentioning this, he misspoke, saying the Astros would send Phil Niekro to the mound and Joe Niekro would pitch for the Braves. Immediately catching the error, Hank checked himself, made the correction and added, without missing a beat, "Honestly, folks, all Niekros don't look alike."

Style, not shtick. Wit, not bombast.

Hank's approach carried a subtle invitation. If you invested a little time in listening to him over the course of a season or the course of many seasons, you came to appreciate him. The clear, conversational way Hank communicated his knowledge and love of the game never was designed to say, "Hey, look at me, listen to me." The result, of course, was that we all wound up listening closely.

Introduction

Leigh Steinberg

When I was a youngster growing up in Los Angeles, the voice of Vin Scully played a major role in my life. His mellifluous tones and vivid descriptions cemented my love affair with the Dodgers.

Radio binds us to a baseball play-by-play announcer in a particularly intimate form. It is a lifeline and pipeline to our ability to re-create a baseball tableau we cannot see. As one would drive through Southern California in the 1960s, it was Scully's voice — coming from car radios, transistor radios, clock radios — that seemed to provide the region with the connection only sports can provide.

When I arrived in the San Francisco Bay Area to attend school at the University of California, Berkeley in the late '60s, it was as a confirmed Giants hater. My heroes were Sandy Koufax and Don Drysdale and Maury Wills, and my especial villain was Juan Marichal.

The thought that I could one day listen to the Giants for entertainment was the most improbable event imaginable. But along came Hank Greenwald, whose wit and wisdom were unique and so entertaining that he carved out a "school" for broadcasters that has attracted many acolytes. It was his ironic sense of humor, dry and deadpan, that provided a joyful form of entertainment for the entire Bay Area. And the fact that my partner Jeff Moorad and I were privileged to give Hank legal representation made it all the more fun.

It's Hank as a person — warm, family-oriented, with a long list of friendships he's cultivated over the years — that is most impressive. His love for his wife, Carla, and the perfect companionship they share, is rare. The patience and pride he's exhibited in his parenting of his daughter, Kellie, who has Down syndrome, has been heartwarming to watch.

For years, he has displayed a commitment to charity and has been active in a variety of community concerns. Unlike many in his profession, Hank puts down roots and believes that he is his brother's keeper.

His one-liners are legendary, but it's his heart that is, and always has been, his most enduring asset.

Now he visits us again, this time in print, sharing a treasury of tales and insights flavored with the same humor and warmth that carried us through each baseball season for nearly two decades. Hank's memoir is a reunion to savor, another chance to marvel at the richness of his storytelling gift.

Former Dodger general manager Al Campanis once said,
"Great announcers work for great teams."

1
"THREE, TWO, ONE. . ."

A t the age of 13 I decided I wanted to become a major league baseball announcer. A playing career was out of the question, as 5-foot-7 first basemen weren't much in demand. At 13 I was the tallest kid in my class, and I thought that was pretty neat until my mother reminded me I was still in third grade. Okay, that is an exaggeration, but let's just say when it came to schoolwork, 90-degree angles to me were the turns you took when you ran the bases.

I had been listening to baseball on the radio since I was 7, when I lived in my native Detroit. It was 1942. The war was on. Less than a year earlier, the United States had been hit for several battleships and thousands of lives by Japan in the top of the first. President Roosevelt, in response to a letter from Baseball Commissioner Kenesaw Mountain Landis, decreed that despite a manpower shortage, baseball should continue because it provided a source of entertainment for war workers at home. I wasn't exactly a war worker, but I was home and it sure provided a source of entertainment for me.

My parents, Ray and Bea Greenwald, were baseball fans. Yet it was Tiger broadcaster Harry Heilmann who got me hooked. There might have been a war on, but life for a young boy in the summer was still easy. Through the age of 10, when the Tiger games were on the radio, I made up a score sheet, poured myself a Vernor's Ginger Ale and listened to Heilmann. It didn't get much better than that.

Heilmann was born in San Francisco. That didn't mean much to me at the time, but it would later as I lived there myself and stumped for his inclusion in the Bay Area Sports Hall of Fame. This was long after he'd made the Baseball Hall of Fame in Cooperstown, in recognition of his great career as a Tiger playing the outfield alongside Ty Cobb. Heilmann won American League batting titles in 1921, '23, '25 and '27. Some thought that was odd. He hit .403 in 1923 and finished with a career mark of .342. There was no questioning his credentials.

I learned much about baseball listening to Harry and, though I didn't know it at the time, much about broadcasting the game. He was a Hall of Famer, and I was a kid, but he was never above explaining the game in ways I could understand. Among the things I learned from him was that every day someone listens to a game for the first time in his or her life, and as a broadcaster you're going to have a great influence on whether that person grows to love the sport.

I also learned the importance of good stories. When you play with Cobb, against the likes of Babe Ruth, Lou Gehrig, Tris Speaker, Jimmie Foxx, Lefty Grove and Walter Johnson, you have a lot of stories. He shared them with me and made me eager to read and to learn even more about the history of the game.

Baseball is such a beautifully generational game. From parents to children, the love of the game is passed on. It was passed on to me and in turn to my kids. A baseball broadcaster has an obligation to pass along that love to a succeeding generation of listeners.

To do this, he must know the history of the game and recognize that it actually predates the founding of ESPN. No sport has as rich a history as baseball. The feats and eccentricities of those who played in the early days deserve to be perpetuated. Baseball history has been made in every decade. All that changes are the players who make it. Any broadcaster who can't make fans out of new listeners isn't really trying.

As much as I loved Harry Heilmann's stories, I didn't realize at the time Harry was a rare breed. In the '40s it wasn't common for former ballplayers to become broadcasters, especially contemporaries of Ty Cobb, Babe Ruth and Lou Gehrig. Of course he had stories. Of course he could pass along the history of the game. To a large degree, he *was* the history of the game.

As I got a older and began to listen to other broadcasters, I came to realize the best storytellers were the guys from the South. When I listened to Mel Allen, Red Barber, Russ Hodges, Lindsey Nelson, Ernie Harwell, Jimmy Dudley and Jim Woods (who, although he was born in the Midwest, had a Southern state of mind), there was just something about their styles and their voices that fit perfectly with a lazy summer day.

Guys from the South had a way of putting things. Even that old Son of the

South, football announcer Bill Mundey, would captivate me on a not-so-lazy autumn day when he described how "Jones carried that ball into the Promised Land of milk and honey for six points for Joejuh Tech."

No mere Yankee could get away with that. I loved hearing the inimitable Barber refer to 6-foot-7 Red Sox pitcher Frank Sullivan as that "big, tall drink of water come stomping out New England way." Mel Allen could say "ain't," and it sounded right. It seemed broadcasters from the South spoke colorfully and not in cliches. How I would come to envy that ability.

M y first break in the business came when I broadcast Syracuse University basketball. The SU program was nowhere near the power it is today, and the games were carried only on the campus radio station. But the 10 people who heard me said I did a swell job. I'd been told I was the first sophomore to do play-by-play at Syracuse. Whether it was true, I sure wanted to believe that it was.

Among those who played for the Orangemen in my sophomore year was Jim Brown. If you thought he was impressive as an All-America running back in college and an All-Pro for the Cleveland Browns, you should have seen him when his muscles actually showed. There were some great games against Niagara, with Larry Costello and Hubie Brown, and the Crusaders of Holy Cross, led by All-America Tommy Heinsohn.

When young people tell me they want to broadcast baseball, I always tell them to get into basketball first. It's fast-paced, there's plenty of scoring, and the games are played in gyms and arenas where the noise level is high and the announcer sounds exciting. In that setting, a newcomer is more likely to make a good early impression. To put it another way, basketball carries the announcer while the announcer carries baseball.

There are basketball announcers who rise to a higher level. Bill King and Marty Glickman come to mind. I'm convinced that listening to and studying their basketball play-by-play styles influenced my style.

King was at the microphone for the San Francisco (later Golden State) Warriors for more than 20 seasons. I sat next to him for eight. Bill came from Bloomington, Illinois, where nothing topped high school basketball. He launched his career after serving in the military, helping prevent the Japanese from retaking Saipan. That the war was over by then also may have helped.

Bill went on to broadcast basketball at Bradley University in Peoria, a town that also turned out broadcasters Jack Brickhouse, Chick Hearn, Milo Hamilton, Tom Kelly and Dewayne Staats. It was King's good fortune to cover Bradley teams that went on to the finals of the NCAA and National Invitation tournaments in the same year, 1950, losing to City College of New York in both. In those days the NIT was the more prestigious tournament, and it was not unusual for teams to compete in both.

When I met Bill in 1962, he was with the Warriors, who were in their first season in San Francisco after moving from Philadelphia. I had been with the Syracuse NATS, who later would move to Philadelphia to become the 76ers. Confused? Haven't you heard of the Rochester Royals, who became the Cincinnati Royals, who became the Kansas City Kings, who became the Sacramento Kings?

Bill was a warm and an unusual-looking man. We hit it off from the start. By "unusual" I mean I hadn't encountered a sports broadcaster with a handlebar mustache *and* a Van Dyke beard. In fact, the last time I'd seen anyone who looked like that, he was wearing a spiked helmet and ruling Germany in World War I. In later years Bill would be walking down the street and old ladies would mistake him for the devil. This was not totally farfetched. He has more than a little of the devil in him.

What made King unique as a basketball announcer was his ability to broadcast away from the ball. Bill understood that every pass (Smith to Jones, back to Smith and over to Jones) wasn't vital. But a double screen away from the ball told him where the next shot would be. He had the ability to make you "see" through the radio what was coming next. He saw that two defenders were switching, and also that the switch had created a size mismatch for the offense.

He would alert his listeners to where the ball was likely to go. You were always a step ahead of the game when you listened to Bill. He never wasted words and always had the perfect ones to fit the occasion. He never attended college, but his vocabulary on and off the air was the envy of us all. He took basketball broadcasting to a higher level. He was the best.

I began listening to Marty Glickman in the late 1940s. He was broadcasting college double-headers at Madison Square Garden, as well as New York Knicks games. I was barely a teenager, living in Rochester, and picked up the games from New York City on WHN, which later became WMGM, which later went back to being WHN. Did you think only ballclubs moved?

Glickman, who spent a half-century in the business, was the first of a long line of broadcasters to come out of Syracuse University. When he enrolled in 1935, that was not his purpose. Radio was still in its infancy, and television was something out of science fiction.

Glickman was graduated in 1939 with a bachelor's degree in political science, having been an All-America running back and a member of the United States track and field team at the 1936 Olympic Games. As Stan Isaacs noted in his book about Marty, his first taste of radio sports came in the fall of his junior year, when a local haberdasher saw possibilities for his store in sponsoring the star athlete on a 15-minute weekly sports show.

Still, it wasn't until 1940 that Glickman's professional broadcasting career got going.

Listening to Marty broadcast basketball was like being inside the old Garden itself. He made you smell the cigars and see that cloud of smoke forming a haze beneath the arena ceiling. You knew the taste of the orange juice and the hot dogs from the Nedick's stand outside the Garden entrance on Eighth Avenue, the place that inspired his trademark call, "GOOD, like Nedick's."

Marty captured the atmosphere of the old Garden so well you could picture those suspicious-looking characters hanging around the pay phones in the lobby, waiting to make that last-second call just before tipoff. And always in the background there was the sound of public address announcer John Condon: "Knickerbocker field goal by Carl Braun, Knicks lead 52-48," or, "That was Zeke Zuwalek, Johnnies lead 21-19." The Johnnies were St. John's University.

There was more to Marty's broadcasts than just atmosphere. As Bill King did, Glickman understood the concept of the "word picture." Dick McGuire didn't just bring the ball across mid-court, "He brings it across on a right-hand dribble." A shot didn't merely miss, "It hits the rim, a bounce to the right." NYU wasn't only going from right to left across your radio dial, "They're shooting at the basket on the 49th Street side of the Garden."

When you listened to Marty you were there, and isn't that the way it's supposed to be? He and Bill King set the standard.

My first opportunity to broadcast baseball came during my junior year at Syracuse. I'd never done it before, and yet I'd done it a million times in my head. Having a large head was a plus. While calling play-by-play for the Syracuse Orangemen was far from the big leagues, it was a start.

If you could broadcast from a ground-level press box behind a screen in back of home plate at Lew Carr Field, you could broadcast from anywhere. It didn't matter if you couldn't see the center-fielder. You knew he was out there somewhere.

The reason baseball is tough to broadcast is simple. Most of the time, nothing happens. If you can make that interesting, you're going to do well. In a nine-inning game the ball is in play less than five minutes. Here's what you're left with:

Another trip to the mound.

Batter steps out to scratch his privates (definitely a challenge to describe).

A beach ball thrown onto the field.

The batter calls the third base coach down to explain the sign. It's only September, so you can't expect the batter to know it by now.

Trying to delay the inevitable, the pitcher stands behind the mound talking to himself. He's not sure he understands the conversation.

While all of the above is taking place, the poor baseball announcer (is that a contradiction in terms?) says to himself, "Why, didn't I take Greenwald's advice and get into basketball?" I know I've said it more than once.

Former Dodger general manager Al Campanis once said, "Great announcers work for great teams." When I read that I felt as if the clouds had suddenly parted and I now had the answer I'd been looking for. At last I knew why I wasn't a great announcer. The sad part was, if his statement was true I probably never would be.

Of course the cynical side of me knew just what Campanis was saying: You're a lot better broadcaster in people's minds when their team is winning.

There was an irony in Campanis' statement. True, the Dodgers had great teams while he was their GM, but their announcer, Vin Scully, would have been great with any team. If Campanis made his remark tongue-in-cheek, I'm right with him. If he was serious, I take issue. Mel Allen and Red Barber worked for great Yankees teams, but with their knowledge of the game and their voices they'd have been great broadcasting chess.

One of the most important things Lindsey Nelson taught me in our three seasons together with the San Francisco Giants was: "Don't get caught up in wins and losses. If you do, and you're with a bad team, you're going to sound the way they play. And you can't let that happen."

As a member of the New York Mets' first-ever team of announcers, along with Bob Murphy and Ralph Kiner, Lindsey knew what he was talking about. Others may have found the 1962 Mets, losers of 120 games, fun to watch. Lindsey did not.

A play-by-play person must learn that, with any ballclub, you cannot depend upon its success for your own. You have to be better in the booth than they are on the field. If you happen to be with a good team, so much the better. But you can't count on that, and you can't coast because of it.

I've always told owners I've worked for, "My job is not to make your ballclub interesting. I have no control over that. Your job is to make the ballclub interesting. My job is to make the broadcast interesting, because I do have control over that." Somehow your heart always races a little faster when you say that to someone who owns the club you work for, but it's a good idea to understand each other from the outset.

Baseball is not an inherently exciting sport. It's an interesting sport, a subtle sport, a contemplative sport. The moments of excitement in a baseball game are very few. These must stand out in a broadcast.

The announcer who tries to make every play seem like the seventh game of the World Series does no justice to the game or to the listeners. An announcer must understand he is not there to assault people's ears. Let the commercials do that. I tell those who want to broadcast baseball, "Your job is not to create excitement. Your job is to capture it."

Over the course of 162 games in a season, no matter how good a team may be, it will lose at least a half-dozen games by seven or eight runs. Think of how many lopsided games a poor club will lose. Those games come with the territory. Just because it's not a good game doesn't mean it can't be a good broadcast. On the contrary, this is where you get a chance to shine, by giving people a reason to keep listening. Baseball broadcasts are built around reporting and entertaining. If your team is behind by eight runs, the reporting side of it isn't going to carry you. So you'd better be entertaining. "If you think this is bad, fans, how about the time in 1912 when the Philadelphia Athletics beat the Detroit Tigers 24-2? Actually, Tiger fans may have had it a little easier then, because there were no broadcasts in those days."

In trying to turn a dull or uneven game into a good broadcast, you reach back for something extra. You talk about the largest deficit ever overcome in a major league game. You talk about the most runs ever given up by a pitcher who still won the game. You talk about the most runs ever scored in the bottom of the ninth to pull out a victory.

Or you can always do what I did when the Giants were getting killed — start rooting for technical difficulties. As a baseball broadcaster, you have the opportunity to turn a minus into a plus. Doing so will make your reputation.

The question I hear most often is, "How do I go about becoming a baseball broadcaster?" The answer is simple. Marry someone whose parents own a ballclub. There's a corollary to that: Be sure your prenuptial agreement says that, in the event of a divorce, you get custody of your in-laws for as long as they own the team.

Some will say having a father in the business isn't a bad way to begin. It's hard to prove that by me. If I'd followed in my father's footsteps, I'd have been a buyer for a group of department stores.

Of course, there are examples of broadcasters whose dads have preceded them in the business. It's not unusual for a youngster growing up in the atmosphere of major league ballparks and broadcast booths to want to be like dad someday. Let's face it, it's a lot more appealing than many other ways to make a living.

Besides, as others are quick to point out, broadcasting baseball games isn't really work.

Having a major league broadcaster for a father is a big advantage:

•You get to go to a lot of games. Dad may not always consider that an advantage.

•You get to eat a lot of cheeseburgers and french fries. Dad definitely sees that as an advantage.

•You get to meet the players and managers. Dad learned long ago that discretion is a good thing.

•You get to go into the clubhouse and the dugout before the games and learn new words. Dad only gets to hear those from mom.

•You get to meet dad's bosses, who are always nice to kids. Dad wishes he were a kid again.

•You get to listen to your dad on the radio. This beats having to listen to dad at home.

•Your friends think your dad is cool because he does the games. Dad thinks you have good taste in friends.

One cannot help the accident of one's birth. To be born into wealth may make you a member of what is called The Lucky Sperm Club, but you can't take credit for that. The same holds true if the old man is a baseball broadcaster. You can only take advantage of what's there, and even then only up to a point.

Offspring such as Joe Buck, Thom Brennaman and Skip and Chip Caray may have been better able to point themselves in a certain direction, but you can be sure they worked every bit as hard as everyone else. Having broadcasters as dads, they knew what it took to get to the top and what it takes to stay there. It might be nice to be a Buck, a Brennaman or a Caray, but it wouldn't have helped if they weren't any good.

The person who qualifies me to discuss this father-son relationship is my son Doug. He, too, has pointed himself toward a career in baseball broadcasting, dashing my hopes for his future as a rabbi. I can hear him now as he reads this, saying, "Nice going, Dad. You'll say anything for a laugh."

No one can say that being Hank Greenwald's son has helped Doug advance his career. He didn't need my help in his march through the minor leagues from Bend, Oregon, to Burlington, Iowa, to Lafayette, Louisiana, to Stockton, California, with a couple of seasons of Hawaiian winter baseball.

Where this eventually will take him is unknown, but, like thousands of other young and not-so-young people, he has his sights set on the major leagues. It's hard to believe that I once was his age and had those same dreams. But what better proof is there that it can be done?

When I was a student at Syracuse I had two objectives: A career in sports broadcasting, and graduating.

It was the second objective that seemed more unattainable. The last thing I imagined back then was being invited back someday to speak. It's amazing how a couple of seasons with the New York Yankees can validate your career.

Whether it's in a college classroom or to a young person individually, I always preach the same message: If you want to go into sports broadcasting, you must understand your business is sports, not broadcasting.

The person listening to your baseball broadcast doesn't care what you know about broadcasting; he cares what you know about baseball. He doesn't care if you know how a microphone works or how stations set their advertising rates. He's listening to hear the game, and one of your objectives is to make that listener feel he knows more about baseball now than he did before he tuned in.

While many universities teach courses in broadcasting, even sports broadcasting, you're not likely to find any teaching baseball. You may make a field trip to a ballpark and even go up to the broadcast booth and meet the announcers. You may even get to sit in a booth and tape-record some of the game. A tip: Try not to be better than the local announcer. Insecurity runs high in the booth.

None of the above teaches you anything about the game itself. The best ways to learn baseball, short of a playing career, are:
• Watch.
• Read.
• Ask questions.

For everything I learned in a classroom, I learned as much or more going to games. Being there is still the best education when it comes to learning baseball or any sport. But "being there" only supplements your formal education. It does not replace it. The more games I attended, the more experiences I compiled.

I was not only learning more about baseball; I was building a frame of reference that would serve me well in later years. Going to as many games as I could, I saw Jackie Robinson play in the minor leagues before he came to Brooklyn. I was there the night in Syracuse when Little Rock manager Frank Lucchesi was ejected and the next inning, still in uniform, climbed the light tower in back of the right field fence so he could watch the game.

Experiences such as these form the basis of your ability to make a broadcast more interesting, especially on a night when the game itself is not. You can tell these stories because you were there. There are things to be learned and experienced in every game you attend.

While nothing beats being there in person, it is not always possible. Thanks to TV, cable and satellites, baseball comes to you. You can still learn a lot from watching on television if you simply turn the sound off and turn on the radio. This will enable you to watch the game and learn something from an announcer whose train of thought isn't being derailed constantly by a closeup of the pitching coach.

The other important part of your baseball education should come from reading. More books are written about baseball each year than about any other activity conducted outside of bed.

Knowing the history of the game doesn't mean knowing what took place in 1910. The Phillies of 1993 were every bit as colorful as the Brooklyn teams of the '20s known as the Daffiness Boys. Babe Ruth hit long home runs, but for years you couldn't go to a National League park without someone pointing way up there where Willie Stargell hit one.

Baseball history is everywhere, with every ballpark and every franchise. The successful baseball broadcaster knows his history. He also knows the difference between history and trivia. It used to bother me when someone said, "I really love all that baseball trivia you talk about on the broadcasts."

"I beg your pardon," I'd reply. "Babe Ruth's record 119 extra base hits in 1921 is not trivia, it's history. The name of Babe Ruth's barber's dog is trivia."

Reggie Jackson's three home runs on three pitches in Game Six of the 1977 World Series is historic. The names of the fans who caught Jackson's homers are trivial.

While it's vital to know as much as you can about the game, it's equally important to know how to use your information. I've seen and listened to too many announcers who seem determined to jam into the broadcast every item they looked up before the broadcast that day, whether it's relevant or not.

Some of the best items I ever aired were ones I kept for two or three weeks, waiting for the appropriate moment. Good baseball broadcasting is not only a question of how much you know, but knowing how and when to use it.

The first baseball broadcast occurred on August 5, 1921, on radio station KDKA in Pittsburgh. The game was between the Pirates and the Phillies, and the announcer was Harold Arlen. Undoubtedly, someone called the station during the game to complain that Arlen wasn't giving the score enough. Announcers have all sorts of ways of reminding themselves to give the score, from Red Barber's three-minute egg timer to giving it after every batter to giving it every 10 seconds.

The fact is, it doesn't matter how often you give the score, someone will complain he didn't hear it. It wouldn't matter if you picked up the phone and called everyone personally: "Is this Mrs. Pinetar at 120 Lois Lane? Hi, this is Hank Greenwald. We're in the bottom of the fifth right now and the Giants are leading, 2-1. Just thought you'd like to know. Nice talking to you."

If you give the score every 60 seconds, and the listener's attention is diverted at that moment, he'll claim you've gone two minutes without giving the score. Give the score. It's important. But assume the frequency doesn't matter. You simply can't win this one.

Despite an academic record that suggests otherwise, I really did learn something in college. One thing I learned became an important part of my work — objectivity. Its importance was impressed upon me by Professor Lawrence Myers, or "Smooth Larry," as we called him. He was smooth in the way he spoke, with a resonant voice we all envied. He was smooth in the way he dressed, with his sport coat and tie. And smooth in the way he looked with that pencil-thin mustache. We hung the nickname "Smooth Larry" on him with affection.

Myers taught an all-purpose course called Radio-TV 168. I never asked if there had been a 166 or 167. There were no courses then dealing specifically with sports. Fortunately, the good professor knew sports, and he knew sports broad-casting. Whenever those topics were discussed, he always reminded us we were reporters, not cheerleaders. As he liked to say, "Root with your heart, not with your mouth."

His words served me well. It was probably the one lesson I never forgot. If you hope to establish credibility as a broadcaster, you must be objective. A great play, for example, can't be dependent on which team makes it. It stands on its own.

In sustaining objectivity I was aided by owners Bob Lurie and Peter Magowan of the Giants. These men saw objectivity as a virtue, something not all owners can claim. I feel for the announcers who are not as fortunate as I was. Sadly, there are owners who want their announcers to see things as "us" against "them." The first time a broadcaster utters "we," he surrenders his objectivity. If it doesn't bother him, I suppose it shouldn't bother me, but it does.

Too many people confuse objectivity with disloyalty. Just because you announce objectively, it doesn't mean you don't want your team to win. Of course you do. There's no way you can be with a group of guys from spring training through the end of the season and not want to see them do well. You fly with them. You ride buses with them. You know them as people, not just players. Even if none of that applied, you still would want them to do well. We all know the more they win, the better announcer you are. But Larry Myers' philosophy still holds. You can "root with your heart, not your mouth."

I must tip my cap to Giant fans for their objectivity. If I had even thought about being a "we" and "they" guy, the fans would have run me out of town. Bay Area fans never tolerated homers as broadcasters. No town's fans should. I was blessed.

In recent years the game has become more difficult to broadcast, a trend that will only escalate. A few years ago we used to joke that someday we'd be saying, "This next pitch is brought to you by . . ." Guess what. We're almost there.

"Tonight's starting lineups are brought to you by . . ."

"This trip to the mound is brought to you by . . ."

"This call to the bullpen is brought to you by . . ."

"The National Anthem is brought to you by . . ."

"This visit to the men's room is brought to you by. . ."

It's coming soon to a broadcast near you.

So much is sold between innings now, it's a rare game when you don't miss a couple of pitches or an at-bat coming out of a commercial. The opportunities for an announcer to say something interesting are vanishing beneath a pile of dollar bills. Hey, so what else is new? It's the American way. Baseball's the American game.

I fully expect to listen to a game soon and hear an announcer say, "There's a foul ball lined into the seats back of third. And when you think FOWL, think of the folks at Gosling's Poultry Farm. Remember, next time you see a foul ball coming at you, it's okay to be CHICKEN and DUCK."

If I thought it was getting to be bad in my last broadcast years, it's only going to get worse.

It's vital to develop a style of your own. Vin Scully is a much-admired broadcaster. A large number of Scully wannabes came along and tried to sound just like him. While it was a great compliment to Vin, he'd have been among the first to tell them that's not how you go about developing your own style. It's one thing to admire what Scully does in his broadcasts, but it's another to copy his voice. You may get a job somewhere, but people will say, "That's the guy who tries to sound like Vin Scully." Your listeners will know who you try to sound like, but they'll never know who you are.

If you like an announcer's storytelling ability, learn to tell stories. If you like his ability to paint a word picture, be descriptive. If you admire his easy-going style, work on sounding like a friend. Do not try to copy someone else's voice. If you don't want people to know who you are, join a witness protection program. There's only one Vin Scully, as there was only one Mel Allen and one Red Barber. Your goal as a baseball broadcaster is to have someone someday say about you, "There's only one. . .," and mean it as a compliment.

He not only kept me in school, but he also got me out. There's not much more anyone can do for you than that.

2
DEAN'S LIST

The note was short and to the point. It said: "Report to the Dean of Men's office tomorrow at 4 p.m."

I knew too well what this was about. It was Monday before Thanksgiving vacation in 1954, and I'd been caught cheating on a midterm exam. I knew Dr. Foster had seen me copying off another student's paper, and although he hadn't said anything at the time, it was obvious now I was in big trouble.

I never figured out if the next 24 hours went quickly or slowly. I thought they went quickly because I was not eager to walk into the dean of men's office. I thought they went slowly because I was anxious to learn my fate.

During that 24-hour period, every possible scenario went through my head. A public hanging in the center of the quad probably was a little extreme, though I wasn't dismissing anything. Expulsion from school was not a pleasant thought, either. I wanted to think my college career would last longer than the first semester of my sophomore year. The only thing I knew for sure was I had 24 more hours.

I swallowed hard and entered the office of Dean of Men, Dr. Carleton L. Krathwohl. What else could he have been with a name like that? Seated beside the good doctor were Dean Eric Faigle and Dr. Eugene Foster. Faigle was the dean of my school, Speech and Dramatic Arts, and Dr. Foster taught the Radio-TV course I'd been taking.

Also in the office was the young man whose paper I'd copied. We were co-conspirators in this. He'd agreed to angle his paper so I could see the answers. Inasmuch as there really wasn't anything in it for him, he must have wondered why he ever got involved.

"I suppose you know why you're here," Dr. Krathwohl said, making clear there would be no formalities.

Given the cast of characters assembled, there wasn't much doubt why I was there.

"Yes," I replied. "I know why I'm here and I would like to say something."

"Go ahead," Krathwohl said.

"First of all, John (not his real name) had nothing to do with this and I feel badly he's here. This was all my doing and I'd hate for him to pay a price for this. I'm responsible for this."

My confession and plea for mercy on John's behalf must have confused Dr. Foster. He had seen me copying and knew John was in on it, but what could he say now? I'm sure it also confused John, who wasn't about to contradict me.

Dr. Krathwohl said, "What do you think your punishment should be?"

"I'll take an F for the exam," I said, figuring I might as well aim high.

"AN F FOR THE EXAM!" Krathwohl shouted, "WHAT DO YOU THINK OF THE POSSIBILITY OF BEING EXPELLED FROM THE UNIVERSITY?"

I sensed the negotiation wasn't going my way at this point and indicated a desire to remain in school.

Dr. K ordered me to return to his office the next morning.

Walking back to my dorm, I knew I couldn't last until the next morning without learning the outcome. It was obvious to me the only compassionate face in that room belonged to Dean Faigle. An hour later, I entered his office in the Hall of Languages. It was the oldest building on campus and was believed to have been built around the time of the pyramids. There was no evidence, physical or otherwise, to suggest anything else.

Dean Faigle was "Syracuse" through and through. He was graduated from the university. He taught there. He became head of the Geography Department and, in 1954, was dean of both the School of Liberal Arts and the School of Speech and Drama. He had a whitish complexion with a hint of red in his cheeks. He had a sharp nose, upon which rested dark-rim spectacles. He also smiled. He was different, an authority figure students actually liked.

It was obvious to Dean Faigle why I was there. It's not easy to sweat in Syracuse in late November. He motioned me to sit down across from him.

"I was most impressed with your plea on behalf of your classmate and your acceptance of the consequences for what you did," he began. "Don't worry. I'm not going to let them throw you out of school."

I'm sure my sigh of relief was audible. Dean Faigle continued, "Now, Hank, this is what's going to happen. You will be given an F for the course and be allowed to take it again next semester. I am not going to send a letter to your parents. I'm leaving it up to you to tell them what happened when you go home for Thanksgiving vacation. I know you'll take care of it."

I left Dean Faigle's office knowing I was still in school because of him and had to do what he said. Facing my parents was another story. It would have been easier to tell them I'd gotten some young woman pregnant.

There were no sprinkler alarms in our house, or they'd have gone off, the way my father was fuming. My mother was in need of a wailing wall, but the nearest one was thousands of miles away.

"Where did we fail you?" she wailed, not wanting the answer I was only too ready to provide.

My parents had determined the course of my life. I was going to be a lawyer, and that was it. Whoever heard of a kid wanting to be a sports announcer? I might just as well have wanted to become a cowboy. They knew what was best, and, by God, I was going to have every advantage they never had whether I wanted it or not.

I was an average student. It was that way in high school, and it was that way in college. I must have heard it a thousand times: I wasn't applying myself.

Why was it always my fault when a course was hard for me? Wasn't it possible you simply didn't understand something no matter how hard you tried?

When I brought home a report card that disappointed them, the standard response was I was going to end up being a truck driver. I should have been so lucky. Truck drivers were making a hell of a lot more money than young lawyers.

If this episode accomplished anything, it convinced my folks I wasn't interested in law and, assuming I made it to my junior year, would major in radio and television. It would be many years before they saw the wisdom of that choice.

I knew what I wanted to be from the time I was a teenager. Knowing that and making it happen are two different things. There is one big advantage to choosing sports broadcasting at an early age. Every game you attend, watch or listen to helps prepare you for your chosen field. All the things I learned about sports as a kid were learned as a labor of love, not a homework assignment. When you learn things in that context, they stay with you. When you cram to pass an examination, you retain the information for the length of the test.

As a C student in high school, I wasn't confronted with many choices when it came to college. There was Syracuse, there was Syracuse and, as I recall, there was Syracuse. Not surprisingly, I chose Syracuse.

Choice or no choice, I couldn't have picked a better place. I knew the school had an excellent Radio and TV Department, although until I won the epic battle with my parents it didn't appear I'd ever get near it. Once that was decided, I was free to pursue my career.

Syracuse was the right school and the right city. For a city of 216,000, it was a great sports town. It had pro basketball with the NBA's Syracuse Nationals; major college football and basketball at SU; an excellent college basketball program at Lemoyne, a small Catholic school; and Triple A baseball with the International League's Syracuse Chiefs. My classrooms would be all over town.

My freshman dormitory was located in an area called Skytop. It was up in the hills about a mile from the campus. Skytop comprised a group of World War II prefabs, each of which housed about 30 men. The first bit of information I learned at Syracuse was that in the event of fire, our dorm would burn to the ground in eight minutes. I had no trouble retaining this.

My first year in college brought me in contact with the greatest athlete I've ever seen. His name was Jim Brown, and he also lived at Skytop. If the university had any idea of what this young man would mean to the school there's no way he'd have been housed in a place that could burn to the ground in eight minutes. It was one thing for me and my roommate, Sherm Levey, to go up in flames, but Big Jim was another story.

Jim's face, with its granite-like features, didn't have to go up on Mt. Rushmore. It was already there. He *was* Mt. Rushmore. Ask anyone who tried to tackle him, or got in his way on the basketball court or lacrosse field. He also was a track and field star and played baseball in high school in Manhasset, Long Island. It seemed Brown could have been anything he wanted. He could have won the Miss America contest if he'd set his mind to it.

I got to know Jim when he played freshman basketball. Sherm was also on the team, and I was the manager. I still have my SU jacket with the basketball on it, and I still can get into it if you overlook the fact the buttons and the snaps are in different ZIP codes.

My relationship with Brown grew because of a man named Marty Handler. Marty was moon-faced with a hawk nose, thick-frame glasses, an ever-present cigar and a heart of gold. He was known as "The Boss," and no one ever needed to ask why. Handler's old friend, Ken Molloy, a Manhasset attorney and a former SU lacrosse star, had asked Marty to be like a guardian to Brown. Syracuse, unlike other schools, had not offered Brown an athletic scholarship. Molloy paid his way in the beginning, and after Brown's eye-opening performances with the freshman football team, the University came to its senses.

A few years earlier, the school had difficulty accepting the social lives of a couple of black football players. Interracial dating was not in vogue in the late '40s and early '50s, and Brown was warned not to be like those "other" guys. This patronizing attitude alienated Brown from the university for many years following his graduation. Years later, when I would run into Jim either at the Super Bowl or an alumni event, he would say to me, "You were there. You remember what it was like." He was right.

Fortunately, a school administration that was not there at the time has made peace with Jim, and the two have embraced each other. There is no way you can separate Jim Brown from Syracuse.

Brown's freshman roommate was an impressive young man from Boys High in Brooklyn named Vinnie Cohen. And that was the way Cohen invariably was introduced. "Impressive young man," of course, would always precede, if not overshadow, the fact that Cohen was also a basketball star. The idea of Brown and Cohen as roommates led to speculation that someday Syracuse might honor the two by retiring their room.

Many who had read Cohen's name in the paper wondered if he was Jewish. Vinnie put an end to the speculation when he said, "I've got enough problems being black."

Black or orange, he had no problem on the basketball floor or in the classroom. Vinnie finished school as Syracuse's all-time leading scorer. He was the No. 1 draft pick of the Nationals, and he earned a scholarship to law school. He later worked for Attorney General Robert Kennedy in Washington and served on the legal staff at Consolidated Edison.

One night, the Syracuse frosh were playing Cornell at SU's old Archbold Gymnasium. One of my best friends from Brighton High in Rochester, Stew Maurer, was the freshman manager at Cornell. As the first half came to an end and the two teams were heading to the locker room, the crowd was beginning to fill the gym for the varsity game to follow. Stew and I stopped to talk. We were really something — two high school buddies, both managers of their respective college freshman teams. Several minutes went by. Stew and I were patting each other on the back when one of the ballboys came up to me. He reminded me I had the keys to the locker room, and all this time the Syracuse squad had been locked out.

Andy Mogish was our freshman coach. Well before anyone knew what lasers were, Mogish could cut you in half with his glare. That night, he exposed me to words taught in no language course in the university curriculum. Mr. Big Shot wasn't so big anymore.

After our first year at Syracuse, I continued to follow Jim Brown's career from a different perspective. I joined the campus radio station, WAER. My days there brought me in contact with more talented people than at any place I have worked. We had producers, directors, engineers, staff announcers, news announcers, sports announcers, classical music announcers, continuity writers and music librarians. It's amazing the kind of staff a station can build when it doesn't have to pay anything. After graduation I worked for a number of stations that tried to operate on the same principle.

The Newhouse School of Public Communications didn't exist when I was at Syracuse. The Radio and TV Department was part of the School of Speech and Dramatic Arts. The University established itself as a place for broadcasters and performers long before my arrival. Alumni included Dick Clark, Peter Falk, Marty Glickman, Sheldon Leonard, Bill Lundigan and Jerry Stiller. My contemporaries included Bob Dishy, Ted Koppel (whatever happened to him?), my old Phillies colleague Andy Musser, Suzanne Pleshette (why didn't I know her?), Dick Purtan (Detroit's premier morning man) and Fred Silverman.

Many others followed us, particularly in sports. Among them were Marv Albert, Len Berman, Bob Costas, Todd Kalas, Sean McDonough, Dave O'Brien, A's broadcaster Greg Papa, Dick Stockton and Mike Tirico.

Working at WAER also introduced me to a classmate named Jerry Hoffman, who became a lifelong friend. Jerry was a native Syracusan who had grown up not far from the campus. As a high schooler he broadcast Catholic League high school basketball games on one of the local stations. On another program he read the Sunday comics. He became Sports Director at WAER in our senior year, and we teamed up to broadcast SU's NCAA Tournament games in March, 1957. We were hot stuff, broadcasting from Madison Square Garden as the Orangemen defeated UConn to advance to the Eastern Regionals. On we moved to the historic Palestra on the campus of the University of Pennsylvania and a Friday night victory over Lafayette.

The following night, we were on the air as Syracuse took the court against North Carolina, coached by the legendary Frank McGuire. This was The Big One. A win against the Tar Heels, and Syracuse would go to the Final Four the following weekend in Kansas City.

The Syracuse coach was Marc Guley, a nice enough man but not exactly inspirational. According to Manny Breland, one of the Syracuse players, "Here we were sitting in our dressing room, moments away from the biggest game of our lives. We were playing undefeated North Carolina, with their All-America Lenny Rosenbluth, the college player of the year. We were tense and in need of some reassurance, some inspiration, anything. All of a sudden the door opened and in came Coach Guley. We were silent as we awaited the words that would send us through that door, charging out onto the court. Coach looked at us and said, 'Well, there's nothing I can tell you now.'

"That was some speech."

Syracuse fell behind by nine points at the half and eventually lost by that margin. North Carolina went on to complete a 35-0 season with a pair of triple-overtime victories, over Michigan State in the semifinal and Wilt Chamberlain's Kansas team in the final.

It would be a long time before I broadcast another game from either Madison Square Garden or the Palestra. Much of my time in college was spent going to games. As much as I was learning about radio and television, I knew sports was going to be my business. I was going to have to talk intelligently about sports, and there were no courses in the Syracuse catalog called Ballgames 101.

I spent many bitter-cold nights waiting for buses to take me to the Onondaga County War Memorial Arena to see the Nats play the Knicks or the Celtics or whomever, and just as many nights going to the Jefferson Street Armory to see coach Tommy Niland's Lemoyne College Dolphins take on Providence with Lenny Wilkens or coach Eddie Donovan's St. Bonaventure team with John Connors.

Syracuse may not be the snow capital of the world, but it's only a short walk from there. It also gets cold. There was something about waiting for a bus on a January night in that town that told me if I'd done better in high school I could have been at UCLA instead. Of course, my grades in college weren't much better. It was hard to concentrate on Robert Frost when you felt more like Jack.

People who live in Central New York are a hearty lot. They tend to look upon snow and cold as a badge of honor. Whatever Mother Nature throws at them, they can take. One night we were watching the weather report on TV, and the weatherman said Chicago was expecting six inches of snow. Marty Handler looked up and said, "Big deal! In Syracuse we call that 'threatening weather.'"

The weather served as a yardstick in other ways. I was standing in the foyer of the War Memorial before a NATS game one night. People were coming in from the snowy street to see the game. The door to the ticket office opened, and Danny Biasone, who owned the team, stepped out. He saw me standing there, came over and said, "The floor isn't wet enough." I wondered why he cared about the floor being wet, not realizing he was measuring how many people had tracked in snow on their way into the arena. I was learning another lesson outside the classroom.

One day I was making my way across the campus. It was cold and windy and must have been 15 degrees below zero. I was heading into the wind like an aircraft carrier about to launch and was probably as well-protected. Hunched over against the wind, with a fur collar pulled over my head, I must have looked like I was on all fours. Dick Abend, a classmate, was approaching from the opposite direction. He eyed me curiously and exclaimed, "My God, it's a bear!"

Ever since, I've been known to friends, primarily in the East, as "The Bear." I no longer wear coats with fur collars, but my posture has done little to suggest I was misnamed. It probably was the first nickname I ever had. It took some getting used to. The Bear. I've been playing golf for nearly 50 years, and it's the only thing I have in common with Jack Nicklaus.

Another of the mistakes I made at college was joining a fraternity. It seemed like a good idea at the time, but it didn't take me long to realize that watching guys throw food across the dining room was an activity I gave up at age 2. Besides, I really didn't care to listen to details of their alleged sexual exploits. Perhaps if I'd had some of my own, their stories might have been easier to take.

I left the fraternity after my sophomore year but took with me three great friendships that have lasted a lifetime.

Dick Dolinsky, Alias The Doll

I still see him in his room, conducting the NBC Symphony Orchestra. He had an unusually large room. More to the point, he had an AM-FM receiver on which he could pick up the symphony's broadcasts. So what if it was Arturo Toscanini conducting? Toscanini. Dolinsky. Close enough. All I knew was that when I entered his room he was waving his arms and there was music. I couldn't do that in my room. When I waved my arms, somebody across the hall waved back.

We nicknamed Dick Dolinsky "The Doll" when we were freshmen going through the ritual of pledging a fraternity. The others in our small group, or "Little Coalition," as we called ourselves, were Abend and Don LaVine.

The Doll was probably the first friend I could converse with who wasn't wrapped up in sports. This is not to suggest he didn't know what was going on. If you pressed him, he could tell you a home run was worth six points and that Allie Reynolds was married to Eddie Fisher. But he didn't need all that.

Dick was a psychology major, and psychologists tend to keep things in perspective. It didn't matter what he said to you, it always made you feel better. Usually he said the same thing: "Well, you'll do what you want and you won't bother me." We never knew what the hell he was talking about, but it sounded profound, and we felt better.

The Doll demonstrated his ability to keep things in perspective one fall day in 1956. The Syracuse football team, coached by Ben Schwartzwalder, was playing host to Army under coach Red Blaik. Syracuse had not been to a bowl game since January, 1953, and, with Jim Brown leading the way, had a shot at the Cotton

Bowl. To get there they'd have to finish as the top team in the East. Army and Penn State stood in the way.

Tickets for the Army game were impossible to get, but all students had tickets, among them Richard Dolinsky.

The importance of the game was underscored by the presence of NBC Television and announcers Lindsey Nelson and Red Grange. When Lindsey and Red had the game, you knew it was big. The Doll took his seat in the student section at old Archbold Stadium. The first half, full of drama and tension, ended Syracuse 7, Army 0.

Everyone awaited the start of the second half. Everyone, that is, except Dick Dolinsky. With the logic only a true scholar could apply, Dolinsky decided this would be a good time to get a haircut. After all, Dolinsky knew he needed a haircut. He figured if everyone else was at the game, there would be no waiting at the barber shop.

Outside, people were still making their way toward the stadium in hopes of catching the second half. Against the tide, one lone figure was seen making his way toward Marshall Street and the barbershop. It was The Doll, adhering to his own philosophy. He was doing what he wanted, and he wasn't bothering anyone.

Syracuse held the lead in the third quarter. With three minutes to play in the game, Army had the ball, first and goal, at the Syracuse three-yard line. The first three plays netted the Cadets only two yards. Now it was fourth and goal from the one. Coach Blaik called time out as he devised the play he hoped would score the tying touchdown and spoil Syracuse's bowl hopes.

Army's Vince Barta took the handoff and plowed straight ahead. There was a tremendous pileup at the goal line. Did he make it, or didn't he? Nobody knew. Twenty-two bodies were in the pile.

I was working as a sideline spotter with a direct line to the press box. My position was on the Army side of the field, adjacent to the bench area. I could see Coach Blaik going crazy, convinced his man had scored. This obviously was no time for objectivity.

The officials began separating the bodies in hopes of finding the football. Was it a touchdown? I didn't know. The officials didn't know. Forty thousand people in the stadium didn't know. Only Dick Dolinsky, sitting in a barber's chair three blocks from the stadium, knew. He was watching on television and saw what no one else could, at that moment.

"I knew he didn't make it," Dolinsky said afterward in his laconic manner. "What was all the fuss about?"

That was The Doll.

In later years he became Dr. Doll when he obtained his Ph.D. from New York University. He taught psychology for 35 years at the University of Toledo. He also taught at Long Island University and was a visiting professor at Princeton.

Dick Abend, alias The Blub

The Blub was a tough nickname, but it fit at the time. Abend was on the chunky side. He was from Utica, about 50 miles east of Syracuse. He brought with him a Ford convertible whose color could best be described as Mary Kay pink. Not surprisingly, he was the one among us who had the most dates.

He also loved sports and saw it as a metaphor for life. He often encouraged me, during a given semester, with reminders such as, "It's only the bottom of the eighth, Bear, you've still got time to pull out a C in this course." Dick Abend was a happy guy in our senior year when Syracuse rode Dolinsky's famous goal line stand to the Cotton Bowl.

The day the Cotton Bowl news was announced, I left town to visit a girl I'd been dating for more than three years. I'd known her from Rochester, where we attended the same high school. She was two years younger and had transferred from Michigan to the University of Buffalo after her freshman year. I thought this was great because Buffalo was a heck of a lot closer to me than Ann Arbor. Unfortunately, it made it even more convenient for her to break up with me the day I arrived.

According to the thesaurus, "distraught" can also mean frantic, distressed, troubled, tormented and upset. I was all of them as I returned to Syracuse late on the night of November 30. I guess I wasn't the only one who'd had a tough night. The same evening, Floyd Patterson knocked out Archie Moore in a heavyweight championship fight. Inasmuch as Patterson and Moore hadn't been dating for three and one-half years, my knockout hurt a lot more.

The next day I told Abend what had happened. Dick was one of those people who saw sunshine on cloudy days. He saw my red eyes, my white face and my blue mood. In an act of rescue worthy of a medal, he turned my outlook 180 degrees. "Look at it this way, Bear. You lost a love but you gained a bowl bid."

One semester, he and I took a sociology course. I didn't even know what sociology was and probably couldn't explain it now, but people thought there was some depth to you when you took a course like that. The class met three times a week and was taught by Dr. Byron Fox. Almost every session, he showed a film. We weren't required to buy a book for his course, but Dr. Fox informed us we had to buy a film guide. Abend and I called him "Twentieth Century Fox."

Dick was never more at home than holding court in a college hangout on Marshall Street with an ever-present girlfriend at his side. He had the ability to look at home wherever he was, with the possible exception of the ROTC drill field.

One day after drill, we piled into his convertible and were heading off for lunch. We were still in our uniforms. The top was down, so we decided to have some fun. Mindful of the motorcades held for General Douglas MacArthur a few years before, I climbed on the back of the open convertible and started waving. Admittedly, one car tends to make for a short motorcade, but a pink one does attract attention.

As we drove through streets near the campus, Abend honked his horn, a couple other guys in the car cheered, and I sat up there and waved. A few people on the sidewalks threw things, but as I recall it wasn't confetti. The highlight of the day was that we avoided arrest.

Somehow I never imagined Dick Abend becoming an attorney. During our days in college I always pictured him going through life in a beautiful car with a beautiful woman beside him. I was right about that part but missed badly about his career. I saw him never having to work a day in his life and living in a place on the French Riviera. Of course, I pictured the same for myself.

Donald D. LaVine, alias The Vine, or D.D.

In my days in college and the many that followed, I have never known a more intriguing person. If that sounds like a bold statement, it was meant that way. It's the truth.

Don LaVine was the guy you saw in an old black-and-white movie, on a fog-shrouded street in Shanghai or Algiers, wearing a trench coat with the collar turned up, smoking a cigarette. He was a man of mystery, maybe a foreign correspondent, perhaps a spy. In real life he was no different. He had the coat and the cigarette and a face lined with intrigue. When you heard him speak, he was Leonard Graves narrating "Victory at Sea" or John Facenda in the early days of NFL Films. I would have killed for a voice like his.

It's difficult to describe someone about whom you feel so intensely. You want every word to be just right. You want to capture every facet of his personality, every nuance, every ingredient. What happens, unfortunately, is you end with a character who sounds more fictional than real, which may be the best way to describe him. Who can say he didn't step out of the pages of a novel? In a more perfect world, Don would have written the novel himself.

I always pictured him at a typewriter, giving birth to another bestseller. He was F. Scott Fitzgerald in many ways, not all of them healthy. He suffered from the curse of talent. Having it is one thing; knowing what to do with it is something else.

LaVine was intelligently funny. You could always see a thought process behind his humor. He could quote the great writers. He had a mind you'd swear went places no man had been before. When he reads this he will say, "Ah, The Bear. Who the hell is he talking about?"

We used to play a game we called Sports Charades. Each player had to relate to a team, a person or a saying connected to sports. For example, I might turn toward the sun and point. That would be West Point. For LaVine, that was too simple. His charades always had more subtlety to them.

One night we were playing, and it was his turn. He was sitting there with one of those small, square pillows you see on a couch. The pillow was on his lap.

"All right, LaVine," I said. "I give up. What is it?"

"Why, Bear!" he said. "Anyone can plainly see it's a base on balls."

On another occasion he stood there with his right arm extended. With his left hand he began slapping the underside of his right arm. That was encouragement for the Syracuse football team the following Saturday. That was Beat Pitt.

That was D.D. LaVine.

In later years we worked together at Radio Station WOLF in Syracuse. I used to get mail there addressed to:

BEAR
WOLF
SYRACUSE 1, NEW YORK

I was working in the newsroom, and LaVine was our traffic reporter. The station had a vehicle that must have landed from another planet. It looked like a space capsule with three wheels on the bottom. It was called an Isetta. We called it a lot of other names because it always seemed to break down. Most of the traffic problems in Syracuse probably were caused by our traffic-mobile. It had to be embarrassing for Don to be seen driving it. Little kids on tricycles passed it. Joggers waved as they went by. Old ladies helped *it* get across the street.

Traffic reports were routine for the most part. At 6:30 a.m. traffic was light. By 7:30 it started to pick up, and by 8:30 it was at its peak. It was the same almost every day.

Don LaVine and sameness are not a good mix. If he was going to do traffic reports, by God, he'd give those folks in their cars something to remember. Every once in a while from the newsroom I would say, "Now for the latest on traffic we go directly to WOLF's traffic reporter, Don LaVine. . . ."

Don: "Here in London this morning, traffic is congested in the Knightsbridge area due to the semi-annual sale at Harrods, which gets underway at 10. Traffic is moving well through Marble Arch and on toward Green Park. There's a bit of backup, however, at Picadilly Circus, where drivers slow down to stare at the pigeon that is dropping greetings from the head atop Lord Nelson's statue. We'll have an update in 30 minutes. This is D. D. LaVine, now back to the studio."

Similar LaVine traffic reports would "emanate" from other parts of the world, leading Syracuse drivers to believe either that they had very powerful radios in their cars, or Haberle Congress beer had more kick to it than they realized.

Life has a way of sending people in different directions. Because I traveled so much over the years, I was the only one of the four of us to have some contact with the other three. The 40th anniversary of our college graduation, 1997, also was the first year of my retirement, and I was free to attend the reunion. I called LaVine, who now was working for an advertising agency in Syracuse. I told him I was planning to attend and would try to round up the others. He said, "Bear, if you're going to be there, I'll be there."

Now that I had the key guy, I could work on the others. The four of us loved each other, but LaVine's presence was what made it worthwhile.

I called Abend in Utica. He was hesitant. His daughter was getting married later that summer. He and Joan had a lot to do.

I told him I could produce LaVine.

"You got LaVine?! I'LL BE THERE."

That took care of Abend.

I called Dolinsky in New York.

"Well you know, Bear, I'd heard about the reunion but I wasn't thinking about going. You should do what you want and you won't bother me. What's that?! You got LaVine?! I'LL BE THERE."

D.D. LaVine. He holds a spell over all of us. He should. There's no one like him.

Throughout my four years in college I kept my focus on graduating. I suppose that's every college student's objective, but it would be more of an achievement for me. I was, at best, an average student. I was getting a great education. It's just that it wasn't all in the classroom. I enjoyed the Radio-TV courses and did reasonably well, but I was thrown for big losses by Genetics, Major Victorian Writers and Aspects of Linguistic Theory. One semester I signed up for a history class that met once a week. Somehow I managed to miss the first five classes.

At the time, I could justify those absences, at least to myself. For example, had I shown up for class I'd have missed on TV Willie Mays' catch off Vic Wertz in

Game One of the 1954 World Series. I can't recall additional excuses, other than to suspect that suddenly I might have found religion and decided to observe the High Holy Days, no matter whose they were.

Finally, in the sixth week I showed up, and to make matters worse, I walked in late. The instructor looked up and said, "May I help you?"

I replied, "I'm in this class."

"What's your name?"

"Greenwald."

"Where have you been for five weeks, Greenwald?"

"I couldn't find the room."

The instructor thought it would be a good idea for me to transfer to another class, one with a room I could find more easily.

My sophomore-year roommate was Tom Lotz. He was taking the same course from a different teacher. I decided to switch to his class. I attended faithfully the rest of the semester. The only mistake I made was forgetting to inform anyone, besides Lotz, I had transferred. I got an incomplete in the course. I was beginning to wonder if I might be able to sign up for a course in truck driving.

Through all of this, I remained close with the athletic department. Arnie Burdick was the sports information director my first three years in school. We called him "The Burr." He called me "Herbie." For some things there are no answers.

Burdick, Marty Handler and I often drove to basketball games when Syracuse played at places such as Cornell and Colgate. There we were: The Burr, The Boss and The Bear.

Before my senior year, Arnie left the University to become sports editor of the afternoon paper, *The Syracuse Herald Journal*, a post he would hold for a quarter of a century.

Burdick's successor was an SU grad named Valjean Arthur Pinchbeck, Jr. For obvious reasons, he preferred "Val." Following graduation in 1952, Val put in time as a naval officer and later was sports information director at Bucknell University in Lewisburg, Pennsylvania. He was only 25 and not far removed from college himself when he took the job. Perhaps that's why he made those of us from the campus radio station and newspaper feel as important as the downtown media or the big dailies in New York.

Val stepped into something big with Jim Brown about to start his senior year. A college sports information director might spend all his days wishing for an All-America. Pinchbeck was about to inherit one. Not only that, there was the Cotton Bowl, and later the basketball team's journey to the finals of the NCAA Eastern Regionals.

The success of the football team and its All-America running back brought a lot of big-name writers to Syracuse to cover the games. Through Val and Marty Handler, who seemed to know everybody, I got to meet, eat with, and help get to the airport people such as Bill Wallace and Gordon White of *The New York Times*, Stanley Woodward, Harold Rosenthal, Irving Marsh and Jerry Izenberg of *The New York Herald Tribune*; Larry Robinson from *The New York World Telegram*; Merv Hyman of *Sports Illustrated*, and of course Lindsey Nelson and Red Grange.

Think about that last name for a moment. Red Grange, No. 77, the Galloping Ghost, the greatest running back of his time. He came out of the Golden Age, the '20s, along with Babe Ruth, Bobby Jones, Jack Dempsey, Ernest Hemingway, Gene Sarazen, Alice Marble, Bill Tilden, F. Scott Fitzgerald, Gene Tunney, and Walter Hagen. Those names were so important we even learned about two of them in school.

For us to meet Red Grange back then would be like some college reporter meeting Jim Brown today. There they were, Red Grange and Jim Brown in the same stadium. I don't recall if they actually met; surely they must have. What wouldn't you give for a picture of the two of them?

I had many memorable moments watching Jim Brown, and it didn't seem to matter what sport he was playing. In his All-America season he scored 43 points against Colgate. This was football. Brown ran for six touchdowns and kicked seven extra points. I was on the sideline at the Cotton Bowl when he scored three touchdowns and kicked three extra points in a losing effort against TCU, 28-27. One of the extra points was blocked.

Next to football, Brown was best known as an All-America lacrosse star. He had also participated in basketball his first three years and track and field before his senior year.

Of all the times I watched him, the most memorable came on a Saturday afternoon in May of 1957, the final day of the school's athletic schedule. The lacrosse team was bidding for an undefeated season, and only Army stood in the way. The match was scheduled for Archbold Stadium, the same field on which Brown had so many triumphant afternoons carrying a football.

Scheduled to take place on the same field about three hours earlier was a dual track meet against Colgate. Although Brown had finished as high as fifth in the national decathlon earlier in his career, he did not participate in track and field as a senior. For that matter, Syracuse had not won a dual meet that season, and this was its final opportunity. Somehow Coach Bob Grieve persuaded Brown to return for one last effort. The track meet was at noon, the lacrosse match at 3 p.m.

I was on the field when the meet with Colgate began. Looking back on it, I'm not sure what I was doing there except making every effort to avoid being on the receiving end of the shot put.

Brown had not practiced any of the events in which he'd been entered. How silly to think it would matter. In short order, he won the high jump. Later, he took first in the discus. Then, in his final event, the javelin, Brown was leading and had one throw remaining when he had to leave the field for the locker room to change for lacrosse. As he ran by he said to me, "If anyone beats my throw, come to the dressing room and get me."

A short time later, the Colgate participant let fly, and his toss landed beyond Brown's. Off I went to the dressing room, near the tunnel entrance to the stadium, to fetch Big Jim. Out he walked in his lacrosse uniform. In one last, heroic effort, he threw. His toss fell just short, but the points he got for finishing second combined with his two firsts added up to 13 and supplied the winning margin in Syracuse's 72-59 win over Colgate. This would have been a full day for most people, but it was Jim Brown we were dealing with.

The largest crowd of the season turned out for the lacrosse finale against Army. Wherever he went on the lacrosse field, two Army defenders went with him. An undefeated season was in reach for Syracuse, and Brown would make sure it happened. He scored one goal and had two assists in a 10-6 victory. It's unlikely an athlete ever closed out his college career in such a manner.

Until that afternoon, I'd always felt that the only sports that really counted were baseball, football or basketball. When Brown left the field following the lacrosse victory, I knew I'd seen something the likes of which I would never see again.

But the day wasn't over. From Val Pinchbeck's office in the Athletic Department, you could look directly into the stadium. It was now late in the afternoon. Val and I were sitting there, along with a reporter from *Sports Illustrated*, marveling at what we had seen earlier. The sun was shining directly at us, and shadows had lengthened across the field as we looked down on the old playground.

Two figures appeared, slowly making their way from one end of the field to the other. We were squinting as we attempted to make out who they were. Finally it became clear. It was Jim Brown walking side-by-side with a boy who couldn't have been more than 10 or 12. We had no idea who the boy was, but we guessed he was just hanging around, the way kids often do after sporting events.

Directly below our window, Brown and the youngster reached the curved end of the field where the stands go up to meet the exits leading out to the campus. Just before reaching the stands, the boy veered to his right and began his climb to the southeast exit. Brown started his slow walk up through the ancient concrete stands where, for the last three years, hundreds of thousands had witnessed his greatness. Before reaching the northeast exit, he waited to watch the boy depart. The three of us looking down from upstairs sat spellbound as Brown walked to the top of the stadium. He turned to face the field, waved and walked out. Was he waving to the boy? Was he waving goodbye to past glories? Did it matter? Pinchbeck and I were speechless, no easy trick. It was left to the reporter from *Sports Illustrated* to break the silence.

"How can I possibly write this? Who would believe it?"

I also was reaching the end of my college days. At least I hoped I was. Going into my last semester, I knew I could graduate as long as I didn't get a D in any of my courses. In addition to the broadcasting courses, I also was taking Major Victorian Writers and New York State Football. The latter actually was a geography course but was so named because the class was made up primarily of football players. It was supposed to be a snap.

The practice back then was to submit a self-addressed postcard to the professor on the day of your final exam. He or she would mail you your grade.

I was a decided underdog going into the Major Victorian Writers final, after running a C-minus at mid-term. Las Vegas had set the over-under at D-plus, which wouldn't do me any good.

I finished the final not knowing what to think. All I could do was wait for that postcard. In this, I was not alone. My friends The Blub, The Doll and The Vine didn't have to sweat as I did, so they kept a vigil with me each day until the mail came. The Cub was there, too, Jerry Hoffman. I was The Bear; he was The Cub. Each day we'd sit outside my place waiting for the mail. Would The Bear make it or not? Those were tense times. Graduation was set for Monday. My parents were awaiting a "go" or "no go" at home in Rochester.

No mail on Thursday.

We gathered again on Friday. At long last, the mailman arrived bearing two postcards. Every day for a week, there had been five guys waiting for the mailman. He never felt so important in his life. I tried to read his face, hoping to detect a clue. No such luck. He was all business. He handed me the cards and was on his way.

My hand was trembling as I looked at the cards. I passed Major Victorian Writers with a C. I flunked New York State Football. I was crushed. How could I have flunked Geography? Of course, I hadn't studied for it. It was supposed to be a snap, and I was too busy studying for the tough one.

Now there was no way I could graduate. A D would have been bad enough, but an F was shocking. How was I going to explain this one to my parents? Of course, by their reckoning I could always fall back on my second career as a truck driver.

Once I regained my composure, I knew there was only one thing to do. Twenty minutes later, I walked into Dean Faigle's office. I did a double take as I recognized seven guys from my Geography class. The teacher had flunked all of them.

Dean Faigle listened to our story. "I can't believe she failed eight graduating seniors," he said, his head rotating slowly back and forth on an east-west axis like a spectator at a tennis match.

"Tell me this," he said. "Was she late for class often?"

As a group, we acknowledged that tardiness seemed to be her habit. The avuncular dean nodded knowingly and told us a story.

"Back when I was head of the Geography Department, she was one of my assistants. The day before she was to teach, she would come to me and ask me to phone her the next morning to make sure she was awake on time. Finally I said to her, 'Do you want me to phone you, or do you want me to nudge you?' She never could make it to class on time."

The eight of us laughed, all the while wondering how Dean Faigle could be telling funny stories while our bachelor's degrees were hanging in the balance. In a way, it seemed like the last meal before our execution.

Then he said, "Let me give her a call and see what I can work out. Come back here at 5 o'clock this afternoon."

Two hours later, full of hope and apprehension, the "gang of eight" filed back into the Dean's office.

"Well, I spoke with her and she's agreed to give you a make-up exam tomorrow at 8 a.m. Good luck to you all."

In retrospect, we agreed that Dean Faigle must have said to her, "You give those graduating seniors another exam and make sure they pass!"

It must have happened that way, because at 8 Saturday morning, two days before graduation, she walked in the room, handed out the exams and said, "One of you call me tonight at 7 for your grades."

She turned and walked out of the room, leaving the eight of us alone.

We designated one of us to make the fateful call. At 7 p.m. he was greeted with a terse, "You all passed," followed by a solid hanging up of the phone. Terse or not, it was Pomp and Circumstance to our ears.

I called my parents and told them it was a "go." They could make the drive from Rochester. I assumed they were pleased, but who knows? The truck driving profession might have lost one of its all-time greats.

Several things stood out in my mind on that graduation day in 1957. There was a sense of relief in knowing I never would have to step into another classroom involuntarily. I could now read *The Sporting News* and know it wasn't at the expense of my schoolwork.

There was the sight of Jim Brown marching into Archbold Stadium one more time in yet another uniform. In addition to his degree, Brown was receiving his commission as a second lieutenant in the United States Army. General MacArthur, with all his decorations, could not have looked any more impressive than Brown in his military attire. Observing him that day, I was left with the feeling that he was not born in the conventional sense. He simply was sculpted, then given life.

Our commencement speaker was the junior senator from Massachusetts, John F. Kennedy. He was youthful looking and energetic. Prophetically, he spoke of a need for more young people to get into politics. He suggested the nation needed an infusion of new blood. Three years later, he would be president. Three years after that, he would be dead.

Graduation time also meant reunion time, and I recall seeing a large group of persons making their way across campus. I asked someone who they were.

"That's the Class of 1932," I was told. "They're here for their 25th reunion."

I stood there for a moment and stared. I was 21 and couldn't imagine what it would be like 25 years later. In 1997, I attended my 40th.

After the graduation ceremonies, I was with my close friend and sophomore roommate, Tom Lotz. Like Jim Brown, Tom was commissioned an Army second lieutenant. Tom was an impressive looking young man, standing almost 6 foot 4, and had been a member of the varsity crew.

I found my parents and, with Tom, went to locate his. Tom's father had been a classmate of Eric Faigle at Syracuse, and the two were longtime friends. They were standing with Tom's mother as we approached.

As introductions were made, Tom's father, knowing of my close call, said, "Well, Bear, you had us worried."

Before I could respond, Dean Faigle said, "Let's just say The Bear had us all worried."

No comment could have punctuated my college days better than that. Dean Faigle first kept me in school, then he also got me out. There isn't much more anyone can do for you than that.

People like Eric Faigle were put on this earth because they were needed. Here was a man who knew there was more to a student than his grade-point average. He saw a young man's potential where others saw only C's and D's. I owe him a lot, and I regret not having been able to write this years ago while he was still alive. I hope somehow he knows where life has taken me and that he's proud — not proud of me, but of himself for believing in a young man's future.

While graduation marked the end of my college days, it only marked a temporary halt to my time in Syracuse. The next two years took me to Vineland, New Jersey, and radio station WWBZ. From November, 1957, to November, 1959, I read egg prices. I also read news and sports and played music, but egg prices seemed to command the most attention.

I wasn't exactly furthering my career in sports broadcasting, but Vineland was convenient to Philadelphia, New York and Baltimore. I spent every free moment driving or taking the train to catch major league games. Mort Berry of the Phillies and Bob Fischel of the Yankees were kind enough to send me season's press passes. They did far more for me than I was able to do for them. Other kindnesses were extended to me by Bob Paul at the University of Pennsylvania and Ed Hogan of the Philadelphia Eagles. Franklin Field and the Palestra were my second homes during the fall and winter, and those Big Five college basketball double-headers were better than anything I've seen since.

Going to all these games enabled me to witness many memorable moments, but I wasn't getting any on-the-air sports experience. My decision to leave Vineland and return to Syracuse was made easier by two things: In 1959, the Syracuse football team was on the verge of a national championship, and the other reason was that I got fired.

There was a tug of war going on at WWBZ, and I was on the wrong end of the rope. The only reason I regretted leaving was that I'd really improved at reading those egg prices. Even now, 40 years later, I'm told I can still be heard mumbling in my sleep, "Large browns 47 cents a dozen. Grade A whites 43 cents."

Now that I was out of work, it seemed Syracuse was the best place for me. At least I knew some people there.

My old friend Marty Handler, The Boss, took me in and said I was welcome to stay until I found a job and a place to live. It was a nice arrangement. Marty was a salesman and was away all week, and on the weekends we went to the football games and partied.

Coach Ben Schwartzwalder's Orangemen continued to roll along undefeated, led by sophomore running back Ernie Davis, who was proving to be an able successor to Jim Brown. Brown, who by then was playing in the NFL with Cleveland, helped recruit Ernie. So did Handler, who, like Ernie, was from Elmira, New York.

I found a job at radio station WOLF doing news and sports. There seemed to be a lot more of both in Syracuse than in Vineland. It was an exciting time to be back. The football team was destined for great things. Its 20-18 victory over Penn State was one of college football's greatest games. Both teams were undefeated and had designs on a national title. Schwartzwalder and rival coach Rip Engle were not exactly close friends, which helped sweeten the pot.

The game was played at Penn State. Syracuse scored early in the fourth quarter to take a 20-6 lead and appeared to have the game well in hand. That lasted only until the next kickoff, which Roger Kaufman of the Nittany Lions ran back 100 yards for a touchdown. The extra point failed, and now it was 20-12. With just over four minutes left, Penn State scored again to make it 20-18 and went for the two-point conversion. To no one's surprise, Kaufman got the call. The Syracuse defense stopped him inches from the end zone.

On the following kickoff, the ball bounced crazily toward the sideline, inside the 10-yard line, when Davis picked it up and inadvertently stepped out of bounds at the 8.

For every championship team there is a defining moment in the course of its season. For Syracuse, this was it. If the defense held and forced a punt, Penn State would be in position to win with a field goal. The Nittany Lions never saw the ball again. Quarterback Dave Sarrette led a drive that produced one first down after another. When the game ended, Syracuse had the ball inside Penn State's 10-yard line. It had to be the greatest non-scoring drive ever.

Syracuse rolled through the remainder of the season and defeated Texas in the Cotton Bowl, 23-14. Perhaps the year was summed up best following a 36-8 victory at UCLA, when a Los Angeles columnist wrote, "If Syracuse's first team is No. 1 in the country, their second team is No. 2."

The station I worked for was owned by a company out of Ithaca, N.Y., called Ivy Broadcasting. Its president was Ellis "Woody" Erdman. Doing business with this man often left you with the feeling that buying a used car from Richard Nixon might not be so bad. I'll say one thing for him — he had big ideas. He obtained the rights to the Syracuse Football Network and in 1960 selected me to do the play-by-play. That was the good news. The bad news was that often he was doing the color commentary. I worked with others as well, including former Cornell coach Lefty James, whose presence added much to the broadcasts.

The games were heard beyond a 50-mile radius of Syracuse, where WSYR had exclusive rights. Woody set up a network of 40 stations throughout the east, and when I started in 1960 Syracuse was the defending national champion. Woody had a similar deal with the NFL New York Giants to carry their games on a network outside of New York City, and I did pre-game and halftime shows.

I spent five seasons broadcasting Syracuse football in an era that bridged the careers of Ernie Davis, Jim Nance, John Mackey, Floyd Little and Larry Csonka. Anyone could sound good broadcasting college football when they played.

While Syracuse had impressive won-lost records during this period, a game they lost is the one I remember most. In 1961 Notre Dame appeared on the schedule for the first time. The game was in South Bend, and legend had it that no team playing for the first time at Notre Dame ever had beaten the Irish. I found out why.

Syracuse held a 15-14 lead with three seconds to play, and Notre Dame lined up for a field goal attempt. Notre Dame kicker Joe Perkowski faced a 56-yard try. He shanked the kick, and the ball rolled out of bounds at the 30-yard line as time ran out.

The teams left for the locker rooms. The bands and spectators were on the field. Suddenly, from out of the past came the thundering hooves of the great horse Silver. Not quite, but close enough. From out of the crowd on the field came the footsteps of F.G. Skibbie of Bowling Green, Ohio. Skibbie was the field judge, and he made a call no one had ever seen before or since: "roughing the holder." The Irish were awarded 15 yards and another crack at it.

First, they had to clear the field and get the two teams back out there. This took several more minutes. Up in the broadcast booth, we were not exempt from the confusion. The explanation of the penalty only added to it.

It was a foregone conclusion that Perkowski, given a second chance, would be successful. He booted it through the uprights, and Notre Dame won in "overtime," 17-15.

Later it was determined that the officials misapplied the rules in allowing Notre Dame another play. At that time the rules stated that play is not extended at the half or the end of the game if a foul occurs when neither team is in possession of the ball. When Perkowski put his foot to the ball on the first field goal attempt, the Irish surrendered possession. Worse, it wasn't a Syracuse player who "roughed" the holder. It was Perkowski, who fell back onto holder Angelo DeBerio, who proceeded to roll around on the ground as if he'd been mortally wounded.

In the aftermath there was controversy in the press. Stanley Woodward of *The New York Herald Tribune* felt Notre Dame should forfeit the win. Red Smith of *The Tribune*, and a Notre Dame alum, thought his boss, Woodward, must have been smoking something funny. Coincidentally, the President of Notre Dame, Father Hesburgh, was a native of Syracuse. The location of one's birth, however, does not always carry with it an abundance of sentiment. The good Father apparently cited the Eleventh Commandment, i.e., possession is nine-tenths of a victory, and Notre Dame wasn't about to surrender possession.

The outcome of the game hurt Syracuse more than most people realized. The contract between the Pacific Coast Conference and the Big Ten had lapsed, and in 1961 the Rose Bowl committee was free to choose a visiting team from anywhere in the country. Syracuse, with Heisman Trophy candidate Ernie Davis, was an attractive commodity.

The Notre Dame game was played on November 18, and the word was out that if Syracuse won, it would be in line for the bid. Obviously, that changed. The Rose Bowl committee went back to familiar territory, choosing Minnesota from the Big Ten. Syracuse went on to the Liberty Bowl and, on a 22-degree day in Philadelphia, defeated Miami, 15-14.

Ernie Davis made history by becoming the first black player to win the Heisman Trophy. While those of us who were close to Ernie recognized the significance from a racial standpoint, we all hoped he'd be remembered for what he'd done on the field. I think Ernie felt the same way. He knew, as did we all, that had it not been for Paul Hornung at Notre Dame, Jim Brown would have won the Heisman five years earlier.

A battle was shaping up for Ernie's services as a pro. The American Football League was fighting the National Football League for the top college players. Davis had been drafted by both the Buffalo Bills of the AFL and the Washington Redskins of the NFL.

Several of us attended the Heisman presentation ceremonies at the Downtown Athletic Club in New York. At the press conference, Ernie was asked over and over his feelings about being the first black player to win the award, as well as the first black player ever drafted by the Redskins. Owner George Preston Marshall viewed Washington as a Southern town, and his regional television audience was from south of D.C. Drafting Davis was a radical move for the socially enigmatic Marshall.

Ernie kept saying he hadn't made up his mind where he was going to play and, in any event, was less concerned about being a black player than a good player. He was being as diplomatic as he could, and for reasons he couldn't talk about.

Ernie and I sat together on the flight returning to Syracuse, and it was only then that I learned his secret. Shortly after we took off from LaGuardia Airport, Ernie said, "Let's go sit in that little lounge in the back."

After we got situated, he said to me in his soft-spoken manner, "Do you remember all those reporters asking me about the possibility of being the first black player for the Redskins?"

I nodded, and he said, "The reason I couldn't get into all that stuff is because I'm not going to play for Washington. My draft rights have been traded to the Cleveland Browns for Bobby Mitchell."

There I sat, stunned. For a few moments all I could think about was Ernie Davis and Jim Brown in the same backfield. Then Davis said, "Now you've gotta promise me you won't use this on the air for another week. Mitchell still has one more game left to play for the Browns and this won't be announced until after that."

I had no desire, or need, to violate a confidence then, or at any other time. Knowing Ernie felt close enough to tell me what he knew was good enough for me.

Unfortunately, Ernie not only wasn't going to play for the Redskins, he wasn't going to play for anyone else. The following summer he fell ill and was diagnosed with leukemia. Evidence of it surfaced during a sluggish performance at an all-star game in Buffalo in June of 1962. In August, he left camp before *The Chicago Tribune* All-Star Game and underwent an examination. The prognosis was not good. We didn't know it then, but he had nine months to live.

Ernie spent most of that time in Cleveland, where he underwent treatment and watched the Browns practice and play. He never suited up.

On May 4, 1963, Davis returned to Syracuse, where he was an honorary captain at the annual Varsity-Alumni spring football game. Ernie's leukemia was in remission. He looked to be in great shape. After the game, a group of us, including Ernie and his girlfriend, went over to Walter White's, an old Syracuse tavern. There was no talk of illness. It was a joyful evening with good friends getting together — for the last time. Two weeks later, May 18, Ernie was dead.

The funeral was held in Elmira. Val Pinchbeck, assistant football coach Roy Simmons and I drove down from Syracuse. Art Modell, the Browns' owner, chartered a plane and flew the entire team in from Cleveland. The line of cars going to Woodlawn Cemetery was estimated at 450 and seemed to stretch for miles. En route, the procession paused in final tribute in front of Ernie's high school, Elmira Free Academy.

More than 35 years have passed since a day that seemed almost as long. Recalling that day brings back much of the grief, but remembering Ernie Davis brings only a smile.

I stayed in Syracuse for another year and a half. Floyd Little and Larry Csonka continued the tradition of great running backs. The reign of Brown, Davis, Nance, Mackey, Little, and Csonka constituted the golden era of Syracuse football.

A young man from Washington, D.C., named Dave Bing arrived at that time to lead the upturn in Syracuse's college basketball fortunes. Bing's backcourt partner, a kid from Lyons, N.Y., named Jim Boeheim, eventually would coach the Orangemen to the college game's elite level.

My days in Syracuse were coming to a close. The NBA's Syracuse Nats were sold to a group from Philadelphia and became the 76ers. Danny Biasone worked hard to keep the team afloat, but the market wasn't big enough to sustain 40 home games. On some nights, when the Celtics or the Knicks were in town, the Nats could have sold 14,000 tickets, but the arena barely held 7,500.

The Syracuse Chiefs won the International League title in 1964 with a team that became the nucleus of the world champion Detroit Tigers four years later. The Chiefs, managed by Frank Carswell, included Mickey Lolich, Denny McLain, Don Wert, Ray Oyler, Willie Horton, Jim Northrup and Mickey Stanley.

In late November of 1964, following the Syracuse-West Virginia football game at Morgantown, I decided to move to San Francisco. I'd been there a couple of times and, like many people, fell in love with the place. I knew there was a point in my career where I needed to find out how far I could go in sports broadcasting. At 29, having made that decision, I did what any level-headed, clear-thinking, mature individual would do. I quit my job and headed for San Francisco, unemployed.

I'd worked with several fine people at WOLF, the most important of whom was Joel Fleming. Joel had been the general manager the first few years I was there, and after he left it was never the same. He showed me it was possible for a man to be your boss and your friend at the same time, and do both well. It's a shame management schools at major universities can't teach what Joel knew. Instead, it appears these schools teach potential bosses how to speak out of both sides of their mouths, to promise things and not deliver, and to take a harmonious and smoothly functioning group of employees and destroy morale based on a need to show who's boss. Management students today should study Joel Fleming.

As I prepared for my move to the West Coast, the last words I recall anyone saying to me came from Val Pinchbeck: "If you're going to starve to death, you might as well do it in a place you want to be."

The reason God made San Francisco so beautiful was so all the locals could take credit for it.

3
HALFWAY TO THE STARS

If I hadn't been a believer in love at first sight, it would have taken me a lot longer to move to San Francisco. Almost from the minute I stepped onto the platform at the old Southern Pacific station one December night in 1962, I was hooked. I was in the mood to begin with, because I've always felt a certain romance about riding trains. I'd just arrived on the Southern Pacific Daylight, still a beauty in the days before Amtrak sterilized rail travel from coast to coast. It was dark when the train pulled in shortly after 6 p.m. on a beautifully clear night. I was young and naive. How was I to know The City had applied her best makeup, or that beautifully clear nights were as rare as World Series parades up Market Street?

I was the perfect candidate to fall in love with a city. I stayed at the Palace Hotel and dined in its spacious, wonderfully lit Garden Court. From there it was a short cable car ride to the Fairmont Hotel to see Ella Fitzgerald. Thirty-seven years later, I still get a thrill walking into the Fairmont.

Atop Nob Hill that night, I saw sparkling views of a city that made me realize no matter how much I loved Syracuse, it was never going to look like this. The few days I spent in San Francisco, I began to love everything about it, from the beauty of the city itself to the funky sounding names of the places. Telegraph Hill, Russian Hill, The Cow Palace, The Presidio and Candlestick Park. In later years, I would come to realize Candlestick Park's name was its only redeeming feature.

I came to San Francisco following a trip to Los Angeles, where I'd broadcast the Syracuse-UCLA football game. I was also covering the NBA's Syracuse Nats, who were on the West Coast for games with the Lakers and Warriors. I arrived on a Sunday night. The Nats were coming in on Monday for their game the following night at the Cow Palace.

Alex Hannum was the Nats' coach. He loved San Francisco, and in less than a year would become coach of the Warriors. I called him that Monday, and he asked me to join him and some of the players for dinner. Alex, Lee Shaffer, Paul Neumann, Dave Gambee and I ended up at Alfred's, an old San Francisco steak house.

A few days later, I met Bill King, the Warriors' broadcaster in San Francisco. Meeting Bill was the start of a relationship in which he would become a mentor, an idol and a cherished friend. Such praise will probably put the friendship in jeopardy, but the world ought to know what I think of him.

I also met an unusual man named Franklin Mieuli, although at the time I had no way of knowing how unusual he was. Franklin was part-owner of the Warriors. He'd been involved in the advertising world and got to know the Morabito brothers, who owned the 49ers. Eventually he bought 10 percent of the club for $50,000, which proved to be a better investment than, say, the Warriors' signings of Dave Lattin and Cyril Baptiste.

Whatever I went on to become in San Francisco, I owe to Franklin Mieuli. When I moved there in 1964, he made sure I met every important person in local broadcasting and hired me himself to team with Bill on Warriors games. When I arrived with no job, he said two things to me:

1. "I don't have anything for you right now, but I'll see to it that you'll never starve."

2. "If you won't hold it against me that I'm Italian, I won't hold it against you that you're Jewish."

Somehow I was left with the feeling I had made the right move.

The San Francisco I first saw in 1962, and settled in two years later, had an aura about it. It was vibrant and fun and made me feel alive. The city was living up to its reputation, not living on it, as it does today. It had a sense of humor that somehow faded over the next couple of decades, then was lost in an era of political correctness.

I loved to read the San Francisco newspapers in the '60s. There were three of them then, the *Chronicle*, the *Examiner* and the *Call-Bulletin*. The *Chronicle* and *Examiner* were morning papers before the *Ex* moved to the afternoon when it merged with the *Call*. The papers seemed to capture the spirit of the city, and columnists got out and around and wrote about the place instead of constantly acquainting us with their families and limiting their world to the perimeter of their houses.

Now it seems as if every word is written in fear of offending someone.

I don't recall exactly when San Francisco developed a foreign policy and began telling other nations how to conduct their affairs. Local government has no qualms about criticizing others, but when someone takes a verbal shot at San Francisco, *oh, my*, do "we" get touchy! Suddenly a city that used to be able to laugh at itself once in a while has become the uptight capital of the world.

It's really something to listen to people boast about how great their city is because, well, ". . .just look at all this natural beauty!"

Am I missing something here? Did these people create all this? I don't think so. More likely, it was a Higher Authority who had something to do with it. But it seems as if the reason God made San Francisco so beautiful is so the locals could take credit for it.

Some people say sports aren't in "the real world." They're right. It's better. The years I spent with ballplayers in locker rooms, on buses and airplanes showed me that people of different backgrounds can joke about, and with, each other without going to war. With ballplayers, almost anything goes when it comes to ethnic humor.

Ballplayers understand it for what it is. I guess sports really isn't the real world. It's only made up of people of different races, religions and nationalities whose ability to get along benefits them and their teams. San Francisco, on the other hand, has become a city of different races, religions, nationalities and sexual persuasions, all of whom are demanding apologies for one thing or another.

To write about San Francisco, I have to separate my private life from my professional life. In my years broadcasting games of the Giants and the Warriors, fans and media people were extremely kind to me. Very little has changed in that regard since I retired. Even people I don't owe money still recognize me.

But while all this kindness has come my way, the way San Franciscans treat each other bothers me. People are so busy protecting their rights, they trample on the rights of others. Far too many seem to hide behind the right of free speech, then threaten to sue others for exercising theirs.

The spirit of the city I fell in love with no longer seems to exist. So how do I cope? For six months of the year, I no longer have to, since my wife Carla and I bought a house in Florida. When we return to San Francisco, I try to avoid the things that get under my skin. I stopped reading columns and articles whose headlines suggest another attempt to pander to some special-interest group. I stopped reading letters on the editorial page, all of which seem to come from someone representing a group that's managed to find something about which to be offended. I don't listen to, or read, anything from anyone in local politics.

Avoiding all these things helps keep my cynicism and blood pressure at acceptable levels. I have attempted to limit my world in San Francisco only to those things I enjoy doing, and the people with whom I like to be. It's not a fail-safe system, but it's sure worth the effort.

Though I paint a dingy picture of present-day San Francisco compared to what I experienced years ago, I see some hope for the future. My hope comes from something I thought this city would never see — a new ballpark. I don't think most people have any idea what this facility will mean here. This point of view, coming from one whose life has been spent in ballparks, may seem parochial, but once Pacific Bell Park opens next year my point will become apparent.

The San Francisco Giants' new home isn't going to cure all the ills of the city. Homelessness will still be a local dilemma, although San Francisco might take a lesson from the city of Miami, which provided old Bobby Maduro Stadium as a homeless shelter. There's always a chance the same could be done with Candlestick.

What Pacific Bell Park will do for San Francisco is generate a feeling of pride, even among those who opposed it. Not everyone can be a visionary, but people certainly can delight in the way this facility will make them feel about their city. Because sports, particularly baseball, cuts across such a wide variety of ideologies, I see the citizens of the city and the greater Bay Area coming together to a much greater extent than they would without the new ballpark.

An Opera House, a City Hall, a Convention Center can be built, and there will be those who care passionately. But build a ballpark and put a halfway decent team in it, and the place gets goofy with pride. I've seen it in Baltimore. I've seen it in Cleveland and in Denver. It will be even more so in San Francisco. A new Opera House or Music Hall tends to define the affluent and the social. A new ballpark tends to define a city.

This project once was the dream of former Giants owner Bob Lurie. If anyone deserved a new stadium it was Bob, who stepped in to help rescue the franchise from a move to Canada after previous owner Horace Stoneham agreed to sell to a group in Toronto. Lurie's attempts to get a new playing field all involved public funding. Despite his own financial contribution to the project, each time it went to a ballot it was defeated.

Unfortunately, those who ran the failed campaigns never could figure out a way to keep Bob from becoming the central issue. Bob didn't help matters by suggesting, if not threatening, to move the team elsewhere.

The opposition's rallying cry was always the same: "Why should we spend our money to build a stadium for Bob Lurie?" On the surface, it was a compelling argument, but one that might have been refuted by three simple arguments:

1. The City would own the stadium, not Lurie.

2. Lurie was not going to own the team forever.

3. Giants fans were entitled to the same comforts and amenities fans in other cities were getting for their money.

Whether the advancement of those arguments would have made a difference, no one can be sure. The point is, Bob Lurie never should have been the focal point of those savage campaigns.

The closest the stadium ever came to voter approval was in November of 1989 when, following the Loma Prieta earthquake, which disrupted the Giants-A's World Series a month before, the measure lost by a only a few thousand votes. Many believe that had it not been for the quake's creating far more urgent needs, the vote would have been favorable.

In 1992, when Lurie realized he had no hope of ever getting a new ballpark in San Francisco, he turned to San Jose. Once again, he met with defeat and put the club up for sale.

Because the prevailing belief was that Lurie would never sell, no one from the Bay Area made an offer. It wasn't until he announced the sale of the Giants to a group in Tampa-St. Petersburg that all hell broke loose. Bob was now an outcast, an ingrate, a spoiled child who, just because he couldn't have his stadium, was moving the team clear across the country.

What people failed to realize was that, traditionally, ballparks *were* built by cities themselves, with taxpayer money. The only privately financed major league facility in existence at that time was Dodger Stadium in Los Angeles. Owner Walter O'Malley had been given the land at Chavez Ravine, and not much, if any, of his money went into the stadium's construction. There was a reason Union Oil had that service station inside the parking lot, as well as the only advertising inside the stadium itself for the first 30 years. There's also the belief that Union Oil was given the oil rights surrounding the stadium. What do you think O'Malley got in return for all that? How about a beautiful new ballpark?

For Bob Lurie to seek public funding for a new stadium was in keeping with standard procedure. In most cases, it remains standard procedure today. When Lurie completed his deal to sell the team to the Florida group, it shocked San Francisco and Major League Baseball, as well. Commissioner Fay Vincent had given Lurie permission to seek a buyer, expecting the club would be sold locally. National League President Bill White, warning a new stadium would have to be built, led a movement to keep the club in San Francisco.

In 1993, a group headed by Safeway CEO Peter Magowan bought the team from Lurie. Magowan, who had been on the Giants' board of directors, resigned to pursue the purchase of the franchise. Just as Horace Stoneham had been halted by Lurie from moving the team to Toronto 16 years earlier, Lurie was stopped by Magowan's group from moving the team to Tampa Bay.

Magowan knew what Lurie knew, what Bill White knew, what those in the public who had been paying attention knew: There was no way the Giants could survive in Candlestick Park, even if you sold the name for a few lousy bucks and called it "3Com Park at Candlestick Point."

Magowan knew the only way a stadium could be built was through private financing. This became the main project of the Giants' hierarchy. In 1996, with a master stroke of political maneuvering, a ballot measure passed overwhelmingly. The Giants had become experts at appealing to every disparate group in the city, and it helped clear this major hurdle. Of course, coming up with the money for this project was another story.

The cost was an estimated $250 million. Magowan told me one day if he could raise $100 million, banks would lend the rest. He hoped to raise $50 million by selling the naming rights to a large corporation. He liked my idea of approaching Ralph Lauren for the money in exchange for calling the new ballpark the Polo Grounds. It was a perfect tie-in with the history of the franchise. Peter even had grown up in New York, and as a youngster watched the Giants play at the old Polo Grounds. The only hitch was, Ralph Lauren might give you the shirt off his rack, but not $50 million dollars.

The big break came when Pacific Bell decided that Pacific Bell Park had a nice ring to it. Sometimes all it takes is for someone to jump in and let others follow. While I was disappointed Ralph Lauren wasn't the one, I was consoled by the notion that Pacific Bell's pledging $50 million dollars meant it might be the first time someone got to send a bill to the phone company.

With the stadium scheduled to be ready for opening day in 2000, Magowan managed to pull off what many, including me, thought impossible. In the four decades since the Giants moved West, too many factions have formed and have gone their separate ways. Now San Francisco has a monument to unity, not divisiveness. This venture will help restore much of the charm and good feeling that existed 37 years ago, when I arrived at the Southern Pacific station, a short walk from the future site of Pacific Bell Park.

It's not that I minded turning 50, it's just that when the season started I was only 43.

4

THE CURSE OF CANDLESTICK

I started with the Giants in 1979. I just missed the glory years, 1921-24, when they won four straight pennants. Fortunately, I wasn't in it for the glory. I had all I wanted the day I broadcast my first major league game, fulfilling a lifelong ambition. Besides, you never know how long you're going to be in this business. As my former partner David Glass commented after he'd been let go, "I always thought play-by-play was a job description. I found out it meant length of contract."

There's a certain irony in my having broadcast 16 seasons for the San Francisco Giants. I still believe they never should have left New York. The day the Giants and Dodgers pulled out of New York City and Brooklyn remains for me one of the darkest days in baseball history.

San Francisco might have been better served had it waited three more years and obtained an expansion franchise. This is no reflection on the merits of the team that came out here. There were some solid players, not to mention the young man in center field. In 1961, major league baseball expanded for the first time, placing American League teams in Los Angeles and Washington, D.C. The original Washington Senators moved to Minneapolis and became the Minnesota Twins.

All this is theoretical, of course, but if San Francisco had received an expansion franchise, it would have been embraced as the city's own, not used goods shipped west from New York. There was this prevalent feeling: "We don't care what you did in New York. You'll have to show us."

The biggest benefit to accrue from a commitment to an expansion team might have been more thought given to a new stadium. If there hadn't been a rush to satisfy Horace Stoneham's demand for a new ballpark with 10,000 parking places, Candlestick Park might not have been born.

What a wonderful thought!

If you were to write the definitive history of the San Francisco Giants, long before the mention of Willie Mays, Willie McCovey, Juan Marichal or anyone else, there would be Candlestick. There's no way of calculating exactly how damaging Candlestick Park was to the Giants franchise, and to the city, but some things are obvious. Mark Twain said, "The coldest winter I ever spent was a summer in San Francisco."

Had Twain seen a few night games at Candlestick, he might not have lived to make that statement.

San Francisco never will have great baseball weather, but Candlestick Point was probably the worst place a stadium could have been built. I won't go into all the political shenanigans concerning the construction of the park at that location, but it was a mistake that haunted the Giants from the day it opened. If the city could find a location for a new ballpark in the late '90s, with all the development that has taken place over the last four decades, it could have found a better place in the late '50s.

The Giants tried to counter the frigid nights by playing more day games. While the sun contributed to a more pleasing aesthetic, it did little to cut down the wind. In fact, the reason the sun shone there many days was that the heavy winds blew the morning fog away. Baseball in the daytime was far more enjoyable for many of us, but as the late afternoon winds increased, it made for some tough conditions.

While it's true the wind also blows at Chicago's Wrigley Field, where would you rather watch a game? The point is, Candlestick has no redeeming features. In addition to the wind, the fog and the cold, it's not even a nice park to look at.

When I started broadcasting there, I used to keep the windows open. It was the macho thing in play-by-play. Originally it was done to pick up crowd noise in the background, before someone got the idea to hang a crowd mike outside. Broadcasters also felt they were more a part of the game if they worked with the windows open.

I felt that way myself when I did minor league baseball in the good old summertime in places such as Syracuse and Honolulu. I maintained the tradition at Candlestick, and I hated it. The cold was one thing. What's an icicle or two hanging from your nose? But I felt like a guy trying to recover a fumble as I pounced on papers and other material flying across the booth. It was Hurricane Harney every night. Harney was the construction mogul who owned the land at Candlestick Point and made a nice deal with the city for the rights to build the stadium. On many nights, you can hear an eerie laugh out there. Some believe he still haunts the place.

It was 1982, and I was in my fourth season broadcasting games with that damn window open. The Giants were playing the Dodgers, and I was fighting my usual losing battle with the elements when I happened to glance to my right. A couple of booths over, there sat Vin Scully, unruffled, unflustered and with the window closed. At once it dawned on me: Here was yet another reason he was going to the Hall of Fame and I was destined to be just another broadcaster. From that moment on, I decided if a closed window at Candlestick was good enough for Vin, it was good enough for Hank.

More important than what that place did to me, and to the fans, was its effect on the players. After all, the fans had a choice. They could have stayed home. There is no doubt in my mind that playing in Candlestick Park adversely affected the performance of Giant players over a period. I've heard all the arguments about how other teams have to play there, too, but you can put up with it when you make only two visits a season. It's far different when you're there for 81 games.

In recent years the team has taken the approach, "Let's make the ballpark work for us." That's nice public relations. But privately, many times, I've heard Giant players, about to embark on a road trip, talk about how nice it was going to be to get some "real baseball weather."

Ballplayers have openly admitted to me that standing out there in the cold and wind affected their concentration. A multimillion-dollar salary doesn't make a player any less human. Mother Nature doesn't know, or care, how much these guys make. Nor does she care when they're at the plate and she's blowing dirt in their eyes.

There are just too many times I have seen players step out of the batter's box at "The 'Stick" to rub their eyes. What a reassuring feeling it must be for that batter to get back in there, hoping his vision has cleared, and see a pitcher getting ready to throw a ball more than 90 miles per hour.

San Francisco fans can only wonder how many other players might have signed with the Giants as free agents but chose another team. In the late '70s and early '80s, both Steve Garvey and Rollie Fingers told me offers from the Giants were comparable to what they received elsewhere. And elsewhere is where they ended up.

The fact remains, the vast majority of decent players the Giants have had in the free-agent era have either been developed in their farm system, or traded for. The major exception to that was Barry Bonds, for whom the money elsewhere might not have been comparable. What made it unique for Bonds was the opportunity to play in the park where he grew up, and in the outfield where both his dad and Willie Mays had played.

Some will argue conditions at Seals Stadium, where the Giants first played in San Francisco, were no better than Candlestick. Perhaps, but it's important to remember Seals Stadium was used as a matter of convenience. It was there, and the Giants had no choice but to play in it until a new and presumably better park was built. I guess it doesn't pay to presume anything.

Can I guarantee the weather at the new Pacific Bell Park will be better? I will, if Giants fans will guarantee me there won't be another 7.1 earthquake in the next 10 years. What I'm willing to bet is it can't be any worse and, in all likelihood, will be better. In addition, it will be far more aesthetically pleasing and far more comfortable, something Candlestick never was, even when it opened.

Here's an ironic twist: The city of San Francisco paid for the construction of Candlestick Park and received virtually nothing in the way of ancillary benefits from baseball. Sure, the city collected rent, some tax money on tickets and other minor benefits. But business in the city got nothing. It has been shown over the years the bulk of the Giants' attendance comes from south of the city.

The park itself is in the southernmost section of the city. If you watch the traffic pattern after the games, you'll see those people turn around and go south again. They don't go into San Francisco for dinner or spend money in other parts of the city. Those in the crowd who don't live south of Candlestick are so frustrated by the time they get out of the parking lot, they just want to go home. Tourists and conventioneers never flocked to Candlestick Park, and business people found it just too inconvenient to go out there for a couple of hours, then back to the office. Besides, after a couple of hours the game would only be in the fifth inning.

It's going to take private investors to do for the city what the city couldn't do for itself, thus benefitting San Francisco both financially and otherwise. The new ballpark's location, close to downtown and accessible to public transportation, will encourage fans to stay in San Francisco after a game. Probably the biggest concerns about the new stadium are parking and traffic. It's interesting that with plenty of parking at Candlestick, the traffic congestion getting out of there is legendary. One hopes there's a lesson to be learned: It might not be a good idea to have thousands of cars leaving from the same place at the same time.

Pacific Bell Park will have limited parking in close proximity. Additional parking areas may be found in time, but those areas won't be adjacent to the stadium. This is good. It means fans may have to walk a few blocks to get to their cars, and I'm told walking is healthy. It also means the cars won't all be leaving from the same place, which is even healthier. Readers in Baltimore, Cleveland and Denver will know exactly what I am talking about.

The biggest benefit will be realized by those who don't bring their cars at all. Caltrain will serve people to the south of the city (Bay Area denizens refer to it as the Peninsula). Bay Area Rapid Transit and ferryboats will take care of fans from the East Bay cities like Oakland, Berkeley and Hayward. And San Francisco locations west of the ballpark will be handled mainly by Muni railway. Ferries and buses from Marin County and other counties to the north will make the hassle of driving to the ballpark a thing of the past. The new park sits right on edge of the San Francisco Bay, making it arguably the most scenic park in the majors. And it is an easy 15-minute walk from the Financial District in the heart of downtown San Francisco.

In all the years I was with the Giants, the times I most felt I was in the major leagues came when I walked into other stadiums (Houston excepted). Now, as a fan, I'll finally get that feeling in San Francisco when I walk into Pacific Bell Park.

When I reported to the Giants' spring training camp at Casa Grande, Arizona in 1979, the first person to greet me was equipment manager Eddie Logan. Eddie's father had held the same job with the Giants in the 1920s, and young Eddie grew up in the clubhouse. One day in 1926, manager John McGraw gave young Logan a couple of nickels for the subway and told him to go down to Penn Station and meet this young kid the Giants were bringing up. The young kid was Mel Ott.

Eddie made sure I got settled at Casa Grande and then gave me some advice: "Don't go walking out in deep right field. There are snakes out there."

I was certain of two things: I wasn't going to walk out in deep right field, and whoever was playing right field was going to play shallow.

Casa Grande was located off Interstate 10 between Phoenix and Tucson and was an ideal location — for testing atomic bombs. No one would have known. During my two-week stay, I soon realized that eating an early dinner was important because the Dairy Queen closed at 9 p.m.

With few distractions, I was able to concentrate on baseball. Joe Altobelli was the manager. I had known him as a player at Rochester in the International League. Joe and I had some things in common. We were born in Detroit, lived in

Rochester and now worked in San Francisco. He had been named Manager of the Year in the National League in 1978, which gave him a nice award to look at when he was fired less than a year later. It's amazing how you can lose your abilities so quickly and then regain them, as he must have when he managed Baltimore to a World Series title in 1983.

Most of my evenings in Casa Grande were spent sitting around talking baseball with Hank Sauer, Jim Davenport, Salty Parker, Wendell Kim, John Van Ornum and Tom Haller. I used to watch Sauer play with the Syracuse Chiefs in 1947. He hit 50 home runs that year, displaying the power that would make him the National League's Most Valuable Player five years later.

Davenport and Haller had been on the Giants' pennant winner in 1962, and Salty Parker was a longtime coach. John Van Ornum had been a minor league player and manager. He became a coach with the Giants and later an advance scout. Somewhere along the line, John's parents must have taught him always to tell the truth, something too many higher-ups in baseball don't want to hear. This resulted in John's making several career moves. My day was always a little brighter when I ran into John, or "VO" as we called him.

Wendell Kim was one of the hardest working guys I'd ever seen in baseball. Like VO, Wendell also played and managed at every minor league level before joining the Giants in 1989 as a coach. He knew early in life his lack of size meant he would have to out-perform and out-hustle everyone else to be noticed. Wendell's departure from the Giants in 1996 resulted from a political tug of war between the front office and manager Dusty Baker. Only one side wins those. Wendell and pitching coach Dick Pole were sacrificed.

My first three years with the Giants seemed to be characterized by low expectations. I remember late one season being told by someone upstairs, "If we can win these last five games, we could finish third."

My heart raced with excitement at the prospect.

It was not until Frank Robinson, Joe Morgan and Reggie Smith came on board in the early '80s that things got better. These three never coveted .500 as a goal. They were used to better things. There were more than a dozen pennants and world championships spread among them, and they provided an attitude adjustment the team sorely needed.

The 1982 Giants responded by carrying the Western Division race down to the final weekend in a contest with the Braves and Dodgers. The Braves beat up on the Padres, while the Dodgers and Giants took turns eliminating each other. Morgan's seventh-inning home run on the final day dealt the Dodgers a death blow.

The Polo Grounds. My favorite ballpark.

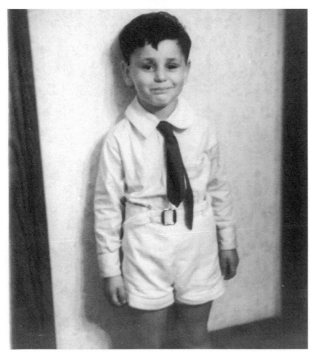

When I had hair, 1940.

With Jerry
Hoffman (right),
NCAA basket-
ball—Syracuse vs.
North Carolina at
The Palestra in
Philadephia, 1957.

Wilt must be standing on a chair.

"Oh say can you see. . ."

"Bill, you just called that referee a what?"

You can see the fans are really behind me.

We all have to start somewhere. A supermarket opening in Vineland, N.J., 1958.

One of us sent copies of this picture to his friends.

Doug and Kellie. Two reasons I enjoy life.

My model railroad. I made the trains run on time.

Johannesburg to Capetown, South Africa, with Carla on the Blue Train, 1982.

Wading ashore at Leyte Gulf, the Philippines, D-Day plus 28 years.

How come General MacArthur looked so great doing this and I was out of breath?

A really ugly American.

One of the world's greatest railroad stations. Kuala Lumpur, Malaysia, 1993.

With my boyhood idol, Hank Greenberg, at the 1984 All-Star Game at Candlestick Park.

The last year I could button my jacket was 1982.

Any momentum from the '82 season was quickly extinguished a few days later when general manager Tom Haller won a power struggle with Robinson and traded Morgan to the Phillies. It's funny how pennants seemed to follow Morgan around. The Phillies went to the World Series in '83.

Reggie Smith left to play in Japan. Robinson continued as manager, with poor ballclubs, until he was replaced in August, 1984. I enjoyed working with Frank. He was a stand-up guy who'd give an honest answer. Some people were intimidated by him, but he enjoyed give-and-take.

One night after a game, I said to him, "This game is tough enough to broadcast as it is without trying to figure out what crazy move you just made." Frank leaned back in his chair and laughed. Robinson might have been a better manager if he'd spent more time on the field before games working with his players. At times he seemed trapped in his office, and maybe he indulged the media more than he should. Perhaps he didn't want to create the appearance of usurping the authority of his coaching staff by instructing players before games. This was unfortunate because many of the players were in awe of his Hall of Fame accomplishments.

When you hit 586 home runs, with 2,943 hits and 1,812 runs batted in, players tend to listen when you have something to say. The one player who seemed to benefit most from Frank was Jeffrey Leonard, who became much more of an offensive threat when the manager taught him how to pull the ball.

In Frank's heyday with the Baltimore Orioles, he was not the only Robinson on the club. He shared his last name with Hall of Fame third baseman Brooks Robinson. The Orioles wore their names on the backs of their jerseys, so there was F. Robinson and B. Robinson. Later, with the Dodgers, Angels and Indians, he was the only Robinson on the team.

In 1984, Frank was starting his third full season as the Giants' skipper. A young pitcher named Jeff Robinson surprised everyone by making the club. Once again Frank became F. Robinson, something that did not amuse him. It was one thing to be "F" to Brooks Robinson's "B," but quite another to rookie Jeff Robinson's "J." Ironically, when Frank was replaced as manager it was young Jeff who asked, "Does this mean I can drop the 'J' from my uniform?"

When the Giants, Dodgers and Braves were in their terrific race for the division title in 1982, the Giants dropped a 4-0 game to L.A. at Candlestick on Friday night of the final weekend. It hurt. The game was scoreless after six innings, with Fred Breining pitching for the Giants. In the top of the seventh, the Dodgers loaded the bases with Rick Monday coming up. Breining had struck out Monday his last time up. Frank Robinson had the hard-throwing Al Holland warming up in the bullpen. Breining was a right-hander and Monday a left-handed hitter. Monday hit a grand slam, and that was the ball game.

Afterward there was a lot of second-guessing about Robinson's decision to stay with Breining, much of it coming from the general manager. The Giants were soundly beaten on Saturday, eliminating them from the race. The grumbling from Friday's loss continued.

The final game was on Sunday, October 3, a famous date in Giants history. On October 3, 1951, Bobby Thomson hit his famous "Shot Heard 'Round the World" at the Polo Grounds to beat the Brooklyn Dodgers in a playoff for the pennant. Eleven years later, on October 3, the now San Francisco Giants won another pennant playoff from the Dodgers in Los Angeles.

October 3 also had meaning for the Greenwald family. It was our son Douglas' birthday. On this particular day he was turning eight, and Giants clubhouse man Mike Murphy invited him to be a bat boy.

It was about an hour before game time and in the Giants clubhouse were owner Bob Lurie, team vice president Corey Busch and Frank Robinson. Doug was decked out in his official Giant uniform as he and I walked over to them. The beleaguered and second-guessed Robinson looked at Doug and said, "Well, aren't you going to get on me, too, about Friday night, like everybody else?"

Doug looked at Frank and replied, "Well, my dad said . . ."

At that moment my career flashed in front of me. Bob Lurie and Corey Busch stood there with their mouths open, and Frank had the look of a man expecting terrible news. The pennant race had not produced as much tension.

". . . that if you brought in Holland to face Rick Monday, Lasorda would have sent up Pedro Guerrero to pinch hit. So Holland wouldn't have faced Monday anyway."

I felt as if we had just won the pennant. I put my arms around Doug and said, "Anything you want, son, it's yours. Anything you want!"

Robinson laughed. Color returned to the faces of Lurie and Busch, and my heart left my mouth and returned to its rightful place.

To make the day even more memorable, Joe Morgan's homer, before more than 50,000 fans, eliminated the Dodgers and gave the Giants another October 3 to savor.

The Giants went on to lose 96 games in the 1984 season, costing Robinson his job. The following winter, Jim Davenport was named manager. Davvy was one of the most popular men who ever wore the Giants uniform. At a press conference announcing his hiring he said, "I'll tell you one thing: There's no way we're gonna lose 96 games this year."

He was right. They lost 100. It was the first time in the history of the franchise, dating back to 1883, that had happened. The Giants reached the century mark on the final day of the season, by which time Davenport had been replaced by Roger Craig.

Truth is, Davvy never had a chance. In the off-season the Giants traded Jack Clark, one of their best hitters, to St. Louis. Jack was an outspoken young man who felt management wasn't committed enough to winning. His displeasure often manifested itself in a lack of intensity, which didn't go over well with his team-mates or the front office

In return for Clark, the Giants obtained four players, one of whom went through the following season with three different names. When he joined the Giants he was Jose Gonzalez, but because the Dodgers already had a Jose Gonzalez, it was announced he had become Uribe Gonzalez. A few days later he became Jose Uribe. While most people thought this was strange, I understood what he was doing.

Had I known what was in store for the 1985 season, I'd have changed my name a few times too. While the Giants were averaging about four hits a game, Davenport kept insisting, "If there's one thing I know for sure, we're gonna hit." The facts proved otherwise. The Giants' .301 on-base percentage was their lowest in 29 years, and their .233 team batting average was, and still is, their lowest since 1900.

In June I marked my 50th birthday. When a person reaches the half-century mark, it usually gives him pause for reflection. It's not that I minded turning 50, it's just that when the season started I was only 43.

While the '85 Giants were trailing in almost every category, their fans were leading the league in apathy. On September 3 at a Giants-Phillies game, I was walking through the press box in the seventh inning when it was announced, "Here's today's attendance. One thousand, six hundred and thirty-two. Sixteen thirty-two."

I said, "Sixteen thirty-two! That's not a crowd. That's my shirt size."

Bob Lurie realized he had to do something. In September he hired Al Rosen as general manager and Roger Craig as field manager. Of all the moves Bob made as owner, these were his best. Once again, here were two men who knew what it was like to win.

Rosen was the American League's Most Valuable Player in 1953 with the Cleveland Indians, and the following year starred on their pennant-winning team, which set a league record with 111 victories (later surpassed by the Yankees, who won 114 in 1998). Craig pitched for World Series winners in Brooklyn and Los

Angeles and was pitching coach for the world champion Detroit Tigers in 1984.

These two were used to better things, and they were able to infuse their ball-club with a winning attitude. In this regard they were bolstered in 1986 by the emergence of rookies Will Clark and Robby Thompson. Veteran pitcher Mike Krukow won 20 games, and the Giants improved their record by 21 games from the previous season. This set the stage for two division titles and a pennant in the first four seasons under Rosen and Craig.

Rosen was a hard-driving man who literally had to fight his way to the major leagues as a player. Here was someone who survived at Okinawa in World War II, only to end up battling anti-Semitism at home in the minor leagues. Al proved equally adept with his fists and bat and went on to an All-Star career with the Indians.

Away from the ballpark, the Giants' GM was a kindly man who could have been anyone's uncle or grandfather. When it came to baseball matters, however, Al's intensity left no one surprised he'd undergone heart bypass surgery. At one time he'd also worked for George Steinbrenner, which might explain a few things. Giants people found it was not a good idea to sit next to Rosen during a game unless you brought earplugs and body armor. Without such protection, you were bound to come away with bruises and an expanded vocabulary. It had been many years since Al wore a uniform, but he was still a competitor.

Roger Craig was just what the Giants needed. Spirits were lower than their .233 team batting average when Craig took over in September of '85. With less than three weeks left in the season, he had them counting the days until the next spring training, convinced they'd win a title. He was one year off.

Roger had seen both ends of the spectrum as a major league pitcher, from Dodger World Series crowns in 1955 and '59 to the expansion Mets of 1962 and '63. He also managed the hapless San Diego Padres in the late '70s, and later served as Sparky Anderson's pitching coach with the great World Series champion Tiger club of '84.

Sparky believed every pitcher he had was the next Cy Young and every hitter the next Babe Ruth. It's likely that sitting next to Sparky in the dugout all season, Roger absorbed some of that positive approach. His first night on the job as the Giants' manager, he marched the entire pitching staff down to the bullpen before the game and began teaching them the split-finger fastball.

Roger and I spent several seasons doing a manager's show on radio, a practice I continued later with Dusty Baker. I loved the fact Roger played with and against so many great players because it gave us much to draw upon. It was easy enough to talk about the Giants when things were going well, and even when they lost a tough game the night before.

It's not so easy when you've lost six or seven in a row. I knew I could always get a smile and a story out of Roger by mentioning, say, Casey Stengel, or some great moment he had witnessed. I wasn't there to put him on the spot. It was, after all, "The Roger Craig Show," not "The Hank Greenwald Show."

One night the Giants were playing the Braves at Candlestick, and I was on television. It was one of those games that just seemed to drag on and on, with numerous personnel changes, and when you looked up it was still only the sixth or seventh inning.

We were away for a commercial, and out of frustration I said, "This is the worst managed game I've ever seen."

Obviously it wasn't intended to go out over the air and, for the most part, it didn't. However, viewers who had satellite dishes could get the raw feed and hear the announcers talking between innings. A great many of my colleagues have been stung as I was about to be.

Somewhere back in North Carolina, Roger Craig's brother was watching the game on his dish. He called the skipper afterward and told him what I'd said. The next day, before we did "The Roger Craig Show," he said to me: "Close the door. I want to talk to you."

Very calmly, and like the gentleman he is, he said, "My brother was watching the game last night and I understand you were criticizing my managing."

I admitted it, although I sputtered some weak-kneed explanation that my comment hadn't mentioned anyone specifically. If I could have found a hole to crawl into right then, I'd have been there.

Roger continued, "I thought you and I were good enough friends you could say something like that to my face. Next time you want to question something, just ask me. Now, let's go do that show."

I was embarrassed and afraid our relationship would never be the same. If my remark the night before changed the way Roger felt about me — and I wouldn't have blamed him if it had — he never showed it. I liked Roger and cared enough about him that I urged him to quit when it became apparent managing was affecting his health. Things weren't going well on the field in 1991 and '92. Roger underwent an angioplasty and was out several days. Naturally his wife, Carolyn, was concerned and wanted him to think about stepping down.

Understandably, Roger didn't want to go out on a losing note. I tried to point out that most people felt losing your life was too steep a price to pay for losing some ball games. Every spring, Roger would come into camp the happiest guy you ever saw, convinced the Giants were going to win another pennant. Sadly, by

August he was looking more and more like Lyndon Johnson when the former president realized the U.S. wasn't going to win in Vietnam.

I wanted Roger to get out while he still had good memories, rather than carry with him recollections of the last couple of seasons. It was advice I would later follow myself. The decision was made for Roger when the Magowan group bought the club from Bob Lurie and wanted their own people in place. It was a move that made Roger look 10 years younger when he paid a visit to the clubhouse in San Diego the following year.

In 1986, Craig's first full season as manager, the Giants' 21-game improvement over the '85 debacle wasn't enough to catch the Houston Astros, who won the division. But it did promise better times ahead. The Astros clinched the Western Division title in the Astrodome when Mike Scott, to whom Roger had taught the split-finger fastball, threw a no-hitter against the Giants. As the Astros were celebrating on the field, Roger ordered his team to remain in the dugout and watch.

"I want you to see this and know what it looks like," he said, "because next year that's what you're gonna be doing."

He was right, but I wasn't there to see it.

The thrill for me was not walking into Yankee Stadium each day. It was walking out of Yankee Stadium and finding my car was still there.

5

TAKE THE "A" TRAIN

J im Haviland had been a United States Marine. When I met him he'd recently concluded a negotiation with George Steinbrenner. Whether the former was good training for the latter — or vice-versa — is open to debate. Jim was general manager of WABC Radio in New York. He had agreed to pay Steinbrenner $30 million for five years for the broadcast rights to Yankees games, beginning in 1987. It was the largest radio contract ever signed by a major league ballclub.

On a cold, gray Friday morning in December of 1986, I made my way along Sixth Avenue to the ABC building. The wind was whipping through the streets with a ferocity that made me feel I was back at Candlestick Park. December in New York, June in San Francisco. What's the difference?

I was looking for work. My appointment with Jim Haviland was at 9 a.m. Following the 1986 season, I'd decided to leave KNBR in San Francisco, where I'd called the Giants' games for the previous eight years. The reasons for my leaving had nothing to do with the Giants or current KNBR management.

Haviland's stint in the Marines made him an early riser. That, combined with a commute from Ridgewood, New Jersey, made for an arrival at the office that often beat the sunrise. He had been busy long before I showed up for our interview.

"Your agent called me an hour ago," Haviland said as he ushered me in.

He was referring to Jeff Moorad, a partner of Leigh Steinberg. Moorad was responsible for a great deal of my sanity.

"Jeff and I were talking and I suddenly realized he was calling me from California," Haviland said. "It's five in the morning out there. I was really impressed."

I thought, "That's nice, but you'd better be impressed with me or it's going to be a long winter."

Eventually we got around to discussing the broadcasting job. He said he was looking for a veteran play-by-play guy and a former player. I knew I wasn't a former player. I also knew I was about to become a former play-by-play guy if I didn't get this job.

Jim was an easy person to talk to. Despite my situation, I felt comfortable in his office. When the time came for me to make my move, I looked at him and said, "I'm not sure which of us has more at stake here. I'm 51 years old and looking for work, and you've just committed $30 million and better come up with somebody good."

A small but rapidly expanding smile crossed Haviland's face. I may have needed him more than he needed me, but we both knew it was a close call.

As our meeting was ending, Jim said, "If Jeff and I can work things out, I think we have a deal."

I took this as a hopeful sign.

Before leaving, I asked Jim whom he was considering for the other job in the booth, the former player.

"I'm going to be meeting shortly with Tommy Hutton," he said.

It was the second-best news I'd heard that morning.

I told Jim, "Whether you hire me or not, hire him."

I'd known Tommy for some time from the National League and had watched him prepare for broadcasting well before retiring. In his last couple of seasons with the Montreal Expos, Tommy had gone around to other broadcasters and asked questions. How do you prepare for games? How do you set up your score sheet? How do you prepare for interviews?

Tommy Hutton clearly was not going to be another ballplayer stepping into a broadcasting job by divine right. Tommy and I spent two seasons announcing Yankees games on radio. I wish it had been longer.

The following March, I reported to the Yankees' spring training camp in Fort Lauderdale, Florida. After eight seasons in Arizona, it was nice to see water. Besides, I hated cactus. It always looked as if it was coming out of the ground for the sole purpose of giving me the finger. Soon enough, driving around New York City, I'd see the real thing.

There's always an uneasy feeling when you walk into a place where you don't know anyone. To my surprise, when I entered the Yankee clubhouse, someone yelled, "Hey, it's Hank Greenwald! I used to watch you when you did the Warriors' games on TV."

It was Dave Righetti, the Yankee reliever, who had grown up in San Jose and had watched my Warrior telecasts during the Rick Barry-Nate Thurmond period in the late '60s and early '70s. When Righetti called my name, several other Yankees sitting in front of their lockers looked up and nodded as if to say, "If Rags knows who this guy is, he must be okay."

I was glad he had a good memory. He had no idea how much easier he made my life that day.

The exhibition schedule hadn't begun, so I watched the team's drills, trying to look as if I thought they were important. Ground ball to the right side, pitcher covers first. You just can't get enough of those things.

My main interest was trying to figure out who everybody was. The Yankees had more coaches in camp than most teams had players. They also had more players than the Costa Rican army. So what if they used duplicate numbers? No one said this would be easy. Each day, the Yankees printed a roster with more names and numbers than the phone book in Vineland, New Jersey, where I had my first job. It reminded me more of a football camp than baseball. This, I later learned, was no coincidence.

George Steinbrenner fancied himself a football coach and loved to surround himself with football people. He once named Lou Saban, the former head coach of the Boston Patriots, Denver Broncos and Buffalo Bills, as the Yankees' president. At spring training, he had former Heisman Trophy winner Howard "Hopalong" Cassady as a conditioning coach. George himself had been an assistant coach at Purdue and Northwestern.

Eventually the weeding-out process began. One battalion of players was sent to the minor league camp. Another must have returned to army duty in Costa Rica.

One day while Tommy Hutton and I were at the ballpark in Lauderdale, the word came down: The Boss wants to see you.

Our first meeting with Steinbrenner was notable because he wasn't wearing a navy blazer, and got my name right.

Throughout the two seasons I was with the Yankees, I had the distinct impression George really didn't know who I was. The reason I say this is I know my parents didn't name me "Big Guy." George gave me the name one day at spring training. I was standing with Harvey Greene, the Yankees' media relations director. George walked by and greeted us:

"Hi, Harvey. Hi, Big Guy."

Harvey realized immediately I had the better of the deal. George's not knowing who I was was something Harvey could only pray would happen to him.

When Tommy and I met with The Boss that day, we talked about broadcasting. To put it more accurately, we listened. Sitting at his desk in the air-conditioned trailer that housed the Yankees' spring-training offices, George was in a reflective mood.

"Your station paid me a lot of money for these broadcasts so I'm out of it now," he said. "It's all yours. If we play lousy you should say it. If the manager makes a dumb move you should say it. If we make a trade you don't think is good you should say it."

Despite all the things we "should say," Tommy and I realized the best thing we could do at that moment was to say nothing.

The Boss did the talking: "I've had too many broadcasters around here who think everything we do out there on the field is great. I pay players a lot of money and they screw up a lot. I want somebody who won't be afraid to say it."

When Tommy and I left the office, we regretted there were no witnesses. Somehow we had the feeling we were more likely to remember that speech than Steinbrenner was.

Since the mid-1970s, I'd had this theory that Billy Martin always was the Yankee manager and everyone else was interim. Bob Lemon, Yogi Berra and Lou Piniella all simply were holding down the fort until Billy was brought back, which was often.

Piniella's first season as Yankee manager was 1987. Lou was an easy guy to like. He had a way of putting you at ease. This was quite an accomplishment for someone who smoked one cigarette after another, who constantly pushed back a lock of hair with his pinky, and who kept putting one foot in back of the other.

Lou was a member of the 300-300 club. He hit .300 and had blood pressure just as high. The source of that high blood pressure was never far away.

There's no way you can manage the Yankees without developing nervous characteristics. Lou and I were sitting in the dugout at Fort Lauderdale after the Yankees had lost six straight exhibition games. Normally I pay no attention to spring training records, but knowing how Steinbrenner emphasized winning, I asked Piniella if he was concerned.

"No, I'm not concerned," he replied. "I'm not concerned. I'm not concerned. I'm really not concerned. If there's one thing I'm not, it's concerned."

I gathered from this he wasn't concerned. The problem was me. I was concerned about Lou.

Hovering over the Yankees at all times was the specter of George Steinbrenner. Tommy Hutton called it "The George Factor." It affected everything: the roster, travel, the coaching staff, office morale. Name it, George's hand was securely wrapped around it.

To be fair, Steinbrenner never bothered Tommy and me, at least as far as we knew. I suspect, though, he'd have liked it better if we never gave a National League score, especially the Mets'. Two of the surest ways to enrage The Boss were (1) mention the Mets and (2) mention Dave Winfield.

Dave was tall, good-looking, affable and had a great smile. He was building a Hall of Fame career, and fans loved him. In short, he was everything George was not. Worse yet, George was paying him a lot of money. In return, this gave George the right to blame Winfield for everything from failure to win the pennant each year to crop failure in Somalia.

One day when we were in Kansas City, The Boss issued an order that every negative statistic on Winfield be included in the press notes. Batting average with men on base, number of men left on base, batting average from the seventh inning on, and so on. (It was no wonder George went through media relations people the way he went through managers. Harvey Greene, like many before him, eventually moved on to better things.) Knowing the press notes had been distributed, George settled back to watch the game on television from his home in Tampa. By the fifth inning, Winfield had two home runs and five runs batted in.

George tried to cut his losses. He called Harvey in the press box, hoping he hadn't passed out those statistics. It was too late, of course; all the media knew who was behind them.

To get to our broadcast booth at Yankee Stadium, Tommy and I had to walk through the team's offices. We always could tell immediately if George was in town. Fear is hard to hide on the faces of employees, and the gloom was more oppressive than New York humidity on an August night.

Several years ago, the movie "White Men Can't Jump" came out, starring Woody Harrelson and Wesley Snipes as a couple of basketball hustlers. The title reminded me of my two years in New York. Anyone who believes white men can't jump has never been in the New York Yankees' office when George Steinbrenner walks in.

Former baseball commissioner Peter Ueberroth said of Steinbrenner, "He can be very demeaning to people. He tends to be abusive to employees at times."

It wasn't the managers or general managers he fired you felt sorry for. He usually found something else for them, and they still were well paid. It was the lower-level employees you felt for. There's no network in baseball for secretaries, as there is for managers. I suspect much of the humidity around Yankee Stadium came from tears shed in the office. As one former employee put it, "When you have all the money you're ever going to need, what else do you have to do? So you wake up each morning and say to yourself, 'Whose balls can I break today?'"

There are people who will swear George Steinbrenner is the kindest, most generous man in the world. It's easy to understand why. A story appears in a New York paper about a police officer killed in the line of duty. George sits down and writes a check that will put the officer's kids through college. A heartwarming gesture, no question. Yet it's a gesture that serves another purpose. It enables Steinbrenner to buy back his conscience, and he can continue to terrorize his employees free of guilt.

If this seems a harsh assessment of the owner of the Yankees, so be it. It's one thing to be a boss. It's another to be a bully.

I learned all I needed to know about George one day as he stood in our booth before a game. He looked down and pointed to Donald Trump, sitting in a box next to the Yankee dugout. George turned to me and said, "There's the kind of guy who helped make this country great."

Hmmm. George Washington, Thomas Jefferson, Abraham Lincoln, Donald Trump. Makes sense to me.

Broadcasting New York Yankees games meant working alongside Phil Rizzuto and Bill White. They did the telecasts on Channel 11, WPIX. These were two men of the highest character. They'd been doing both radio and TV before Tommy and I were hired, and it could have been uncomfortable for us had Scooter and Bill been any less than the gentlemen they were.

I'll never forget listening to Rizzuto right after Casey Stengel abruptly ended Phil's playing career in August, 1956, and outrighted him to the broadcast booth. It was only a few days after joining Mel Allen that, in the middle of Mel's play-by-play, Phil blurted, "OH MY GOD! He's going to steal home on the next pitch!"

Because the Yankees hadn't traded Rizzuto to another team, Stengel hadn't bothered to change his signs. Right on cue, the Yankee runner broke for the plate, and Rizzuto's broadcasting career was off and running. It didn't stop for another 40 years.

I first saw Bill White at the Polo Grounds when he came up as a first baseman with the New York Giants in 1956. I was still in college, and White's build and the way he carried himself reminded me of my college classmate Jim Brown. Bill had a successful major league career with the Giants, Cardinals and Phillies, then became an excellent broadcaster. When you listened to Bill White, you felt you knew more about baseball than you did the day before. Bill went on to become President of the National League, a post for which he was greatly overqualified.

It's customary for broadcasters to be referred to as "voice of the (fill in the team)." For years Mel Allen was the voice of the Yankees, and to me he always would be. Mel no longer was doing Yankee broadcasts during my two seasons there. But he was there every day, broadcasting highlights on the big screen at Yankee Stadium as host of the popular TV show *This Week in Baseball.*

As a high school kid in Rochester and later at college in Syracuse, I used to picture myself as Mel Allen, sitting in the booth at Yankee Stadium. Now I was there, and Mel Allen was there. Whenever we saw each other we would visit. In this business it's not often you allow yourself moments of reverie, but standing there with Mel deserved such a moment. Given my feeling for Mel, one thing was difficult for me. I hated it when people introduced me as "the voice of the Yankees." That title should have been retired when Mel Allen did his last Yankees broadcast. There was only one "voice of the Yankees," and it wasn't me.

Mel was part of the roll call of great Yankees names people thought of every time they walked into the Stadium. There was Babe Ruth, Lou Gehrig, Joe DiMaggio, Mickey Mantle, Yogi Berra and on and on. One reason it was easy to broadcast the games was that the club had so much history.

I don't think Yankee fans ever got enough of it. And during my time, 1987-88, that was about all we had to talk about. The club hadn't won anything since 1981 and wouldn't until 1996, long after I returned to the Giants. Every night, on that big screen in center field, there was Ruth hitting another homer, DiMaggio hitting in his 56th straight game, Gehrig saying, "Today, today, today. . . "

Yankees history was everywhere, and it was only right to perpetuate it. First and foremost when you think about the Yankees, you think about Babe Ruth. Sorry, George. It doesn't matter that some of Ruth's records have been surpassed. He still reigns as the dominant baseball figure of the 20th century. The Babe spent five seasons in the American League before he started hitting home runs in earnest. This means from 1919 through 1935 he averaged 41.4 a season. That includes his final year, when he played only through May and finished with just six.

Millions who pour into Yankee Stadium are awestruck as they look out at that field where so many of the great ones played. It is a tremendous thrill. But the thrill for me was not walking into Yankee Stadium each day. It was walking out of Yankee Stadium and finding my car was still there.

Make no mistake, I love New York and have from the first time I went there in

1944. Having said that, I still believe New York is a tough town. I didn't realize how tough a place it was until I was moving there. We were flying over New York harbor when I looked down and saw the Statue of Liberty with both hands in the air. That's a tough town.

But I loved working there. New York fans really care about baseball, and you love to broadcast to fans who care that much. It pumps you up. Fans in every city usually know all there is to know about their own team. In New York, they know all there is to know about every team. It keeps you on your toes.

Tough town or not, the fans were good to me. I'd been on the air only a few weeks, and they already were mentioning me in the same breath with Mel Allen and Red Barber. So what if they were saying, "Well, he's certainly no Mel Allen or Red Barber."

Practically the first people I met when I joined the Yankees at spring training in 1987 were the media people covering the ballclub. In New York, that's a lot of people. Unfortunately there were no rosters with their names printed each day, and they didn't wear numbers on their backs. Getting to know them proved easy enough, though, and they made a couple of rookies from the other league feel welcome.

While Tommy was commuting from his home in Palm Beach Gardens each day, I was on my own at dinnertime. I recall one night walking alone into Gibby's, a steak house in Fort Lauderdale. A group of writers was about to have dinner and spotted me as I came in. Marty Noble of *Newsday* came over and invited me to join them.

That set the stage for what became a warm relationship over the next two seasons. There was rarely a get-together for dinner on the road to which Tommy and I were not invited. It struck me as being different from my days with the Giants, where the newspaper people seemed to go in one group and the broadcasters another.

Though I no longer see many of the New York gang, I won't forget the likes of Noble, Steve Buckley, Dan Castellano, Murray Chass, Joe Donnelly, Michael Kay, Moss Klein, Bill Madden, Mike Martinez, Tom Pedulla, Bill Pennington, Phil Pepe, Claire Smith, Suzyn Waldman; and columnists Dave Anderson, Ira Berkow, Joe Gergen, Stan Isaacs, Steve Jacobson, Mike Lupica, Phil Mushnick and Bob Raissman. It was always fun to reminisce and talk baseball with Maury Allen, Red Foley and Jack Lang. My New York experience was only two years, but they were years to treasure.

Another who made New York unforgettable was a Cuban export named Dulio Costabile. Perhaps the only way to explain Dulio is to suggest that shortly after he arrived in this country, the United States placed an embargo on anything else coming here from Cuba.

Dulio is a freelance TV cameraman who works baseball telecasts from both Yankee and Shea stadiums. He operates a camera and manages both ballclubs at the same time. He's also the world's foremost authority on Cuban baseball, a title he comes by with some merit. It's believed Dulio was on hand in 1878 when Jose Marti threw out the first ball at the opener between the Habana Leones and the Cienfuegos Elefantes.

Señor Costabile worked two booths away, on the other side of Rizzuto and White. He trusted me immediately when he discovered I knew that Fulgencio Batista was not the center fielder for the Yankees' Columbus Triple-A farm club. Dulio would spin his stories about the great Cuban ballplayers Martin DiHigo, El Tiante Sr. (father of Luis), Dolph Luque and others. I would sit and listen. I had no choice. I couldn't get a word in anyway. Seeing Dulio at the ballpark meant you were going to hear words you'd never heard before, and for which there might be no printable translation. To this day, he remains so revered in his native land his picture appears in the Spanish dictionary: look up the word "loco."

When it came to the Yankee players during my two years with the club, it didn't take long to understand why Don Mattingly and Willie Randolph were a cut above. It was one thing to see them on TV occasionally when I was broadcasting National League games, but another to watch them every day. These two were Yankees the way I remembered the Yankees of my youth.

In the three seasons before I came to New York, Mattingly hit .343, .324 and .352. Over the same stretch, he hit 89 home runs with 368 runs batted in. Watching him prepare for a game each day, it was easy to see how he did it. You can talk all you want about quick wrists, bat speed and good eyes, but Mattingly had more. His work ethic was unmatched. The more success he had, the more he pushed himself to do better.

Don was not a glamour boy but a working man. He was listed as 6 feet tall but seemed shorter. Perhaps it was that crouch at the plate. There was an intensity in his eyes that never seemed to leave. He had that rare ability to be all business while remaining cordial at the same time.

Every day Mattingly took extra batting practice. He worked constantly off the batting tee. It got so that Lou Piniella had to chase him out of the batting cage for fear he'd wear himself out before the game began. Piniella said, "It's one thing to want to do all that extra stuff in April, May or late September, but this is August and it's 95 degrees." To Don Mattingly, anything less than a supreme effort wasn't enough.

It was not always possible to appreciate what Willie Randolph was doing. He had this habit of making things look too easy. Unless you're rolling in the dirt and eating half the infield as you go for a ground ball, you don't get noticed as much. Those who noticed Willie most were pitchers, who saw base hits turn to outs, and managers, who knew when they wrote his name in the lineup they didn't need to worry about second base.

Randolph was one of those players who always seemed to be involved when something good was happening. He either was making the big play in the field, hitting to right field to send Rickey Henderson from first to third, or keeping an inning alive with a two-out base hit to save an at-bat for Mattingly or Winfield.

Randolph defined the word "graceful." You could picture him fielding a ground ball with his glove hand while carrying a tray of dishes with the other. You knew he wouldn't drop either.

I never saw anyone swing harder than Dave Winfield. With his bat speed and long arms, he could swing and miss and circulate enough air to make you feel you were at Candlestick Park. He didn't always miss. In his eight full seasons with the Yankees, Winfield averaged 101 RBI. They were not all meaningless, no matter what George Steinbrenner would have you believe.

The first Yankee home game I broadcast, Winfield hit one into the upper deck in left field. I didn't know you could do that. Everything about him was big. He hit big home runs. He had the world's biggest smile. He stood 6-foot-6. His teeth were 6-4.

Watching Winfield at the plate, I felt he was capable of hitting .350 a year if he didn't swing so hard. There were a lot of base hits to the opposite field to be had; seldom did he ever take advantage of that. On the other hand, he's going to Cooperstown some day. So who can say he should have done anything differently?

Playing for the Yankees has its rewards and drawbacks. The pay is good, but the abuse from the man at the top can be devastating. The tension between Winfield and Steinbrenner will resolve itself when the doors of the Hall of Fame swing open and only one of them enters. Guess which one.

After my first season in New York, Jim Haviland, the man who hired Tommy and me, was gone as general manager of WABC Radio. ABC, which owned the station, was bought by Capital Cities, Inc., which began bringing in its own people. Haviland's replacement was Fred Weinhaus, who believed a penny earned should go into his own pocket.

Our first meeting with Weinhaus took place just before 1988 spring training in Fort Lauderdale. It seemed he had a hard time grasping that we had been hired for the sole purpose of broadcasting baseball. "Haven't you two ever thought about doing other things in the off-season, like sports shows?" he asked (implying "for the same money").

"No," I said. "I always felt play-by-play was the essence of our business."

I don't think that was the answer Weinhaus and Capital Cities were looking for.

My contract with WABC was for two years, with an option held by the station. My best option, it appeared, was to start looking for something else. No sooner had the 1988 season begun than an item appeared in one of the New York papers. "A source close to ABC" had suggested that Tommy and I wouldn't be back next year. Naturally, the source was Fred Weinhaus.

Billy Martin returned to manage the Yankees in 1988. By now, this was a common occurrence. We began to mark Billy's eras as Yankee manager the way we did the Super Bowl. The '88 season marked the start of Billy V. It was not a long era.

I was not thrilled by the thought of Billy's return. I liked Piniella. He was friendly. He was honest. He was easy to talk to, and he could get us on the golf course at the Kansas City Country Club.

I knew Billy from his days as manager of the Oakland A's. The Giants and A's played each other frequently at spring training in Arizona, and we chatted often before games. It was not unusual to encounter him as he was making his rounds at night. Sometimes I wished I hadn't. It wasn't pleasant watching A's traveling secretary Mickey Morabito restraining Martin as he was about to go after a bar patron as if the guy were an umpire.

In Billy's earlier Yankee managing stints, there was always some controversy surrounding him. This was easy enough for anyone who managed under George, but sometimes it was hard to tell who was Billy's worst enemy, George or Billy himself.

There are a lot of people who just can't drink. Not all of them get to manage the New York Yankees — at least not yet.

As Billy V began, there was no question he was a highly motivated man. Unfortunately, revenge, hatred and a constant need to demonstrate one's masculinity are not the healthiest motivators. Sometimes Billy even felt the need to take on someone else's battles. In May, the Yankees flew cross-country to Oakland. Taking on his old team should have been incentive enough, but with Billy there had to be more.

The Yankees permitted hard liquor on their charter flights. This was good and bad. It was bad for the obvious reasons that drinking hard liquor can be bad. It was good because if you drank enough of it, you no longer noticed how bad the food was.

I wasn't sure what Billy was thinking as I walked down the aisle of the plane and neared his seat. He grabbed my arm and said, "Come here."

There weren't many other places I could go with my arm locked in his hand, so I stopped.

When Billy managed Oakland, part of his deal included a house in an exclusive area of Danville known as Blackhawk. He continued to live there after his days with the A's, and was familiar with the circumstances of my decision to leave San Francisco.

"Now listen to me," he said, still gripping my arm. "We're going out to the coast and I'm gonna beat those A's and then when we go on to win the pennant I'm gonna get those Giants for you in the World Series."

I could have lit a cigar with the fire in his eyes. I tried to settle him down.

"Billy, it's okay. I never had a problem with the Giants but if you play KNBR in the Series, that's another story."

I don't think Billy could understand that not everyone was as motivated by revenge as he.

My experience with Billy Martin went much better than I expected. Billy seemed to feel he could trust Tommy and me, probably because broadcasters are more closely associated with the ballclub. I recall a day early in the season when he told me, "If you're ever in a room where I'm being interviewed, don't ever ask me anything. Just be quiet. Then, when it's all over and those other guys have left, I'll tell you and Tommy the truth. You have to understand there are just a lot of things I can't say in front of them."

Looking back on those days, I'm not sure Tommy and I ever learned anything from Billy we could use on the air. I think Billy's willingness to tell us "the truth" was another example of trying to get back at people.

We got along reasonably well, despite Billy's hatred of the National League. He always called me "National Leaguer." I took it as representative of his dislike for the other league, and didn't take it personally. Besides, it was better than "Big Guy," and, unlike George, Billy did know who I was.

To George, I remained anonymous. One Sunday afternoon, the Yankees were playing the A's at The Stadium. One of the guests in George's booth was Oakland owner Walter Haas.

I knew Walter from my days in the Bay Area, and during a break between innings I walked down the corridor to say hello. Naturally, there were guards blocking the entrance to The Boss' booth.

Just as naturally, they didn't know who I was, either. They asked me what I wanted. Just as I was explaining, Walter turned around and spotted me. As we exchanged waves and I was about to return to the broadcast booth, I could see George, sitting next to him, turn and whisper in his ear. Walter said something in return. It didn't take much to figure out the exchange.

George: "Who was that?"

Walter: "That was Hank Greenwald, your broadcaster."

George: "Oh."

It seemed as if every 10 feet in Yankee Stadium, there was some security type asking me if I had a pass. After a while I felt as if I were in school again, walking the hall en route to the bathroom. Finally, I decided to take my American League pass and tape a picture to it.

"I'll fix these guys," I vowed as I took an old Giant media guide, cut out a square-inch picture of Jeffrey Leonard and fixed it to my pass.

Leonard often wore a dour expression, and his Giant teammates nicknamed him "Penitentiary Face." This was unfortunate because, as somber-looking as he could be, Jeff also had a great smile and laugh. He loved to intimidate, but loved it when you gave it right back to him. I chose his picture as the ultimate test of whether the security people paid any attention to my pass, or whether they were simply programmed to ask. Jeffrey Leonard is black.

The next time I was stopped and asked for my pass, I took it out. The security person looked at it, looked at the picture, then looked at me.

"Okay, go ahead," he said, and that was it.

It was right about then that I began wondering if my parents had been completely honest with me. The only time I was ever questioned about the pass, I was entering the press gate in Arlington, Texas. The lady checking credentials looked at me and exclaimed, "Are you sure that's you?"

"That's me, all right," I said. "I don't usually take that good a picture."

I continued to use that pass for the remainder of my first season, before deciding on a new approach for 1988. Nothing had changed in terms of my anonymity, so I decided this season to use a different picture every day. I also began clipping the pass to the lapel of my coat. I went through a lot of pictures: men, women, black, white, Kentucky Derby hopefuls, you name it. It worked. Nobody stopped me anymore. I had my pass. It didn't matter who I was or what I looked like.

Under Billy Martin, the Yankees were sailing along. At one point, they had a five-game lead. And then it happened.

On a hot Friday night in Arlington, the Yankees lost to the Rangers. I was back in my room reading, and as Friday night dissolved into Saturday morning, the fire alarm went off in the Sheraton Hotel. I looked at my watch. It was 1:20 a.m. I didn't think much about the alarm, because they frequently go off in hotels, followed by an announcement proclaiming it was a false alarm.

This time it wasn't.

As instructed, I made my way down to the lobby, curious as the next person to find out where the fire was. There were about 400 people, in various stages of dress, already in the lobby when I arrived. Outside I could see at least three fire trucks and several official cars, all with lights flashing. It looked like one heck of a "come as you are" party.

I was near the registration desk when I saw Yankee trainer Gene Monahan and his assistant, Steve Donohue, making their way through the crowd. I thought someone had been injured and they were coming to help. Then I noticed something strange. Right behind them was Yankee third base coach Mike Ferraro. This struck me as odd because, generally speaking, when there's a hotel fire in progress there isn't usually a need for a third base coach. A late-inning reliever, maybe, but not a third base coach.

The three men snaked their way through the crowded lobby and around in back of the registration desk. I watched the three Yankees as they moved toward a door behind the desk. When they reached it, it opened. There was Billy Martin in a back office with blood running down his face.

I naively wondered what that had to do with the fire. As it turned out, it had nothing to do with the fire and everything to do with an escapade at a topless club called Lace.

Billy and Mickey Mantle had been at the club, and as the evening wore on, Mickey at least had the good sense to go home. Meanwhile, Billy got into it with a couple of guys in the men's room. The two guys were bigger than Billy in every way, including one Billy was reluctant to acknowledge. The two men took the Yankee manager out into the alley, where he became an unwilling blood donor.

When he finally regained his senses, Martin figured he'd better get back to the hotel before anyone saw him. If there was one thing he didn't need, it was to be the center of another controversy. Besides, he probably figured, there wouldn't be many people around the hotel lobby at that hour of the morning. He could sneak in and fix himself up as best he could. He knew he could always make up a story about the appearance of one or two cuts.

Wouldn't you love to have been in the cab with Billy as it approached the hotel, only to be met with fire trucks, police cars, lights flashing out front, and 400 people standing in the lobby?

Billy was no stranger to the Sheraton Hotel in Arlington. He once managed the Texas Rangers. He knew there was a back entrance, and he used it. The fire, which turned out to be minor, had shut down the elevators, and Billy couldn't get to his room. So help, in the form of the Yankee trainers and Ferraro, was on its way to him.

As luck would have it (bad luck), George Steinbrenner was on this trip. George came strolling into the hotel and was alerted to the problem. By now, rumors were beginning to circulate among media in the lobby that something had happened to Billy. George immediately called for Harvey Greene. Harvey wasn't around. He had a date. On any other night, that would have been the big story. Only a Billy Martin escapade could top it.

Now George had to endure the role of spokesman because many of us wanted to know what was happening. The Boss was doing his best to be vague while continuing to wonder where the hell Harvey was.

It was well after 2 a.m. when Harvey Greene and his date, oblivious to the goings on, entered the lobby. Quickly he realized something was up and started to ask George. Steinbrenner looked at his media relations director and barked, "Harvey, get your ass in bed!"

Greene replied, "That's what I've been trying to do!"

The fiasco at Lace marked the beginning of the end for Billy. It wasn't much longer before Lou Piniella was brought back to pick up the pieces.

Lou's return to the dugout wasn't much more than two months along when George began an infatuation with Dallas Green. The former Phillies manager and later Cubs general manager was known as a disciplinarian (whatever that means in today's baseball world), and the thought appealed to the Yankee owner. Rumors that Lou would be replaced by Green in 1989 began appearing in the New York papers, and before long it seemed like a done deal.

As the Yankees reached Detroit on the final weekend of the season, Piniella was not happy. He called Harvey Greene and asked him to set up a dinner at the London Chop House for Saturday night, and to invite all the coaches, writers and broadcasters, and send the bill to Steinbrenner. What was he going to do to Lou, fire him?

I was sitting next to Harvey when the bill came. He looked at me and said, "What do you tip on $2,400?"

One of the highlights of the evening came when the singer at the London Chop House took her break. At the urging of several in the Yankee party, Suzyn

Waldman picked up the microphone and began to sing. Suzyn was a radio reporter who covered the ballclub and who now does some play-by-play. She was an accomplished singer, and what she accomplished that night was upsetting the regular singer, who realized Suzyn was a better performer. It was no contest, and the house vocalist was not amused.

There were several toasts during the course of the dinner. Pitching coach Stan Williams gave one: "Here's to Greenwald. He's the only one of us who knows where he's going to be working next year."

The dark cloud that Fred Weinhaus at WABC placed over my head in spring training began to lighten about halfway through the season. I got a call from Jeff Moorad. He told me the Giants and KNBR had agreed on a new five-year contract, with one important difference. This time, the Giants insisted on the right to hire the announcers. This was a reflection of the falling out I'd had with station management and my decision to leave. Jeff told me the Giants wanted to know if I'd be interested in coming back.

As much as I loved working in New York, it had never been my desire to leave San Francisco in the first place. Now Weinhaus was making it apparent he would hire anyone who would do Yankee games for less money and work year-round. Yes, I loved working in New York, but one fool at WABC was enough.

By retaining the right to hire the announcers, the Giants paved the way for my return to San Francisco. The Giants and I both knew I'd never again have anything to do with Bill Dwyer at KNBR.

Bill was the general manager of the station, a position he seemed to feel gave him the right to hassle people, including my wife. It was not uncommon, when we were in his company, for him to say, "Hey Carla, next time Hank goes on the road I'll give you a call."

He wasn't dumb enough to call, but his intent was to make both of us uncomfortable, and he succeeded.

On another occasion, a dinner for Giants general manager Al Rosen, Dwyer came up behind Carla and, through the back of her blouse, tried to snap her bra.

She exclaimed, "Bill, don't be so gauche!" And walked away.

For me, walking away wasn't as easy. It took a few more years before I reached the point that no job was worth what I was going through.

I wasn't alone in all of this. I saw what Dwyer had done to David Glass, one of my colleagues on the Giant broadcasts. David came in as an enthusiastic young man, a hard worker with a great sense of humor. It took Dwyer almost no time to turn him into a nervous wreck. He would call Glass moments before we went on the air and say things like, "I had some calls complaining about your work yesterday, but I don't want you to worry about it." Or, "I just read what so-and-so said about you in the paper this morning. Try not to think about it."

Poor David. Just before we signed on from spring training, he said to me, "I'm going to do something and please don't laugh. Bill Dwyer wants me to recite poetry."

Dwyer had decided he wanted Glass to sound more learned, to quote poetry about springtime and tie it in with baseball, because "Vin Scully does things like that."

I don't know how Glass lasted five years. It wasn't that he was incompetent. The wonder was he didn't end up in a mental institution.

Now the same thing was happening to me. When I hired the firm of Steinberg and Moorad to represent me, Dwyer bellowed, "I can't tell you that you can't have an agent, but let me tell you no goddamn agent is gonna tell me what I'm gonna pay you."

Dwyer was determined to get me to quit. He couldn't fire me because he'd have to explain why. What was he going to say, my wife shrugged off his advances? The Giants were pleased with my work, and the fans were great to me. Dwyer would do the only thing he could, which was make my life miserable. He succeeded.

In 1986 I was working with Phil Stone, who replaced Glass. My contract called for me to do innings 1,2,5,8 and 9. Stone would do 3,4,6 and 7. One day I received a memo from Dwyer saying from now on, I would switch innings with Stone because it wasn't fair that all the excitement seemed to be happening in my innings.

In spring training that year, I received a note from Dwyer's right-hand man, Jay Barrington. Jay smoked a lot, drank a lot and said, "That's right, Bill," a lot.

In Jay's note, he said Stone was finishing up the Los Angeles Clippers' NBA season and would miss one spring training broadcast. Jay asked if I would work the game alone, and insisted it would be the only time it would happen.

Two weeks later, when it happened for the third time, I called Jeff Moorad. He said, "Tell Barrington you will work, as your contract states, innings 1, 2, 5, 8 and 9, and he either will find someone else to do the other innings or pay you extra to do them."

When I called Barrington, who was at the hotel in Scottsdale that Sunday morning, he said, "Aw, Coach, you can't do that to me." He called every guy "Coach" and every woman "Babe." He also knew I'd just ruined his Sunday, because now he was going to have to call Dwyer and tell him what I said.

It was a brutally damp and windy morning when I showed up at Scottsdale Stadium and saw, on the field, asking for a Giants media guide, Barrington. He was in a short-sleeves shirt and sandals, no socks. (The press box at the old Scottsdale ballpark was one long row of chairs, enclosed on three sides, with a roof.) He asked me again if I'd work the game alone. I gave him the same answer.

It was about 15 minutes before game time when Barrington finally reached Dwyer on one of our broadcast phones. I was sitting right there, along with our engineer, Vern Thompson. This was what we heard of the conversation: "But Bill! But Bill! But Bill! Oh God! I can't work the whole game alone."

When Barrington got off the phone, he was trembling. He looked at me and said, "You are hereby suspended from KNBR until further notice and I'm going to have to ask you to leave the booth."

I said, "Jay, there is no booth here. It's one long row of seats. If you want me to move down a couple chairs, I'll certainly do it."

I spotted Carla, who was sitting in the stands below us, and I went down to tell her what had happened. We agreed it would probably be a good idea if I notified the Giants that Dwyer's flunky was about to broadcast their game. I walked toward the Giants' office, and there were Bob Lurie, the team owner, and Al Rosen, the general manager.

"Aren't you supposed to be on the air?" they said, almost in unison.

"I've been sent to my room," I said, and proceeded to tell them the story.

Smoke was beginning to escape from Rosen's ears as he made his way up the stands to the press box.

"Get me Dwyer!" he yelled.

By the time he slammed down the phone, I had been reinstated. Barrington was far more relieved than I was, but he wasn't out of a jam yet. He was assigned innings 3,4,6 and 7.

The weather wasn't getting any better, and the dampness and wind weren't helping anyone dumb enough to show up in a short-sleeves shirt and sandals, no socks. When the seventh inning finally ended, Barrington couldn't get out of his chair fast enough. I grabbed his arm and reminded him the Giants and the Milwaukee Brewers were tied going into the eighth, and if this game went into extra innings, the 10th would be his. Sure enough, he ended up sitting through four more innings. Mercifully, it ended in the 11th. It had been a perfect day.

Bob Lurie was not pleased with what was going on and asked if we could fly to San Francisco to meet and try to work things out. The next day, we gathered in Dwyer's office and agreed a more cordial atmosphere would be helpful. That lasted about as long as it takes to say, "Play ball."

The memos, faxes and phone calls never stopped coming. I couldn't walk into a hotel room without the light on the phone flashing, and a message to call Jay Barrington.

When I showed Lurie and Rosen the memo about switching innings with Stone, they got on the phone to Dwyer and put an end to that.

Every year, Major League Baseball sent a letter to all teams asking their cooperation with CBS Radio. The network broadcast a Saturday Game of the Week, and in the fifth inning would use an announcer from the visiting team to call the top of the fifth and the home-town announcer to call the bottom half. It gave fans around the country a chance to hear the various announcers. I had participated many times without any problems. The Giants called to ask if I would go on.

The team was in Cincinnati. It was August of 1986, and I had returned from lunch to find a FedEx memo from Barrington. Obviously it was from Dwyer, but he had pledged a more cordial atmosphere, so he had Barrington sign the memos.

In the latest, I was given hell for agreeing to participate in the CBS broadcasts. I was told that no one had given me permission, and I had no right to accept. This was just the latest ploy in Dwyer's effort to get me to "quit."

It's amazing how a person's life suddenly can turn around. You hear stories like this all the time, and, if you're like me, you get skeptical. But about an hour before leaving for Riverfront Stadium, I was reading Red Barber's book, *The Broadcasters.* In one chapter, he wrote that his father had told him, "Son, don't let any man put you in fear of your job, or make you believe it's the only one you'll ever have."

I'd never experienced a moment like that. Reading that line made clear what I was going to do. There was nothing those bastards could do to me anymore. I would no longer be in fear of my job and would go on to something else if necessary. It was necessary, and it turned out to be the Yankees.

Now, two years later, I was coming back to San Francisco. Lurie, Rosen and Dwyer were at the press conference announcing my return. All had nice things to say about Hank Greenwald.

One of them was lying.

"That's the toughest thing I ever did in broadcasting."

6

EVERYTHING'S COMING UP ROSEN

Before a spring training game in Miami in March of 1988, I ran into Frank Robinson, who was working for the Baltimore Orioles. Frank had a big grin on his face as he saw me approaching. He said, "They got rid of you and me and they finally won something."

In 1989 I returned to the Giants, and, despite my presence, they would win again.

When I arrived in Scottsdale in March, I went to the practice field at Indian School Park. Willie Mays was standing there, and I went over to say hello. The two of us had done a pre-game show together in 1986, and I hadn't seen him in a couple of years. As we stood talking, a photographer from the *San Francisco Chronicle* asked if he could take our picture.

The next day the picture appeared in the paper. Like many people, I'd often wondered just how far I'd come in the course of my career. When I saw the picture and read the caption, I no longer had to wonder. Here we were, with a caption that read, "Two old friends greet each other at spring training. Giants broadcaster Hank Greenwald and Willie Mays (right) catch up on things at practice."

I read that and thought, "'Willie Mays (right)!' Willie Mays (right)! They have to identify which one of us is Willie Mays! I must be doing better than I thought."

As usual, Roger Craig had forecast a pennant, and this time he was right. Of course, winning a pennant is rarely easy, and this would be no exception.

The Giants were tested early, embarking on an 11-game road trip in May that took them to Chicago, Montreal, Philadelphia and New York. After winning three of the first five games, the Giants moved into Philadelphia's Veterans Stadium on the night of May 15. Scott Garrelts of the Giants and Don Carman of the Phillies pitched the first nine innings without giving up a run. Garrelts allowed only three hits and struck out eight, while Carman surrendered four hits and walked seven.

The closest either side came to scoring was in the 10th, when Will Clark just missed a home run to right field and had to settle for a double. Clark was later thrown out at the plate by Von Hayes on Candy Maldonado's single to right. Clark came up again to lead off the 12th, and this time he wasn't going to leave one short. He put the ball into the right-field seats, and the Giants led 1-0.

Seconds later, Kevin Mitchell hit a homer to left, and there was a mini-celebration in the Giants' dugout, as the score was now 2-0. Little did they know how premature that celebration was.

In the bottom of the 12th, with Craig Lefferts pitching for the Giants, Hayes led off and struck out. Pinch hitters Dickie Thon and Steve Lake followed with singles, putting the tying runs at first and second. Lefferts got Steve Jeltz to pop up for the second out, and the Giants needed one more out to win.

Outfielder Bob Dernier, who entered the game in the top of the 10th, stepped to the plate. He promptly ripped one down the left-field line and into the corner. It was obvious the tying runs were going to score as Mitchell went after the ball. Suddenly the ball, following the contour of the wall, shot out of the corner and, hugging the base of wall, went past Mitchell and out toward center field. Dernier circled the bases with an inside-the-park home run, and the Phillies won the game, 3-2.

Al Rosen had been sitting near the Giants' dugout on the third base side. He went off like a Roman candle. As he shot up the steps toward the exits, those in his path were in mortal danger. A baseball season often takes unusual twists. The winning pitcher for the Phillies that night was Steve Bedrosian, who had given up the two home runs in the top of the 10th. A month later, Rosen acquired Bedrosian from the Phillies in exchange for infielder Charlie Hayes and pitchers Dennis Cook and Terry Mulholland. When the deal was done, Rosen said, "I just got the pitcher who's going to be on the mound when we win the pennant."

When the Giants won the pennant in early October, the pitcher on the mound was Steve Bedrosian.

It took the Giants until September 4 to make up for that night in Philadelphia. They had a six-game lead by then, but Houston and San Diego were coming on strong. The first of a seven-game road trip in Cincinnati wasn't off to a good start. The Reds jumped on starter Kelly Downs for seven runs in two and one-third innings and led 8-0 going to the seventh.

Will Clark and Terry Kennedy homered for the Giants to make it 8-2. Craig began replacing some of the regulars at that point. Going to the top of the eighth, Clark, Kennedy and Robby Thompson were out of the game. Ernie Riles, who had taken over for Thompson, singled, and Mike Laga, who had replaced Clark, hit a two-run homer. Suddenly it was an 8-4 game, and interest was picking up.

The Giants were still down by four going to the ninth when Greg Litton, pinch hitting for Pat Sheridan, singled. After Candy Maldonado lined to second, Donnell Nixon singled, and pinch hitter Bob Brenly reached on an error to load the bases. The tying run was at the plate. Chris Speier came off the bench and singled to center, scoring Litton and leaving the bases loaded.

Now it was 8-5. John Franco relieved Norm Charlton, who had started the inning, and wasn't having any more success. Bill Bathe, who replaced Kennedy behind the plate, delivered a base hit to center, scoring Nixon and Brenly. Now it was 8-7. It was Rob Dibble's turn to come in from the bullpen, the Reds' third pitcher of the inning. Up stepped Riles, whose base hit to center brought home Speier and tied the game.

In the Giants' dugout at that moment were players in various stages of dress. Those who came out of the game early, and had been in the clubhouse changing, were running back to see what was going on.

With Bathe now at second base representing the tying run, Craig sent in Scott Garrelts to run for him. The Giants now had Garrelts at second and Riles at first, and Laga coming to the plate. Four runs were in. Top of the ninth. Score tied 8-8. Laga bounced one between first and second. Reds first baseman Todd Benzinger, moving to his right, couldn't get it. Second baseman Luis Quinones, moving to his left, couldn't get it. The ball went through into right field, and Garrelts scored. The Giants had wiped out an 8-0 deficit and led 9-8, and I was becoming a really good announcer.

Unfortunately, the excitement didn't end there. In the bottom of the ninth against Bedrosian, Quinones flied to center to open the inning. Then it got ugly. Bedrosian walked Paul O'Neill, and Barry Larkin looped one into right field for a double, sending O'Neill around to third. Cincinnati now had the tying run at third and the winning run at second and only one out. Craig ordered an intentional walk to Benzinger to load the bases.

Up stepped Chris Sabo, whose error in the top of the ninth had contributed to the Giants' rally. Now he had a chance to make up for it with a base hit to drive in the winning runs. These were the moments Al Rosen had in mind when he made the trade for Bedrosian back in June. The tall, bearded right-hander, known as Bedrock, got Sabo to pop up to short for the second out. Next, it got down to Bedrosian and pinch hitter Dave Collins. You can imagine how disheartening it would have been to lose in the bottom of the ninth after that great comeback. Not to worry, mate. Collins hit one on the ground to Riles at second, and the Giants had atoned for that frustrating night back in Philadelphia.

Throughout the season, I'd been watching a man bravely attempt to rehabilitate his pitching arm. His name was Dave Dravecky, and he'd undergone surgery the previous fall to remove a cancerous tumor from the deltoid muscle in his left arm. Dave was probably the only one who thought he would ever pitch again, and every day he worked harder to make his dream a reality.

He had strong religious and political beliefs, which, to some, made him a curiosity. Politics aside, however, it was his faith and his determination to pitch again that made this one of the great stories of 1989. Or any other year. After a couple of tune-ups with Giants farm clubs, Dravecky realized his dream when he returned to the major leagues on August 10.

Only twice in the years I broadcast major league baseball did I have tears in my eyes while on the air. (This doesn't count the tears I shed watching another useless pitching change, or a 2-1 game dragging on well beyond three hours.)

The first teary episode was in July, 1980, when Willie McCovey came to bat for the final time of his 22-year career. The sight of this dignified man striding to the plate, combined with the stirring ovation from 40,000 fans at Dodger Stadium, had me swallowing hard. It was an overwhelming tribute from the fans of a team he'd helped defeat so many times.

Nine years later, I was looking down from the radio booth at Candlestick as Dave Dravecky walked through the door leading to the Giants bullpen to warm up. Just the sight of Dravecky climbing onto the mound out there, and wondering what was going through his mind, was enough to cloud my eyesight. Suddenly, fans down the right field line began to applaud. Then, section by section, as more and more fans began to notice he was about to start his warm-ups, the ovation grew.

No one knew what to expect when the game began. How many innings could he pitch? How effectively? Dravecky set the Reds down in order in the first inning. He continued to put zeros on the board as the Giants scored single runs in the second and third and Matt Williams' two-run homer in the fifth made it 4-0. Going to the eighth inning, Dravecky had faced 23 batters, two over the minimum. In the eighth, Todd Benzinger's single and a double by Scotti Madison put runners at second and third with two out. Luis Quinones' three-run homer suddenly made it 4-3. Roger Craig stayed with Dravecky, and he got Jeff Richardson to ground out to end the inning.

The fans knew Dravecky was through for the day. He walked off the mound to a standing ovation. Admiring teammates hugged him and shook his hand as he entered the dugout. Bedrosian finished up, and once again Dave Dravecky was a winning major league pitcher. If this was a high point in the season, a low point was just around the corner. Dravecky made his next start five days later in Montreal. His wife Jan, daughter Tiffany and son Jonathan would not be on hand for this one. The game was not being televised, but I was sure they'd be listening to the radio. As he had in the game at Candlestick, Dravecky shut out the Expos through the first five innings as the Giants built a 3-0 lead.

Damaso Garcia led off the bottom of the sixth with a home run, and Andres Galarraga was hit with a pitch. The next batter was Tim Raines. As Dravecky delivered his first pitch he collapsed, and the ball shot off in the direction of the Expos' dugout on the first base side. Our broadcast location in Montreal's Olympic Stadium put us closer to Toronto than we were to the field, but it was obvious Dravecky was in great pain as he lay on the mound, surrounded by teammates and trainer Mark Letendre.

There are times in the broadcast business when you have to choose your words carefully. This was one of them. Suspecting that Jan Dravecky was listening to the radio and couldn't see what was happening, I didn't want to use the word "collapse," although Dravecky looked as if he'd been shot. I said he appeared to stumble and was being looked at by the trainer. The last thing I wanted to do was speculate on someone's injury to the point of creating panic in the player's family, without knowing the facts.

Dave Dravecky had just thrown the last pitch of his major league career. That pitch snapped a bone in his left arm, an arm that had been living on borrowed time. Less than a year later, the cancer returned, and the arm was amputated. On the night he lost his career, he won his last major league game. Today Dravecky travels the country serving as an inspiration to young boys and girls with physical disabilities. Cancer took his arm. Nothing could take his heart.

The Giants went on to win the Western Division title and would play the Chicago Cubs, winners in the east. It was the second division championship in four seasons of the Al Rosen-Roger Craig era. This was heady stuff for Giant fans, who, until 1987, hadn't had a division title to celebrate since 1971. Following a bitter seven-game playoff loss to the Cardinals in '87, the Giants were eager to take that next step and win a pennant. Of course they weren't as eager as the Cubs, who hadn't won a pennant since the year MacArthur took the Japanese surrender on the battleship Missouri.

The Giants and Cubs split the first two games of the series in Chicago, with the Giants beating Greg Maddux in the opener. That last part probably sounds as strange to you as it does to me. Games three, four and five were at Candlestick, and they turned out to be three of the most tension-packed games I've ever seen.

In game three, the Cubs took a 4-3 lead with a run in the top of the seventh. After the crowd of 62,065 took its stretch, Paul Assenmacher came on to pitch. With one out, Giants center fielder Brett Butler singled and when the count went to 1-0 on Robby Thompson, Cubs manager Don Zimmer brought in right-hander Les Lancaster. Thompson promptly hit a two-run homer, giving the Giants a 5-4 lead. The Cubs managed to get the tying run on in the ninth, but Bedrosian locked the gate, and the Giants led the series two games to one.

Somehow, 13 more people managed to squeeze into the park for Game Four. The score was tied 4-4 in the bottom of the fifth. Will Clark, who had doubled, was at second, and Matt Williams was facing Cubs left-hander Steve Wilson. Williams fouled off what seemed like 10 pitches before blasting a two-run homer.

The Giants carried their 6-4 lead into the top of the ninth. Kelly Downs had pitched brilliantly in relief of starter Scott Garrelts, working four scoreless innings and allowing only three hits, the last of which was a two-out single in the ninth by Ryne Sandberg.

With a count of 2 and 0 on Lloyd McClendon, Craig once again called on Bedrosian. McClendon came though with a single to right, sending Sandberg to second. Now the tying runs were on base, with Mark Grace coming up. Grace and the Giants' Clark, the two first basemen, provided this series with an extra layer of drama. Clark would finish the series 13-for-20 (.650) while Grace went 11-for-17 (.647).

What made Grace tough to pitch to was his ability to spray hits around the whole field. Bedrosian knew Grace wouldn't be trying to hit one out of the park when a shot to the gap in left center would score two and tie the game. Pitching carefully, Bedrosian walked Grace, loading the bases for Andre Dawson.

I don't know whether broadcasters are supposed to have favorite players, but Andre Dawson was mine. Here was one guy I'd have paid to watch. From the time Dawson came up with Montreal, it was obvious he was something special. He had a grace in center field that made me feel guilty about comparisons to Joe DiMaggio. At the plate, he had such a quick bat, the ball was gone before you realized he had swung.

Andre was also mortal. After years on the AstroTurf in Montreal, his knees were examined more times than those of the Rockettes. Far too often, he underwent surgery. It was a shame. Andre had it all, but the baseball gods never intended it to be easy. Those surgeries probably will keep him out of the Hall of Fame.

Dawson may have been the player I most enjoyed watching in my years as a baseball broadcaster. But now, in the ninth inning of Game Four of the National League Championship Series, he was the player I most wanted to see make the final out with the bases loaded.

Dawson struck out. Bedrosian had won a Cy Young Award when he was with the Phillies. He was now a Cy of Relief.

The Giants were one game away from winning the National League pennant. The Cubs knew, win or lose, they were going back to Chicago. The Giants didn't have to pack their bags quite yet, and, whether they would need to at all was up to them. Oddly, there seemed to be more pressure on the Giants.

If the Cubs kept the NLCS alive and it returned to Wrigley Field, it would revive horrible memories of 1987, when the Giants led the Cardinals three games to two, only to see St. Louis win the last two, and the pennant, at Busch Stadium.

Game Five was played on Monday afternoon, October 9. Not all Giants pennants can be won on October 3, and when they don't come that often you take them when you can. I remember thinking of other October afternoons when I was a kid and important baseball games were being played. There were no play-offs in those days. There wasn't even television. Games played in October meant only one thing — the World Series. How strange it was that the first World Series game I ever saw was on October 3. The year was 1945, and I watched my Detroit Tigers play, of all teams, the Chicago Cubs. Forty-four years later, this made me one of the few people alive who had seen the Cubs play in a World Series. I wasn't eager to see it again.

Rick Reuschel, who took the loss in Game Two, was the starter for the final series game at Candlestick. Known as "Big Daddy," Reuschel stood 6 foot 3 and was built in such a way that hitting his weight would have been a good thing. In fact, he looked a lot like me, except he was eight inches taller and could pitch. Reuschel began his big league career with the Cubs and had been around the block a few times. If I was one of the few people alive who'd seen the Cubs play in a World Series, I might have seen Reuschel pitch in it. No matter his age, he could still pitch. He won 17 and lost 8 during the regular season with an impressive 2.94 ERA, and he had more than 200 career victories.

Cubs manager Don Zimmer selected right-hander Mike Bielecki, an 18-game winner who had started against Reuschel in Game Two.

The Cubs took a 1-0 lead in the third inning when Ryne Sandberg's double scored Jerome Walton. The Cubs threatened again in the sixth with runners at first and third and one out. Reuschel got Marvell Wynne to fly to Pat Sheridan in short right and Luis Salazar to ground to Thompson.

Meanwhile, the Giants were doing little with Bielecki, who shut them out through the first six innings. Things brightened in the bottom of the seventh when Clark opened with a triple and Mitchell's sacrifice fly tied the score, 1-1.

In the top of the eighth, the Cubs threatened again when Walton drew a walk and was sacrificed to second by Sandberg. Wynne's grounder to second moved Walton to third and brought up Grace. If anyone was going to beat the Giants on this day, it wasn't going to be him. Grace was intentionally walked, bringing up Dawson. As great a player as he was, this just wasn't going to be Andre's series. Reuschel got him on a comebacker, and the crowd of 62,084 began breathing again.

Bielecki disposed of pinch hitter Ken Oberkfell and Jose Uribe to start the eighth. With two out and nobody on, Maldonado pinch-hit for Reuschel. Big Daddy had pitched well enough to win, but something drastic was going to have to happen for him to do so now.

The game of baseball takes many twists and turns, and you never know when something bizarre is going to happen. Who'd have guessed that Mike Bielecki was about to walk his only three batters of this game, or that he'd be left in that long?

Zimmer finally brought in Mitch Williams to face Clark with the bases loaded — not exactly the time for a pitcher whose nickname was "Wild Thing." When balls left Williams' hand, even folks in the press box ducked. But he was left-handed, and he threw hard. Clark, meanwhile, was about to experience the defining moment of his career. It was the moment every kid dreams about in those days when he's too young to know how much pressure comes with it. Clark was hitting over .600 in this series. In his mind there was only one possible outcome to his next at bat. His smash up the middle into center field scored Maldonado and Butler, and the Giants took a 3-1 lead.

Back in 1979, when Lindsey Nelson told me not to get caught up in wins and losses, it was far better advice than I realized. There's no way I'd have made it through 18 seasons broadcasting major league baseball had I allowed myself to let winning and losing determine the quality of my work. On the other hand, there is a human element to be considered. Going to the top half of the ninth inning, whatever my head was telling me was being vetoed by my heart. I wanted the Giants to win the pennant. I wanted it for Bob Lurie and Al Rosen. I wanted it for Roger and the players. I wanted it for the fans, who had endured too many cold nights and windy days with too little reward

Deep down, I also wanted it for myself. I suppose every broadcaster relishes the opportunity to describe a pennant-winning moment, but there was more to it than that. Ever since I was a kid, I could name, year by year, every pennant-winning team in both leagues. I wanted to add "1989 San Francisco Giants" to the list. My fantasy needed three outs.

There's an old saying in baseball: "Never count outs." If you're leading after seven innings, you don't start saying, "We only need six more outs," and so on. Going to the ninth in Game Five, with Bedrosian coming out of the Giants' bullpen, the math was staring everyone in the face.

Luis Salazar was first up for Chicago and grounded to Matt Williams. Two outs to go. Up next was Shawon Dunston. Bedrock got him on a fly to Mitchell. Now the fans were ready to show their sheer joy, rising as one in expectation of the final out. This was the one that, more than any other, validated the cliché about the game not being over until the last man was out.

Curtis Wilkerson came off the bench to pinch hit for Joe Girardi. Wilkerson, a switch-hitter batting left-handed, looped a single into left field. This accomplished two things. It quieted the crowd and demonstrated the fragility of a two-run lead by bringing the tying run to the plate.

Zimmer had saved Mitch Webster for this very spot. Like Wilkerson, Webster was also a switch-hitter. But unlike Wilkerson, who was a singles hitter, Webster had the power to tie the game. The good news was that he didn't. The bad news was that he singled to center, sending Wilkerson to second and putting the tying runs on base. It also brought the top of the order to the plate in Jerome Walton, who would earn rookie of the year honors that season. Walton wasted no time showing why, as he came up with the Cubs' third hit in a row, a single to center that scored Wilkerson and sent Webster, the tying run, to second.

Besides Mark Grace, the only other Cub you wouldn't want coming to the plate in this situation was doing just that. It was Ryne Sandberg, hitting .421 in this series with eight hits in 19 at-bats. For Giant fans, the agony had crept ahead of the ecstasy, which they expected would have arrived by now.

Were the Giants one out away from winning a pennant, or were the Cubs one hit away from taking the lead? My mind went back three years to the American League playoffs. The Angels were one strike away from their first pennant, and Boston's Dave Henderson hit a series-winning home run for Boston. Then there was the World Series that year. The Sox were a strike away from their first title since 1918 when the Mets rallied to win. Just when you think the tension can't get any higher, it goes up another notch.

I tried to put all negative thoughts out of my head and reminded myself that whatever I said at that moment would probably be played over and over again, no matter what happened. I did not find that a comforting prospect.

Fortunately, we didn't have to wait long to find out. Bedrosian's first pitch was a slider. Sandberg reached for it and grounded it to second. There were few sights more comforting for the Giants that year than a ground ball hit to Robby Thompson. This one was no exception. Robby backed up a step to play it on a big hop and calmly threw to Clark. It was over.

How wonderfully symbolic the final out would go in the scorebook — 4 to 3, Thompson to Clark — the two whose arrival in 1986 marked the upturn in the fortunes of the ballclub.

The ball settled in Clark's glove, and Steve Bedrosian stood on the mound, about to be mobbed. As Al Rosen had forecast back in June, "I just got the guy who's going to be standing on the mound when we win the pennant."

It was good to let the crowd noise tell the story of what had just happened. I needed time to collect my thoughts. I was in shock at having lived long enough to see the Giants win a pennant. The last time it had happened, 27 years earlier, I'd been working in Syracuse.

As great as I felt at that moment, I also felt a tinge of sadness for the Chicago Cubs. Twenty-seven years of waiting is a long time, but 44 years is a lot longer. I was a boy of 10 when I saw the Cubs play in the World Series. Now, as a kid of 54, I would get to see the Giants.

If there's one thing the 1989 World Series never seemed like, it was a World Series. For one thing, I slept in my own bed each night. For another, the Giants played the Oakland A's, a team they'd faced nine times in spring training, the last three at Candlestick and the Oakland Coliseum. If there's anything that can remove the mystique of meeting a team from the other league for baseball's biggest prize, that's it.

Of those nine games, the A's won eight. Call me irresponsible. Call me unreliable. But I think it's safe to say the Oakland team won the World Series in spring training. The Giants' track record versus the A's was never very good, and that year it was the worst. You can talk all you want about how spring training games don't mean anything. That's true when it comes to the regular season, but when it came down to October the Giants probably would have preferred to play anyone else. The pattern had been established, and while handicappers might have conceded one game to the Giants, the A's four-game sweep wasn't a big surprise. That made it 13 times in 14 games the A's had beaten the Giants that year.

Another reason this never felt like a World Series: Our broadcast location for the games at Oakland was at field level, behind the screen in back of home plate. If nothing else, this made me realize how far I'd come in the 32 years since I did play-by-play baseball at Syracuse University from a field level box, behind the screen in back of home plate. At Lew Carr Field in Syracuse, at least we were enclosed. Broadcasting the World Series at Oakland, we got rained on. In my college days, when I imagined what it would be like to broadcast the World Series, this wasn't exactly what I had in mind.

After the Giants lost the first two games in Oakland, the Series shifted to Candlestick for Game Three. The location wasn't all that shifted. Moments before the game got under way, instead of the usual call of "Play ball," Mother Nature shouted, "Let's get ready to RUMM-BULLLLLL!" When Roger Craig said he needed to shake things up after those first two games, this was probably not in his plans.

When the earthquake hit, I was standing in the press box next to Duane Kuiper, the former Cleveland and San Francisco infielder who now was part of the Giants' broadcast crew. I was happy to be back at Candlestick, if only because I'd be working from a booth that was above the field and enclosed.

As the stadium began rocking to and fro, I was no longer sure the booth would remain elevated, or enclosed. Kuiper and I looked at each other and agreed the press box and stands above us might go right over. About 15 seconds later, the shaking stopped. A cheer went up from the more than 60,000 fans in the park, as if they were saying, "Good one!" There was no question these folks knew a "good" earthquake when they felt one.

One of the worst possible scenarios at the time of an earthquake is to have 60,000 people in one place. The potential for panic can only be imagined. In this regard it was fortunate that two local teams were playing in the 1989 World Series. It's possible the least amount of panic at that moment was in the stands. Ninety-five percent of the people there were from the Bay Area and had experienced earthquakes before. In the aftermath, they remained calm and orderly.

The greatest panic was in the press box, where 95 percent of the media were from out of town. It was evident they had a lot to learn about earthquakes, including lesson No. 1 — you can't outrun them. This didn't stop many of the media from trying. Quite a few fled past Kuiper and me and headed for the door. Another few seconds of shaking, and the door would have come to them.

In another act of cruelty foisted upon the Giants, Candlestick Park survived. Other parts of the Bay Area were not as fortunate. Sixty-eight people lost their lives, and damage was well in the millions. The fans, not knowing what had happened elsewhere, expected the game to be played. The scoreboard lights were out, as was power in other areas of the park. The quake hit at 5:04 p.m. Pacific time, so there was still plenty of daylight. That, too, was fortunate. When Fay Vincent, the last of the non-owner commissioners, learned of the damage in other parts of the city, he decided to postpone the World Series. Too bad he only postponed it.

Eleven days later, the Fall Classic resumed. Two days after that, it was over. For the regime of Bob Lurie, Al Rosen and Roger Craig, winning the 1989 pennant was as good as it got. Shortly after the Series, voters in San Francisco narrowly turned down another stadium measure, one that might have passed had it not been for the earthquake. For the next three seasons, the Giants were just another ballclub. This and other factors took a toll on Lurie's patience, Rosen's nerves and Craig's heart. In June 1992, when voters in Santa Clara County turned down a quarter-percent tax hike that would have funded a new stadium in San Jose, Lurie put the team up for sale. Once again, no one in the Bay Area took him seriously. In early September, Lurie announced the sale and impending move to St. Petersburg, Florida, in the Tampa Bay region. Naturally the news was met with shock waves of indignation. Some contended the team belonged to San Francisco. How could it be allowed to move?

To me, that sounded like an empty cry from a city that hadn't been terribly interested in doing anything to support it.

I was not among the indignant. When you own a team that plays in the worst outdoor ballpark in the major leagues, and people don't like coming to it, and the area you're in won't build a new stadium, and no one in the area is willing to buy the club, and it's your money going down the drain, by God, you've got a right to sell or to move the team somewhere else.

I still had two years left on my contract, and I started wondering what it might be like to move to St. Petersburg. The idea began to take on more and more appeal. Here was the retirement capital of the United States. Among other things, for the first time in my years in baseball, I'd be going to a city where the groupies were my own age.

The Magowan group made all this academic. Its purchase of the ballclub meant the franchise would remain in San Francisco for a few more years, pending construction of a new stadium.

Peter Magowan didn't waste any time putting his imprint on things. He knew a new stadium was a must, and it would have to be privately financed. Magowan's ability to get this seemingly impossible task headed toward near-completion was remarkable, and worthy of a statue in his honor. The city will have reason to thank him more than it realizes.

Many holdovers from the Lurie era were quickly phased out. This is not unusual under new ownership. Al Rosen moved to Palm Springs. Roger Craig knew he wasn't wanted, and he retired. Two of my fellow broadcasters, however, wcre left in limbo. Duane Kuiper and Ron Fairly were guys I looked forward to working with. In those days I was doing both radio and TV. I worked with Fairly on radio and Kuiper on television.

Because we did far more radio then, I spent a lot more time on the air with Fairly. We had been together four seasons since my return from New York. In the lame duck days of the Lurie administration, no new hiring or contract extensions could be undertaken. When Magowan took over, I expressed the hope my colleagues would be retained. Peter made it obvious he was not a fan of Fairly's work. He said nothing about Kuiper. There wasn't much doubt in my mind about Ron's future with the Giants. I loved working with him. He cared strongly about the game, he could add nuances I was incapable of detecting, and he had some great stories. We had four years invested in each other. Ron had been there for six, including the two years I was in New York. I didn't look forward to starting new with someone else on the radio.

Magowan's feeling about Fairly presented me with a dilemma. I knew Ron wanted to come back, and I knew he wasn't looking elsewhere. Was it up to me, as a friend and partner, to tell him, or was it up to Magowan or whomever he designated?

I made the mistake of thinking the Giants would handle it properly. After all, hiring and firing were the team's responsibility. When I had spoken with Magowan, it was November of 1992. Each time Ron called the club to find out what it was going to do, he couldn't get a straight answer.

Duane Kuiper was being strung along as well. I urged him and Ron to look elsewhere. As tough as it is to pick up and start over somewhere else, why should anyone let himself be toyed with over a question that wasn't that difficult to answer? Kuiper said he might have a chance to go with the new Colorado Rockies, who would begin play in the National League the following season. I said he had to think of himself and his family first.

At this point, both guys were dealing with Larry Baer, a club vice president who was said to have communications skills from his previous job at CBS in New York. While Baer proved to be an asset to Magowan in many ways, the one thing he couldn't do, or wouldn't do, was communicate. Larry Baer was a product of Harvard Business School, where apparently they teach people to say things such as, "I hear you. I know where you're coming from. . ."

Harvard also must teach its business students that unless they're under oath, they don't always have to tell the truth if they can talk around it or make something up. Maybe I should look at the bright side. With Harvard Business School tuition around $25,000 at the time, I figure Baer saved Fairly, Kuiper and me at least 75 grand combined. A few years later, I'd get my education firsthand.

Kuiper did the wise thing and accepted the job with the Rockies. Ron was still clinging to the hope of coming back, and the Giants took another three months to tell him he wasn't. Fortunately, he was able to hook on with the Seattle Mariners.

Magowan was eager to hire Dusty Baker as his manager. There had been much campaigning for Dusty in the local media, and I hoped that if Magowan hired him he was doing it because he really wanted him, not because of pressure from outside. I believe Peter felt Dusty was the right man for the job, and history certainly supports him. Dusty proved to be the biggest asset the Giants had.

In the years I was around baseball, there wasn't one aspect of managing a ballclub that appealed to me. If anything, "manager" is a misleading term. He's not part of management, and he's obviously not a player. In short, a manager has no status and no protection. He's so far down the pecking order, he's at the whim of the marketing, promotions and public relations departments, all of whom get first crack at his time. If there's time left over, he gets to deal with the players and the game that day. That Dusty Baker has maintained his sanity over the years is testimony to training only the Marine Corps can provide. The 1993 season marked the arrival of Barry Bonds, who had become a free agent after leaving the Pirates. Bonds had many skills as a ballplayer and few as a person. The fact that I often marveled at things he did on the field was totally diminished for me by other things he did on the field, and the way he conducted himself elsewhere.

Barry seemed obsessed with trying to outdo his father, Bobby, who had five seasons in which he hit 30 home runs and stole 30 bases. For whatever reason, Barry was so determined to surpass Bobby, his stolen-base attempts were both shameful and meaningless. Players on opposing teams often wondered what he was doing, while his scornful teammates knew only too well. In 1993, when Barry finished with 29 steals, it provided many of us with the only solace that came with finishing second to the Braves by one game. In 1996, after reaching 40 homers, he decided he wanted to do what Jose Canseco had done before him, and have a 40-40 season. It never bothered him that his attempts, besides being outright selfish, also distracted those batting behind him. When he attained his 40th stolen base in Denver, two days before the season ended, he was the only one who seemed to care.

When Canseco became the first to reach the 40-40 mark in 1988, it generated a wave of publicity throughout the game. Asked to comment on the accomplishment, Mickey Mantle said, "Heck, if I had known it was such a big deal I'd have done it a few times myself."

Does anybody doubt that Willie Mays and Hank Aaron could have done it a few times if stolen bases were that important to their teams?

Despite Bonds' stolen bases, the fact is he is not a good base runner. Too often, he allows himself to get picked off in crucial situations, and he often is hesitant on the bases. In time, Barry Bonds will be elected to the Baseball Hall of Fame, and deservedly so. His hitting and defensive play speak for themselves. So does his behavior.

The 1993 Western Division race was as exciting as you'd want. For the Giants, it was just as disappointing. Winning 103 games, only to lose to the Dodgers on the final day of the season and finish one behind the Atlanta Braves, was tough to take. On the other hand, the Giants were 10 games in front of the Braves on July 22, and that's impossible to overlook. It was then the Braves did something unfair. They acquired Fred McGriff in a trade with the Padres. Pitching staff or no pitching staff, if ever someone turned a club around in half a season it was McGriff. He arrived on July 20; Atlanta won 51 and lost only 17 the rest of the way. McGriff's 19 homers and 56 RBI in only 68 games were just what Bobby Cox's club needed.

Meanwhile, the Giants began to sink. Their 10-game lead was wiped out in only 43 games, and when they lost to St. Louis on September 10, the Giants and Braves were tied. Dusty's team was starting an eight-game losing streak that saw them fall four games behind with only 17 left. It was a tribute to Dusty's skills as a leader that he was able to hold the club together and rally the players one more time. With Billy Swift and John Burkett en route to 20-win seasons, and with strong support from Jeff Brantley and Rod Beck out of the bullpen, the Giants won 14 of those last 17, including a three-game sweep of the Reds and a four-game sweep of the Padres.

The Giants regained a tie for the lead on September 28 when they beat the Colorado Rockies, 6-4, only to fall a game back the following day. On Thursday the 30th, the Giants opened the final weekend of the season, a four-game series in Los Angeles. Swift defeated Tom Candiotti in the opener, while the Braves lost to Houston. The teams were tied again with only three to play. The Giants knew they had to sweep the remaining games with L.A. because the Braves had the good fortune of playing host to the Rockies, to whom they had not lost all season, in their final three games. Swift's win Thursday night was his 21st.

Now it was Burkett's turn. In Friday's game, he managed to escape with his 22nd win, 8-7, over Ramon Martinez. Meanwhile, the Braves' Steve Avery beat Colorado, 7-4, for his 18th win. Both teams won again on Saturday, with Rod Beck saving the Giants' 5-3 victory. It seemed as if Beck had pitched in every game of the last two weeks.

On Sunday, as the Giants were taking the field in Chavez Ravine, they were aware the Braves were putting the finishing touches on Greg Maddux's 20th victory and completing a 12-game sweep of the expansion Rockies for the '93 season. This meant the Giants could not win the division outright on the final day. A win would only force a playoff, and a loss would end the season.

As his starting pitcher, Baker selected rookie Salomon Torres, who was held in high esteem by the front office. Torres was the name that always seemed to come up when other teams wanted to "help" the Giants out by unloading someone they no longer wanted. Such altruism was rejected at every turn. Torres, from the Dominican Republic, had made his major league debut on August 29, defeating the expansion Florida Marlins. He followed it up a few days later with a win over Montreal. He brought a 3-4 record into the season's ultimate game, having lost to the Rockies in his most recent start.

Baker's choice was a gamble, but no less risky than his other two options, left-hander Jim Deshaies and Scott Sanderson. Sending Deshaies against the powerful right-handed-hitting Dodger lineup would have tempted fate. Sanderson, an impressive-looking pitcher when he came up with Montreal 15 years earlier, had become a medical marvel. At this point in his career, his back stood a better chance of making it to Cooperstown than he did. His chief weapon now seemed to be taking so much time between pitches that hitters would swing at anything out of sheer boredom. I stood second to no one in admiring Sanderson's courage, but he would not have been my choice for Game 162.

No matter how much any of us would have preferred a different outcome, nothing will change the Dodgers' 12-1 thrashing of the Giants. Salomon Torres was the losing pitcher, and, to this day, Dusty is second-guessed. There actually are people who believe Torres gave up most of the Dodgers' 12 runs, if not all them. It's funny — I was at that game, and I don't remember anything like that. In fact, when Dusty took Torres out of the game in the fourth inning, it was 3-0. The Giants picked up a run in the fifth to make it 3-1. When a team has won 103 games, a 3-1 deficit is not what you'd call insurmountable.

However, by the time Mike Piazza and Cory Snyder homered off Dave Burba in the fifth, it was getting there. It was now 6-1, and things only got worse. To blame Dusty Baker for starting Torres is, as the great sportswriter Stanley Woodward once wrote, "like blaming the Johnstown Flood on a leaky toilet in Altoona."

The Giants' battle with the Braves for the 1993 National League West title was guaranteed in advance of being the last great division race. The following year, the geniuses who preside over the game divided each league into three divisions and produced a playoff format that included a wild card, the non-division-winning team with the best record. Now a team no longer had to win its division to get into the playoffs. The wild card would prove to be the Viagra of baseball. It didn't matter how you got there; all that mattered was that you made it.

While the 1993 season was a great one for the Giants, it was a difficult one for me. After Ron Fairly's departure, I no longer had a steady partner in the booth. What I had was a steady stream of partners, a situation that infuriated me by showing what little respect there was for the radio broadcasts. While it's true that I did several games with both Ted Robinson and Barry Tompkins, "several" out of 162 still leaves an awful lot. Most of the time, I had no idea who would be sharing the booth with me until the day before. It wasn't unusual for Larry Baer to inform me, "Oh, I got (Astros owner) Drayton McLane to sit in with you for a few innings in Houston."

It sure made me feel better knowing that if I had to get up and run to the men's room, I could turn over the mike to the owner of the Houston Astros.

The net result of all those guest broadcasters was I spent more time preparing for them than I did for the game itself. Bud Black, Enos Cabell, Bob Costas, Drayton McLane, Tommy Hutton, Al Hrabosky, Duane Kuiper, Garry Maddox, Gary Matthews, Willie Mays and Willie McCovey were just some of the men I worked with — all fine people. I'd have been happy to share a booth with almost any of them all season long, but a game here and a game there on a rotating basis was no way for anyone who cared about the broadcasts to operate.

One day in Houston, it came to a head. I was going to have Cabell, who'd done some cable TV games for the Astros, sit in with me. I'd also been asked to come over to the CBS Radio booth in the top of the fifth inning. When the time came, I turned to Enos and said, "Have you ever done any play-by-play on the radio before?"

Enos looked at me and said, "No."

"Well," I said, "You're going to do it now."

Enos looked as if he'd just taken a fast ball to the groin without wearing a cup. I left the booth and walked next door. The CBS Radio "Hometown Inning" called for the visiting broadcaster to do the top of the fifth. My CBS inning went 1-2-3, on only six pitches. I quickly returned to the Giants network booth, where Enos looked at me and said, "That's the toughest thing I ever did in broadcasting."

When I returned to San Francisco, Larry Baer was not happy and let me know about it. I said, "If you don't want people in there who can't do play-by-play for even six pitches, don't give me any."

It was obvious what little respect Baer had for the radio broadcasts, or for me.

Of course I could do the games with different people, but much of the time they were poor broadcasts with the guest announcers talking over pitches, oblivious to what was happening on the field. On TV, you can get away with that, but on radio, fans don't like to hear the crowd reacting to something and not knowing what's happening on the field. Baer didn't seem to care. All he knew was, for that day at least, he had solved a problem.

The 1994 season marked the end of the six-year deal I signed with Bob Lurie when I returned from New York. Before spring training began, Baer and I arranged a lunch to talk about the future. I told him the travel was getting tougher on me every year and I didn't know how much longer I could keep doing this. When he wondered what the club could do about it, I asked if I could stay on the concierge floor of each hotel on the road. The concierge floor usually is a little quieter, and you can eat breakfast and grab a newspaper without having to go downstairs. Given all my years with the Giants, it wasn't a lot to ask for. Baer agreed. I suppose I should have requested that this begin with the coming season, instead of with the new contract. That way, I'd have found out a year earlier he had little intention of honoring it.

In the course of a baseball season, a team checks into a hotel about 25 times. In 1995, it seemed all I ever heard from Reggie Younger, the Giants' traveling secretary, was, "There aren't any concierge rooms available" or, "You'll have to discuss it with Larry." In fairness to Reggie, he was doing what he was told.

Looking back on it, I should have confronted Baer earlier. It wasn't until we opened the 1996 season in Atlanta, and I got the same treatment, that I phoned Larry back in San Francisco and threatened to quit. This time I made sure he "heard me" and "knew where I was coming from."

The next day, Reggie came to me and told me, in effect, that concierge rooms all over the National League suddenly seemed to have opened up. If Baer hadn't recognized I was serious, this remarkable moment in hotel history probably never would have taken place. Faced with the reality of some embarrassing publicity, Larry decided it might not be a good idea to nickel-and-dime me.

The Giants did honor my request for my own row on the charter flights. Of course, this didn't cost them anything. Much of the time, many of us had our own rows anyway. What I resented were the times when the team had an important series, and people you never saw all season, media and others, decided to jump on the bandwagon. What little comfort I found on airplanes disappeared.

When Baer and my agent Jeff Moorad negotiated my final contract, I told Jeff I wanted only two more years, 1995 and '96. I couldn't imagine going any longer. The truth was, I couldn't imagine surviving two more years. Once Carla and I bought the house in Florida, however, at least I could see light at the end of the dugout tunnel. While I only wanted two years, Baer insisted on four. Even Jeff couldn't understand why I'd be willing to walk away from the nearly $1 million those last two years would bring me. I knew Jeff wasn't thinking about agent's fees.

The best thing I ever did in business was hire Leigh Steinberg and Jeff Moorad, who, along with their associate Scott Parker, were like family. If Jeff was concerned about those last two years, it was to make my retirement more comfortable. My goal was to live long enough to have a retirement. "Four more years" might make a nice campaign slogan, but I wasn't running for office. "Two more years" sounded better to me.

Baer continued to insist on four. Finally, it dawned on me: They couldn't stop me from retiring after two years, so what was the difference? Besides, if conditions got better for me, I might even stay on. Excuse me for laughing in retrospect.

When the 1996 season got under way, Jeff and I began to discuss an appropriate time to make an announcement. We agreed late August seemed right. This would give the Giants plenty of time to fill my spot. I planned to draft a letter to Peter Magowan and told Jeff I would go over it with him before I sent it. Once we agreed on it, I hand-delivered it to Shirley Casabat, Peter's executive assistant.

Peter had always been a Hank Greenwald advocate. He demonstrated his loyalty as far back as 1986, when I left KNBR because of Bill Dwyer. As Chairman of Safeway Stores, Peter pulled his advertising off the station's Giants broadcasts for a year. When I returned in 1989, he and Safeway were prime supporters of an Easter Seals dinner in my honor at the St. Francis Hotel. Safeway had always been generous in its support of Easter Seals, which had done so much to help my daughter Kellie. What puzzled me was why Peter, as President of the Giants, would have authorized that four-year contract, only to have Larry Baer give me so much grief over a modest provision. If I had even the most remote thought of staying on those last two years, that killed it. Peter was a "hands on" guy when it came to the Giants. Certainly he must have known what Larry was doing. Maybe I'm wrong. I hope so.

Before making a formal announcement of my retirement, I had to tell the guys I worked with. Lee Jones and I went back to 1979, when I started broadcasting Giants games. Lee was far more intelligent than the rest of us, proof of which was his decision to stop traveling several years ago and work only the home games. You could talk about almost anything with Lee; he was interested in many subjects. I thought he would have made a good professor. It was always a comforting sight to walk into the booth and see "Lee J."

In l985, Mike Marshall of the Dodgers collided with Duane Kuiper near second base and helped launch Duane's career as a broadcaster. What a break it was for me. Over the years, we did a lot of games together on TV and radio, and I loved every minute. It was easy to see how he came by his nickname, "Smoothie." The man has no rough edges. Knowing I was scheduled to work a game with Kuip put me in the best mood I'd be in all day.

The good news about working with Mike Krukow on the air was the same as the bad news. You never knew what he was going to say next. I loved it and feared it, but it was always fun, and that's a big part of what a baseball broadcast should be. No one worked harder than Mike to refine his ability as a broadcaster. You only needed to tell him something once.

During our time together on the air, Mike called me "The Captain." If I was "The Captain," he was a Green Beret. If you have to go into battle somewhere, Krukow's the guy you want next to you.

Ted Robinson was hired to replace Ron Fairly. I wasn't happy about Fairly's departure, and my attitude didn't do much to make Ted feel welcome. I wasn't very professional about it, but neither were the Giants in the way they dealt with Ron. It was only when I realized I had sunk to their level that I got over it. I began to enjoy Ted's company, both on and off the air. In the time we worked together, we became good friends. He knows he can confide in me, and I feel the same about him.

Raul Velez began to engineer our road games my last two years with the Giants. Raul could make anything electronic look simple. Engineers twice his age came to him for answers. Raul is a terrific young man with an unlimited future. Breaking the news to these people wasn't easy, but it was a relief. Except for those who needed to know, I had kept my intention to retire mostly to myself. Now that it was being announced, it began to seem real. For the first time, I started to enjoy the season. There were only five weeks left, and the thought of my career coming to an end didn't bother me at all. As many of my colleagues in the business reminded me, I was going out on my own. In that regard, I think some even envied me.

When the season ended, Jon Miller was named to replace me. I'd known and admired Jon for many years. His reputation as a fine broadcaster was well established. I related well to him, as we both put any scale we stepped on to the ultimate challenge. I never felt it would take a big man to fill my seat in the Giants' booth, but I'm flattered the Giants did. With Kuip, Ted, Kruk and Jon, the broadcasts are in good hands for years to come.

In those last days at Candlestick, many well-wishers stopped by the booth.

Most understood my desire to do other things with my time, such as spend more time with my family. Others spoke of the joys of retirement. It seemed as if they all brought me cigars.

One fan made me a humidor large enough to hold all of Cuba. It now occupies a prominent place in my house in Naples, Florida.

One of the things I enjoyed most was hearing fans recall exactly where they were when I described a certain play or told a story. You don't think about such things when you're broadcasting a game. You're not often conscious of any impact you might have on people, except for your desire to be informative and entertaining. It's not until you reach the end of the line that you're made aware of what you meant to those on the other end of the radio. I thought back to all the times I was ready to leave the house for the ballpark and couldn't do it until I checked one more fact or story. At the time, you wonder to yourself: Is it really worth it? Does anybody care? How satisfying it was to find the answer was yes.

On September 15, the Giants graciously held a ceremony for me between games of a double-header with the Pittsburgh Pirates. Carla, Doug and Kellie were at my side. Doug was home from his first season broadcasting baseball at Bend, Oregon, in the Western League. It couldn't get any more symbolic than that. Duane, Mike and Ted were the masters of ceremonies, and each offered reminiscences. Lee Jones presented me with a beautifully engraved humidor (a man can't have too many humidors), and I almost broke down when we hugged each other. As the ceremonies continued, I was of two minds. Part of me wanted to get it over with, while the other wanted it to go on forever. I listened as others spoke. If it was possible to eavesdrop at your own funeral, this must have been what it would be like.

Art Spander, a gifted columnist and old friend, spoke and did the impossible, for Art. He kept it short. Inwardly, I blessed him. KNBR's Tony Salvadore, a true baseball fan, presented me with an inscribed piece of crystal with a beautifully made baseball on top. Peter Magowan said such nice things, I wasn't sure who he was talking about. Knowing of our plans to attend the Olympics in 2000, Peter presented Carla and me with two round-trip tickets to Sydney. Peter's feelings toward me were evident once more. Others might have made those tickets one-way. Peter also introduced me, and it was my turn to speak. It wasn't until late the night before that I finished polishing up everything I wanted to say. I thanked Bob Lurie. I spoke of the guys I worked with on the air, of Dusty Baker, of Mike Murphy, the Giants' equipment manager, who's in every baseball person's hall of fame as a great human being. I thanked the fans for putting up with me for 16 seasons, and I thanked Peter for his loyalty over the years.

Then there was my family. What could I say about them? I thought about all the times I had to leave them at the start of another road trip. I hated that part of the job. I looked at them and said, "It was only the sight of them standing there at the airport, at the end of another long road trip, that enabled me to keep going."

I was thankful to have finished on my feet, and the ceremony was over. There was still the second game of the double-header to play, and it was back upstairs for me. Ted and I were working together, and, as the second game went into the 10th inning, I turned to him and said, "Did you ever have one of those truly memorable days in your life that you hoped would never end? As we head into the 10th inning, I think this is going to be one of them."

Two weeks later, I did my final game. I loved the idea that it would be at Denver's Coors Field, a real ballpark. I was touched that 48,000 turned out that day, until someone reminded me the Rockies drew 48,000 for every game. Bud Geracie of the *San Jose Mercury-News* flew in to write about my last broadcast. I was scheduled to work with Ted and Mike. Duane, who was off that day, asked to do one last inning with me, a gesture I'll never forget.

When the game reached the top of the ninth, Mike Swanson, the Rockies' media relations director and one of my favorite people, had it announced to the crowd that this was my last game. Maybe he was as happy as I was. We'd played a few scoreboard tricks on each other over the years. The fans gave me a nice hand, and the Jumbotron board showed me waving. Thanks to Swanson, the fans in Denver could see why I now worked solely on the radio. Mercifully, the Giants' 12-3 loss to the Rockies came to an end. We all sat around on a lengthy post-game show and reminisced. Lon Simmons, the longtime Giants announcer who had returned in 1996 after his years with the A's, joined us. My colleagues seemed intent on breaking me up. I'll admit I came close; after having watched the Giants the last two seasons, tears were not hard to come by. We finally made our farewells and signed off.

One of my joys in life is riding trains. I'd never taken the California Zephyr from Denver before. Knowing the season would end there, I'd made plans, months earlier, to do so. I knew I needed some time for reflection and didn't want to fly back on the team charter. I would stay in Denver overnight and take the train the next morning.

It was only a 15-minute walk from Coors Field back to the hotel. As I crossed the intersection in front of the ballpark, two women came over and introduced themselves. They were part of a group from Sacramento that had come to see Coors Field and the Giants' final series of the season. They were walking back to their hotel to meet a bus that would take their group to the airport. As we walked and chatted about the Giants, the ballpark, the game and the season, I felt euphoric, unable to recall many other times when I didn't have a care in the world.

Eventually we reached their hotel and said goodbye. They wished me well and disappeared into the lobby. As I stood there waving, I thought, what a perfect way to end it — walking with a couple of fans, talking baseball.

All it takes to make you realize how fortunate you are is to look at those who have it worse.

7

A STAR IS BORN

She approached the microphone, put her two-minute speech in front of her and began. Carla and I sat there in the auditorium of Benjamin Franklin Middle School, recalling the days we wondered if Kellie would ever talk at all. What a long road it had been, and what a longer one lay ahead. There were 900 persons in the auditorium that June day in 1992, but only two who could share such a moment. Carla and I had shared many moments along the way, not all of them good. On such a special day, however, memories of sadder days were washed away by tears of pride and joy.

Kellie delivered her speech with poise I could only envy. I seldom enjoy speaking in front of audiences; she seemed to relish it. When I speak, sometimes every face seems to be the enemy. When she spoke that day, every face seemed to belong to someone who loved her. Kellie thanked her teachers and her principal. She talked about her friends in the special education department and throughout the school.

The superintendent of San Francisco public schools was sitting on the stage, and we hoped what he saw in Kellie that day would encourage strides in special education. Not many San Francisco public schools provided it. Kellie was, and is, an example of how far a child born with Down syndrome can progress.

We had no reason to suspect anything out of the ordinary was about to take place when Carla entered the hospital the night before Kellie's delivery. The birth, by Cesarean section, would be the following morning, April 20, 1978. When the time came, Carla was taken into the delivery room and soon we learned we were parents of a little girl. How wonderful! Our son Douglas, who was 3½, now had a sister. Everything had gone smoothly. Or so we thought.

When the doctors told us our new baby had Down syndrome, we knew it wasn't good, but we weren't sure what it was. It wasn't until we heard such words as "Mongolism" and "retardation" that the full impact really hit. Along with it, Kellie was born with a hole in her heart, a condition common to Down syndrome babies. We were stunned, angered, saddened.

In the midst of trying to deal with our own feelings, we had to think about how to deal with family and friends, all eager to know how things turned out. Neither Carla nor I have a large family. Each of us was an only child. Carla's mother was in town from Seattle for the birth of her second grandchild. Difficult as this was going to be for her, at least she didn't have to hear about it on the telephone. I would take care of everyone else.

There are times when you feel worse for the people with whom you must share your bad news than you do for yourself. This was going to be one of them. I called friends in San Francisco and other parts of the country and told them as matter-of-factly as I could. I told them what I knew and that we would deal with things as best we could.

Telling them what I knew was one thing. Telling them we would deal with things was premature at best. Probably the most difficult part of informing people of Kellie's birth and condition was they didn't know quite what to say.

What are you supposed to say to someone who calls to tell you: "My wife just gave birth to a daughter with Down syndrome"?

Do you say: "Congratulations"? Do you say: "I'm sorry"? Do you say: "I don't know what to say"?

Rather than subject them to that awkward moment, I tried not to give them a chance. Before most of them could say anything, I just kept going, informing them we were both fine and would take things one step at a time.

Doctors told us the hole in Kellie's heart could be repaired surgically. In addition, the chambers of her heart had failed to form properly, and she would need surgery for that, as well. Although Kellie was almost seven pounds at birth, she would need to be considerably stronger before an operation could take place.

I was more concerned about our daughter's heart problems. Down syndrome, by itself, is not life-threatening. Understandably, Carla was not yet able to separate the issues. The problems surrounding Kellie's birth were a devastating blow to her. Like most parents-to-be who are unaware of the sex of their child, we mouthed the same platitude about not caring what it was as long as the child was healthy. Inwardly, of course, we wanted a girl. That would have made it perfect.

When Kellie was born, we had our girl, and she was far from perfect. What we didn't know then was that it would take Kellie just a little longer to get there.

When word of Kellie's Down syndrome circulated, we began receiving advice, solicited and otherwise. Several people felt we should institutionalize her immediately. They told us it would burden us the rest of our lives. Our lives would be hell. We didn't need this. It would affect the life of our son.

Some of these admonitions were coming from people we knew well and cared about. One thing we knew for sure: We needed counseling.

We spoke with our pediatrician, Dr. Alan Johnson, and with a geneticist. Our crash course in Down syndrome was under way. We were told such children will develop skills but will do it more slowly. We were told to treat Kellie the same way we would any other child. We were told not to project. In other words, not to look at kids who were 15 and think, "That's what my child will be like." Just take it one step at a time. Most important of all, we were told if we decided to raise the child, to get her in a development program as quickly as possible. This would prove to be the best advice of all.

With all of this running through our heads, Carla and I came to one conclusion. Institutionalizing Kellie was not going to be the first option. That was the last option, the one you could always take when all else failed. Placing this newborn child in an institution would not be fair to her, or to us. We didn't want to look in a mirror knowing we hadn't at least given it a try. It frightens us now to think we could have made the wrong choice.

After bringing Kellie home, we spent many nights wondering if we were capable of dealing with the situation. Those who forecast our lives would be hell often were correct. On top of everything else, Kellie had what was called "failure to thrive." She was not tolerating formulas and not gaining weight. This was of considerable concern to us because the doctors didn't want to do the heart surgery until she was stronger.

Much experimentation took place before we finally found a formula she seemed to accept, but even then the weight gain was painfully slow. The doctors informed us that without the surgery Kellie most likely would not make it to age 3.

Carla began to take Kellie to the Infant Development Program at The San Francisco Easter Seal Society when she was 17 days old. Carla drove her there twice a week, all the while dealing with our 3½-year-old son and a husband who never seemed to be at home. She was proving correct everyone who believed women are indeed the stronger sex.

The time at Easter Seals proved to be the most valuable period in Kellie's early development. People are often amazed when we say she started at 17 days. Not weeks or months. Seventeen days! With a child like Kellie, early involvement is essential. The staff of the Infant Development Program began working with her, stimulating her senses and reactions. They were giving her the chance to develop, something that would never have taken place had she been institutionalized. She was interacting. She was with people who believed in her potential, not her limitations.

The Easter Seals experience was as beneficial for Carla as it was for Kellie. The other mothers whose children were involved in the program became her support group. Being with them also gave her an opportunity to put things into perspective. All it takes to make you realize how fortunate you are is to look at those who have it worse. With the exception of her heart problems (a big exception) Kellie was not physically disabled. There were blessings to be counted.

There were many nights that first year, however, when blessings were the furthest thing from our minds. Rarely did Kellie sleep through the night. She would wake up more than once, and nothing we did seemed to calm her. We went through all the usual checkpoints. We changed her diapers, fed her and changed her again. Eventually she cried herself to sleep. She wasn't alone. Somehow, her brother Doug, in the next room, was able to sleep through all of this, an ability he would take to a higher level as he got older.

Meanwhile, we would go on, almost night after night, supporting each other and trying to comfort Kellie at the same time. She would finally settle down at 2 a.m., and by 3:30 she'd be crying again. We were walking in our sleep, not knowing how we were going to make it. The part of the wedding vows that went "for better or for worse, in sickness and in health" was certainly coming into play.

Just as one of us was ready to crack, the other would somehow gain strength. I don't know how it happened. It just seemed to work that way. Some unknown force, it seemed, made sure one of us was always able to cope.

We were being tested, and we knew it. Through all of our sleepless nights and emotional challenges, we never doubted our decision to raise Kellie at home. It only took one little smile from her to remind us we'd done the right thing.

Although Kellie was not making the physical progress we'd hoped for, she was developing in other ways, thanks to Easter Seals. She could not talk, but she was learning to express herself. Neither Carla nor I realized the extent of this until one day we had her in a stroller at a local shopping center. It was Christmas season, and Kellie was nearly eight months old. We were in line to have her picture taken with Santa when the lady behind us asked, "Is your little girl using sign language?"

What a proud moment that was for us. Our daughter was communicating by use of her fingers that she wanted "more," and someone recognized what she was doing. It's amazing how big little things can be. Something like that strengthens and encourages you. It's that little sign that says, "Stick with it, you're doing the right thing."

We weren't as successful in helping Kellie gain weight. Periodically the doctors would monitor her heart. They would wait as long as they could before operating in hopes she could build up her strength.

It's strange how misdirected things can get at times. As much as we tried to build up Kellie, I was the only one who was gaining weight.

During this time our son Doug was developing a relationship with his sister. He was now 4 and had accepted the fact that his "brother" was really a girl. Carla and I had picked out names beforehand. If it had been a boy we'd have named him Blake. When the big moment arrived and we told Doug we had a girl named Kellie, he informed us he wanted "Blake boy" instead. Fortunately, at that age kids tend to get over things quickly. Doug, a quick learner, was grasping the advantages of not having to share a room.

We wanted the two of them to have as normal a relationship as possible. All parents know the importance of that balancing act when it comes to attention for each of their children. Kellie was going to need far more than the normal amount, and it was up to us to make sure Doug didn't get short-changed.

On April 20, 1979, Kellie was a year old, and Carla and I had picked up 10 or 15 years more ourselves. Looking back over the first 12 months, we conceded the days had gone quickly but the nights lasted forever. At Kellie's birthday party we were thankful we were all still there to celebrate. At this stage of her young life, Kellie was now able to sit up unsupported for as long as one minute. It was another milestone. Carla and I marveled at it the same way we do now when I sit up that long after drinking wine at dinner.

A few weeks later, following a catheterization, we were told the deterioration of Kellie's heart had reached the point where surgery had to be performed soon. I was in my first season as a Giants broadcaster and was about to leave on a two-week road trip. We were told the operation could be done Monday, June 11, the day after I returned and an off-day. It had been one thing for Carla and me to know someday Kellie would need open heart surgery. It had always been in the abstract. Now, suddenly, a date was set. It was staring us in the face, and we were frightened. June 11, 1979. Would this be a day of joy or sadness?

We met with Dr. Johnson and Kellie's cardiologist, Dr. Robert Popper. They were sensitive but honest. This would be no ordinary operation. The fact that she had not developed physically, as they had hoped, would work against her. On the other hand, if successful, the surgery most likely would make her a new person. It had to be done. Carla and I knew that without it she had no chance.

If we lost her, we knew it would be in the attempt to give her a better life. Intellectually, we could live with that, no matter our emotions. Our biggest concern was Doug. How could we explain this to him if his sister didn't make it? How could we deal with the inevitable questions, such as "Where is she now?" We prayed we weren't going to have to answer that, and that we'd have the strength to try if we had to.

There was another problem. Doug was scheduled for some minor surgery himself later that summer. Going into the hospital is never minor to a child. How would it affect him if he knew his sister had gone into the hospital and never returned?

Where was the book that had all the answers?

Carla took me to the airport on the morning of May 29. Kellie was in her car seat. This trip would take the Giants to Los Angeles, Chicago, St. Louis and Pittsburgh. For Carla and me, it would be the longest two weeks of our lives. Once the date was set, the anxiety and suspense started to build.

In a way it was easier for me. I had more to distract me, preparing for and broadcasting games. For Carla there was no such escape. Every time she held Kellie in her arms, she had to wonder how long she'd be able to do this. She continued to take Kellie to the Infant Development Program at Easter Seals. She was going to continue to give her every chance as long as she could.

I called home each night from the road. Baseball trips are long enough under ordinary circumstances, but this one seemed interminable.

The San Francisco Giants at that time had several players who were known as "born-again Christians." These were people who often verbalized their beliefs by giving credit to a Higher Authority for their successes and accepting God's will for their failures. Some people felt that leaving on-the-field outcomes in God's hands made these players less competitive, but I can tell you it never stopped Gary Lavelle from buzzing a hitter who was taking too much of the plate.

Any group that spends as much time together as a baseball team does is going to be close-knit. The players had seen Kellie, and they knew what she was about to undergo. I'll never forget finally returning to San Francisco and catcher Marc Hill saying to me, the night before the surgery, "We'll pray for your daughter."

I believed him, and to this day I believe those prayers helped. During that two-week trip there was something else that helped me get through it. It was the presence of Lindsey Nelson. He knew from firsthand experience what it was like to raise a child with Down syndrome. His daughter Sharon was then in her 30s. Lindsey was the most calming influence imaginable during that time, and for the three years we worked together as broadcasters. He was kind, worldly, professional and, most of all, a gentleman. Knowing what he had been through in his life was making mine a lot easier.

The man selected to perform Kellie's surgery was Dr. Bob Szarnicki. Sometimes you hear someone described as "a bear of man, but with the hands of a surgeon." That's Bob Szarnicki. He was an offensive lineman during his football days at Columbia. I figured if he could protect a quarterback he could probably take care of our daughter. The fact that Kellie's other doctors recommended him highly didn't hurt, either. Dr. Szarnicki told us the operation had a success rate of slightly over 60 percent. While we would have preferred better odds, such as 100 percent, there was no turning back.

On the morning of the surgery we went to the blood bank to donate. Kellie would need blood, and several friends were also willing to help out. The surgery was scheduled for 7:45 a.m., and we were advised not to show up at that time. It was going to be a long operation.

It's remarkable how we could have been nervous wrecks for the previous two weeks and so calm when the day finally arrived. I guess we felt everything possible was being done for Kellie, and that sustained us. It was either that, or we were just too numb to feel anything. We got to the hospital around 11 a.m. It was not until 12:45 that Dr. Szarnicki emerged from surgery and proclaimed, "I've done a perfect job."

If I have tears in my eyes writing this, I'm sure Carla and I must have cried like babies upon hearing those words. It's contrary to the conservative nature of doctors to say such things, but there were no words we'd have rather heard. Besides, who goes to Columbia to be conservative? All we knew was that Kellie had survived the surgery, although the next few days would be critical.

Carla and I celebrated the way we often did, by going to Perry's Restaurant on Union Street in San Francisco. In the nearly 10 years it had been open, Perry's was home to many of our happy occasions. None was happier than this.

The biggest job facing the doctors now was keeping Kellie calm while she recovered in the hospital. In addition to her limited use of sign language, one of Kellie's chief means of communication was kicking her feet. This is not unusual and is a practice often employed by baseball managers in debates with umpires. In Kellie's case, however, it was not a good idea following her surgery, as she had all sorts of tubes and wires attached to her.

After a couple of days, she did what any 14-month-old would do. She tried pulling them out. Because these devices were monitoring her vital signs, it became necessary to apply gauze restraints to her hands and feet. The important thing to us, and to the doctors, was that she was active. While the restraints were needed, the fact she was fighting them was a good sign.

One of her doctors' long-range concerns was that Kellie might ultimately get too heavy. Who could have imagined such a thing? All the time we were praying for her to gain weight, so she could have the operation. Now they were concerned she might gain too much weight. Her tendency to gain weight over the years has left little doubt she really is my daughter.

It could be said that Kellie really has two birthdays. April 20, 1978 was the day she was born and June 11, 1979 was the day she was given life. From the later date, she became a new person. Now, with a fully working heart, she was becoming far more responsive and physically active. To this day, Carla and I marvel at what that surgery did for her. And for us.

At the same time Douglas was developing as well. Each time I returned from a trip with the Giants, I brought him a baseball cap from one of the teams in the National League. By the time the 1979 season was over, he had them all. Now that I was home until the following spring, he said to me, "Maybe next year you should work in the American League so you can bring me the caps from there." It was evident to me his mind was expanding faster than Major League Baseball.

Carla vigilantly continued her round-trip drives to Easter Seals and the Infant Development Program. It was during this time that someone contacted me about serving on the Easter Seals board of directors. Once baseball season got under way, there was no way I could attend meetings. I told them they could use my name if they felt it would be of any benefit.

Carla had a better idea. She felt the board would gain more from having a parent familiar with the programs, as she was, and she offered to serve instead. She filled that spot for many years and made far more valuable contributions than I ever could. She served on the California state board, as well. Carla is much more of a joiner than I am. She's been involved with several nonprofit organizations and attended as many meetings as I attended ball games, it seemed.

She often chastised me for not being more civic-minded. Finally, I reminded her of the nonprofit organization I was quite involved with. It was called the San Francisco Giants. Unlike Carla, I'm not comfortable at meetings or events where the only reason I'm invited is because of my "celebrity" status.

While she likes to mix, I like to touch people's lives, presumptuous as that may seem, on a one-on-one basis. It's far more satisfying to me to talk with young people who dream, as I did, of becoming a sports broadcaster. When I was a young man, Hall of Fame broadcaster Curt Gowdy sat down with me one day and shared his expertise and experiences. He didn't have to do that, but he took the time. I never forgot that.

Whenever someone has come up to me and wanted to talk about broadcasting, I've tried to make time for that person. I don't mean the fools who ask me how I can stand to work with so-and-so, but the ones who are serious. I love to talk with parents of youngsters who have concerns about their kids' wanting to get into such a competitive field. Unless a parent is planning to leave his or her child a few million bucks, what field isn't competitive? Everyone should contribute to society in the way he or she is most comfortable. For me it's one way, for Carla it's another. The important thing is, we do it.

As Kellie continued to flourish, Carla and I were becoming less fearful of the future. We now had a daughter who was lively and adorable. Parents tend to use words like "adorable." We knew Kellie would develop more slowly than other kids her age, but she was developing, and every achievement was a source of great pride.

If we were to establish any form of normalcy as a family, it was important we take Kellie as many places as we could. If people stared at her because she looked a little different, so be it. She was part of our family, and where we went, she and Doug went when appropriate. Five months after Kellie's surgery, we took the kids to Hawaii. Kellie was now 1½. We were on the beach one day and noticed Kellie was picking up sand and eating it—— yet another sign she was capable of normal activity.

When you look back over a period of 20 years, you tend to think how much things have changed. What you often forget is how much things had changed 20 years ago from what they were before. In Kellie's case, that meant a lot. Despite those who felt from the outset she should be institutionalized, more enlightened attitudes prevailed in 1978, and more advanced techniques for her development were available. We were fortunate such help was available at the time she was born. When we say "such help," we are really talking about people. People develop techniques. Dedicated people administered the procedures that accelerated Kellie's progress.

It was people who shared with Carla and me Kellie's achievements, whether they were physical, mental or in the area of speech development. Every time someone says we've done such a wonderful job with Kellie, we're mindful of all those who helped give her a head start.

Because Carla and I are only-children, neither of us wanted our child to say the same. It was a wiser decision than we could have imagined at the time. It would have been a wise decision for us under most circumstances, but even more so once Kellie was born. Having a brother such as Doug is of tremendous benefit to Kellie, and will remain so in the future. I was 43 when Kellie was born, and Carla was 35. The probability is inescapable that someday Doug will have to make decisions on her behalf. Doug has already played a vital role.

There is a plus side to having your children compete with each other. In our case, it was a source of mental stimulation for Kellie. While she was continuing with her speech therapy with Dyanne Krasow, underwritten by the Elks Club, she was also getting plenty of it at home, thanks to her brother. While records suggest Kellie's first word was that old favorite, "dada," I'm inclined to believe her first full sentence was, "He's kicking me!"

It's probably not historically accurate, but it's the one we seemed to hear most often at the dinner table, where the two kids sat opposite each other. In time, as Kellie began attending public school and became more aware of the world around her, she added another accusation: "He's giving me the middle finger!"

As a young child, Doug had a remarkable way of doing things at the dinner table his mother and I never saw. What we did see was his sister responding. Even at a time when putting two connected sentences together was a big thing for her, Kellie always seemed to do better when accusing her brother.

By being a normal, teasing, playful sibling, Doug was making her reach for something extra when it came to verbalizing. While mom and dad kept asking her questions that could be answered "yes" or "no," he was doing things that forced her to respond in phrases and sentences. We could never seem to catch the little rascal if he was kicking her under the table or giving her the middle finger, but whatever he was doing was fostering a normal, healthy, competitive relationship, and we loved it.

A big breakthrough for Kellie, and for us, was being able to place her in nursery school when she was 3½. It was the same one Doug had attended earlier, San Francisco Living and Learning Center. To have Kellie "mainstreamed" at this early stage of her life was another important step. It gave her the opportunity to interact with normal children, and it gave them the same opportunity with her.

This was a bold step for the nursery school itself because those who ran it risked reaction from parents who might not want their kids mixing with someone who was retarded. There's a certain irony to the fact that while it's kids who go to school, it's often the parents who need educating. A school assessment reported, "We find Kellie to be an extroverted, responsive, socially aware child who has easily and smoothly adjusted to being mainstreamed."

Special time was set aside for the class to sit as a group to discuss handicaps and focus on their feelings about Down syndrome. Living and Learning Center was assisting in the enlightenment of the next generation of parents.

By this time, Kellie's personality was becoming more clearly defined. Whatever limitations she might have were not known to her. As far as she was concerned, there was nothing she couldn't do or didn't want to try. Like many kids her age, she loved to perform. Some do it because they love it; some do it for the attention. In her case, it was both.

It never bothered her to get up in front of people and sing, although her singing seemed to improve with the size of the group singing with her. Unfortunately, it seemed more difficult for her to focus on what she was supposed to be doing if her parents and brother were on hand.

One Christmas season, her nursery school class was performing at a nearby senior citizens home. Carla, Doug and I attended. As the "little angels" took their places on the stage, a lady seated within earshot of us pointed at Kellie and said, "I've seen that one before. She's a real ham." Kellie didn't disappoint her. Just as the kids were getting ready to sing, Kellie spotted us in the audience. For all to hear, she shouted, "Hi Mom! Hi Dad! Hi Doug! Out for dinner?"

Kellie was getting used to the finer things in life and, yes, we were taking her out for dinner afterward, if we could get her mortified brother out from underneath his seat.

In 1984 we took our kids overseas. Doug was born in Sydney, Australia, while Carla and I were living there in the early '70s. When we left to return to the U.S., Doug was six weeks old. We felt it was important for him to see where he was born, and we promised him that when he turned 10 we would take him there. It was now time to make good. Kellie was 6½ when we departed on this six-week odyssey. We left the day before Thanksgiving and returned New Year's Eve. This way, the kids missed only about three weeks of school. Our plan was to visit several places in Australia and spend a week in Fiji.

Our first stop was Cairns, in Northern Queensland, the gateway to the Great Barrier Reef. QANTAS, the Australian airline, had just instituted nonstop service from Honolulu to Cairns. Inasmuch as we may have been the only people who ever took that flight, it was soon discontinued. From San Francisco to Honolulu and then to Cairns makes for a long day, though you're never quite sure what day it is.

We were staying in an apartment-style hotel, which enabled us to order food sent up from downstairs. We could hardly keep our eyes open that first evening and decided to eat in our unit. As a rule, dinner at the Greenwald home was never a quiet activity. That night in Cairns was an exception. It was too quiet. We soon discovered the reason. We looked at Kellie, and what we saw was a little girl fast asleep with her fork raised inches from her mouth.

Falling asleep at dinner became a frequent occurrence for Kellie during our stay Down Under. The Great Barrier Reef and the beaches of Queensland gave us ample opportunity to enjoy the outdoors. It was easy to feel good, and tired, at the end of the day. Kellie was long past the days when "failure to thrive" was a problem.

By now she'd caught on to the trick of gaining weight: EAT. The problem was, her father was finding it more difficult to carry her back to hotel rooms when she fell asleep in restaurants. Gradually we worked out a system. I would carry Kellie, and Carla would put her hand in the small of my back to keep me going. Doug provided encouragement. What a family!

It was during this vacation that we came to realize just how much Kellie's communication skills had developed. From the days of asking for "more" with sign language, she learned a smile and a simple request could work wonders. This became clear to us one day in Fiji. The four of us took a boat excursion from our hotel to a little atoll called Beachcomber Island.

It was about a three-hour trip, and when we got there my first inclination was to look for Gilligan. There was a small hotel on the island with an outdoor bar not far from where we were sitting on the beach. Kellie got up and wandered off in the direction of the hotel. The next thing we knew, she was sitting at the bar having a drink.

Astounded and embarrassed, we went to investigate. There was no great mystery. Kellie had simply said to the bartender, "I'm thirsty," and he gave her a glass of orange juice. Our 6½-year-old daughter with Down syndrome had mastered the technique of hustling a drink. Carla and I were rapidly concluding there was nothing wrong with Kellie except she'd been born to retarded parents. While Doug was given to doing things independently, Kellie was more of a people person. En route to Beachcomber Island, there was entertainment provided on the boat. It wasn't long before Kellie was sitting in with the Fijian band and attempting to play guitar. Fortunately, Fijians are the warmest and friendliest people in the world. The guys in the band were loving it.

We were pleased Kellie was an outgoing child. We felt her personality would make things easier for her as it tended to make others less conscious of her Down syndrome. Carla and I wanted her to be thought of as a person first. We knew, however, we had to temper lack of inhibition with a sense of propriety.

This remains an ongoing effort. Kellie's inclination is almost always to participate. If there's a wedding, a dinner or some other social event, she's always ready to give a toast, sing a song or make a speech. Not everyone is as receptive as the Fijians, nor should they be.

While Kellie was obviously enjoying herself on our South Seas vacation, so was Doug. We often discussed Australia with him, and he, in turn, would ask us questions. What was the name of the hospital where he was born? What was the doctor's name who delivered him? Answering his questions at home was one thing, but being able to show him was even better. When our plane touched down in Sydney, he had a wistful look as if to say, "There really is such a place."

One day, while Carla and Kellie were off together, I took Doug to King George V Hospital. We went inside and checked the directory, and there was the name we had told him: Doctor John Solomon. He looked at it and nodded, satisfied it all checked out. We went to visit the maternity ward, and I tried to locate the waiting room where I cried when Dr. Solomon told me I had a son. While the intent of our hospital visit was to be a significant day for Doug, it was equally so for me.

Because Kellie required so much attention, it was important, from time to time, to do things exclusively with Doug. Much of the time it was at ball games, where I could take him in the clubhouse or down on the field. Sometimes Carla and I would get a sitter for Kellie and take Doug somewhere with us. It was not always easy being Kellie's brother, but he never complained. She embarrassed him at times with her uninhibited ways, but he was a good brother and deserved our full attention whenever possible.

By the age of 10, Doug had been well into baseball for some time. He often related things in terms of baseball. While in Sydney, we took the ferry over to Manly to spend an afternoon at the beach. We weren't alone. Going to the beach is not an occasion in Australia, it's a way of life.

We were sitting on the sand, people-watching and enjoying the beautiful afternoon. Two adorable little boys, probably no older than 2, were running around. Carla wondered if they were twins. We waited till they returned to their parents, and Doug walked down to where they were sitting to investigate. Moments later, he came running back to us and shouted, "It's Kent Hrbek and Tom Brunansky!" which meant, of course, they were indeed Twins.

Baseball had its hooks into our son, just as it had with his father many years before. At times, especially in Doug's teens, Carla worried that he wasn't interested in anything else. When I suggested we could try interesting him in drugs and gangs, she conceded baseball had its virtues.

Like her brother, Kellie loved going to baseball games. She could sing "Take

Me Out To The Ballgame," and it was becoming evident the line she liked best was, "Buy me some peanuts and Cracker Jack." There was the social aspect, as well, and it wasn't long before she seemed to know almost every usherette, ticket taker and, especially, vendor. She was an active child.

Carla took her to a lot of games but didn't get to see many. It wasn't long before Kellie decided she wanted to sing the National Anthem before a game. Over the years, I'd been exposed to a great many people making fools of themselves at Candlestick Park trying to do the same thing.

For some reason the Giants seemed to take delight in finding people who either couldn't sing or whose rendition of the anthem was longer than the games. Kellie began lobbying everyone, from manager Roger Craig to team vice president Pat Gallagher. A solo performance, though it probably wouldn't have been much worse than many of the others, was out of the question. Twice a week she had been participating in group singing at the San Francisco Community Music Center, and it was finally arranged to have her and her group perform the anthem. This prudent decision satisfied her and enabled her to realize another ambition.

Kellie was 9 when we moved to New Jersey. It was 1987, and I had begun broadcasting Yankee games. It didn't take long before Don Mattingly, Willie Randolph and Dave Winfield became as familiar to her as Will Clark, Robby Thompson and Chili Davis. Kellie was becoming a Yankee fan and loved going to The Stadium. This was more than could be said for Carla, who feared driving anywhere in New York, let alone the Bronx.

The Yankees became Doug's American League team, but the Giants remained number one in his heart. Summer nights, he stayed up until all hours listening to WFAN, just to get the late scores from the West Coast.

One Saturday, the Yankees had a special promotion with the Disney people, and there was a party after the game in one of the stadium clubs. Various Disney characters were there wearing Yankee uniforms. George Steinbrenner was on hand. Sure enough, Kellie recognized him and started toward him. I chased after her, not knowing what she might say and not eager to find out.

"I know you," she said. "You're George Steinbrenner. You're the owner of the Yankees."

George said, "Not me, sweetheart. You've got the wrong guy."

Kellie: "Oh, then you must be the owner of the Mets."

Even George had to laugh at that one.

Getting settled in New Jersey was not easy for Carla or Doug. We rented a house in Park Ridge for six months, starting in April. Carla began looking for a placc to buy. Surely she would find something before the lease was up. Wrong. Our lease was up October first. That meant Doug would have to start eighth grade in Park Ridge. When you're 13 years old and move clear across the country, it's tough enough, but to start a new school in eighth grade is even tougher.

Meanwhile, my broadcast partner Tommy Hutton and his family rented a place in nearby Washington Township for one year. Their problem was they wanted to go back home to Florida when the season ended, and in order to keep their place for next season had to maintain the lease. They wanted to sublet, and we needed another place to live, so we moved in and assumed their lease. Unfortunately for Doug, he had to change schools after only one month.

In New Jersey you're required to attend public school in the town where you live, or the nearest school to it. So he started eighth grade again, this time in Westwood, New Jersey.

Kellie was having no problem at all. Schools with Special Education classes were few, and she was bussed each day to Vilano School in Emerson. Carla was not happy with the Special Ed program in New Jersey. Coming from California, we were spoiled by what was available. We monitored Kellie's homework closely, and almost every day it seemed she brought home the same assignment. Even allowing for the fact we had no expectation of Kellie's attending Harvard, we felt she was not being pushed enough. More likely, it was Kellie who was doing the pushing. She was an outgoing child and, at times, aggressive.

One day she brought home a note from school. It read in part: "Dear Mr. and Mrs. Greenwald. Kellie had a rather difficult day today at school. While the children were in line waiting to enter the classroom, she and one of the boys began pushing each other. In the course of this activity she reached down and grabbed his penis."

Needless to say, Carla and I were taken aback. The three of us were seated at the kitchen table, and we began to question Kellie. Our daughter has a way of limiting her answers if she thinks she's in trouble, so it was not easy "uncovering" the truth. We started out simply enough.

Mom, dad: "What happened with you and Jimmy in line today?"

Kellie: "Nothing."

Mom, dad: "Your teacher said you and Jimmy were pushing each other in line. Were you doing that?"

Kellie: "No."

Mom, dad: "Your teacher said you grabbed his penis. Did you do that?"

Kellie: (silence)

Mom, dad: "Well, did you?"

Kellie: (more silence)

Mom, dad: "Kellie, for the last time, did you or did you not grab Jimmy's penis?"

Kellie: "Most of it."

Did you ever try to keep from laughing out loud when that was the last thing you wanted to do? Carla and I attempted to suppress it the best we could and only succeeded in emitting squeaking sounds. Hearing this, Kellie said, "Why are you crying, Mom and Dad?" At this point we were practically under the kitchen table, we were laughing so hard. It was no use. We just gave Kellie a big hug and decided if we ever wrote a book, that story would have to be in it.

Shortly after we took over the Hutton's lease in Washington Township, Carla found a house. It was in Woodcliff Lake, and the people selling were willing to vacate in December. So it was that poor Doug started eighth grade at yet another school, his third in four months. If 13 is an awkward age, it seemed we were making it as awkward as we could. How he survived is testimony to his good nature. The following year he started high school, and a year after that, we were back in San Francisco and he was in yet another school. They say kids are resilient.

It was becoming apparent that if we were going to have another reporter in the family, it was going to be Kellie. She could ask questions like Ken Starr, and some were almost as embarrassing. It was impossible to go anywhere without her introducing us to anyone she encountered, whether she knew them or not. We would get on an elevator, and by the time we got from the ground floor to the second, everyone on board knew who we were.

"Hi, I'm Kellie," she would say, extending her hand.

"Hi Kellie, I'm Bill."

"Bill, this is my mother Carla, my brother Doug and my dad Hank. He's the broadcaster for the Yankees."

There's no place to hide on an elevator, but that didn't stop me from looking. We tried to explain to Kellie such introductions weren't always appropriate, but she loved her family and never missed an opportunity to share them with others. Kellie's usual line of questioning upon introducing herself was: "Are you married? Do you have children? Do you have grandchildren?" The questions weren't always in that order.

In the fall of 1988, all four of us went up to Boston for the Syracuse-Boston College football game. We stayed at the Sheraton Boston Hotel, the same place I stayed when the Yankees came in to play the Red Sox. After the football game, we entered the hotel and spotted Tommy Lasorda and a group of men sitting in the coffee shop. Naturally, Kellie recognized him and we went in to say hello.

Tommy gave both kids a big greeting, remembering Doug from the times I brought him in the visitors' clubhouse at Candlestick. Kellie determined that because we were in Boston, Tommy must now be managing the Red Sox. In fact, Lasorda and former Sox star Bobby Doerr were in town for the annual Jimmy Fund dinner to raise money for children's cancer research.

The following morning, when we came down for breakfast, Carla and the kids went to check out the buffet while the hostess seated me at a table. Sitting at the next table was none other than Joe DiMaggio. I knew Joe from San Francisco, and I'd seen him a few times during the last couple of years at Yankee Stadium. We visited briefly before the rest of the family came to sit down. I made the introductions and prayed Kellie wasn't going to say something other than "hello."

I mean, this was Joe DiMaggio, perhaps the most famous man in America. This was one person whose privacy you respected. Kellie was remarkably restrained, and throughout breakfast we minded our own business. Finally, we finished and it was time to leave. We got up and were saying goodbye to Joe when Kellie struck.

"Hey, Joe. Are you married?"

I almost died right then and there. Of all the things one might possibly think to ask Joe DiMaggio, this wasn't exactly it. With the remarkable grace that characterized his Hall of Fame career, Joe got up, gave her a hug, and said, "No, sweetheart, I'm waiting for you."

Kellie hugged him back, gave him a little kiss, and we departed. It was left to 14-year-old Doug to put things in perspective. Leaving the coffee shop, he said, "Just think, Joe DiMaggio is the only guy who's been kissed by both Marilyn Monroe and Kellie Greenwald."

When we moved back to San Francisco in 1989, Kellie entered Benjamin Franklin Middle School, the same school where she would later deliver her graduation speech. She was also active in after-school programs at the Recreation Center for the Handicapped. She loved to perform when they put on plays. Kellie never met a microphone she didn't like. As she progressed into her teenage years, she was occasionally asked to speak to kids in other schools about having Down syndrome. It was pleasing to us she was helping normal kids become aware that people like Kellie had thoughts and feelings just as they did.

Around that time, there was a show on television called "Life Goes On." One of the stars was a young man with Down syndrome named Chris Burke. Patti LuPone and Kellie Martin were also on the show. Obviously we were attracted to the program and watched it every Sunday night. It not only dealt with Down syndrome, but had a girl named Kellie (same spelling) in the cast. What more did we need? It was a marvelous vehicle to demonstrate to so many people around the United States the capabilities of a child with Down syndrome.

"Life Goes On" may have contributed to a greater enlightenment, but life did not always go on so smoothly for Kellie. During her time in middle school and later at Lincoln High School, she would come home and tell us about kids making fun of her and calling her names. We knew, of course, Kellie was an easy target, and she didn't always help her own cause.

We were losing the struggle to keep her weight down, and, despite our efforts to make her conscious of personal hygiene, she often looked as if she'd just finished a game of tackle football. Kellie was also a good agitator. When we investigated her complaints at school we found, often as not, she had started it. She was becoming street smart in ways her parents and her brother never experienced. Our precious daughter was becoming one "bad" girl.

Around this time, one of Kellie's teachers suggested we have a talk with her about sex. He recognized in the less protective environment of a public high school she should be made aware that potentially harmful things could happen. We knew Kellie was aware of the word "sex," but, as with so many things, we were never sure how much she knew. She liked to throw that word around, and often when I hugged Carla, Kellie would say, "Oh, you're gonna have sex aren't you?"

Then she would laugh. Judging from the number of times she said that, she seemed to attribute to us powers more consistent with wishful thinking than reality.

When we discussed the topic with her, she would say she liked boys but didn't want to have sex, or babies. Given that she was barely into her teens, we were glad to hear this. We just hoped no one would try to take advantage of her.

There are things about Kellie I suppose we'll never understand. There are things she says that astound us and make us wonder how her mind generates these things. Even recognizing that much of her life has revolved around baseball, how do we account for her asking, to our absolute amazement, "Dad, does Lou Gehrig still play for the Yankees?"

One night Doug and I were talking baseball, and Kellie dropped the name Ed Vosberg. Now Ed Vosberg hadn't pitched for the Giants in seven years. I'd forgotten he'd even pitched for them at all. Where did she come up with that name?

One night during spring training before my last year with the Giants, we were having dinner. Doug was on spring break from Boston University and was with us. We were playing a word game with Kellie about names of baseball players. We gave her little clues and would see if she could guess the player. She was good at it, especially if the answer was Robby Thompson, one of her favorites. This time the clues were: He played for the Yankees. He hit a lot of home runs. He was an outfielder. He wore No. 3. Kellie still couldn't figure it out. Finally we gave her another clue. He was the greatest baseball player in history. Kellie's eyes lit up. It was obvious she now had the answer.

"Dan Gladden!"

While acknowledging Dan might be the first to agree with her, Carla, Doug and I were laughing too hard to tell her otherwise. Dan Gladden hadn't played for the Giants in 10 years. Where did she come up with an answer like that?

One evening in San Francisco, the four of us were in the car going out for dinner, Kellie's favorite social activity. She was in the back seat with Doug.

"You're my favorite sister, and I love you," he said.

"I love you too, Doug," Kellie said, "but not in the biblical sense."

I almost drove off the road. Of course, now that she got a big laugh with that line, Kellie went on to milk it the rest of the night. But the question remained: Where did she come up with that, and how would she know to use it in that context? We couldn't get the answer out of her.

Such things continue to mystify Carla, me and especially Doug.

When I was with the Giants, I left for spring training around the first of March. With the kids in school, this limited the time I could see the family during the month I was in Arizona. If spring break coincided with my time away, it was fine. Otherwise Carla took them out of school for a few days so we could all be together. After Doug went off to college at BU, Carla investigated putting Kellie in school in Phoenix for a month. But the public school system there put such a high price tag on their special education program, it was hardly worthwhile.

In 1993 I was walking out of Scottsdale Stadium when I ran into former Giants shortstop Chris Speier. He asked how my family was, and I told him how Carla had tried in vain to come down for the whole month but couldn't get Kellie in school. Chris said, "My wife and I run a school right here in Scottsdale. If it wouldn't bother you that it's a Catholic school, we'd love to have Kellie. It would be a good experience for the kids in our school to interact with someone who has Down syndrome."

Although it would be another year before we could take Chris up on his offer, I couldn't wait to tell Carla. I guess any time someone expresses a genuine interest in your child, it means a lot to you. It also meant for the first time since I started with the Giants, Carla could come to Arizona for the whole month.

Chris and Aleta Speier had six children of their own. They might have felt they were running a school even before they started one. Now, instead of six, they had about 85 kids to look after. The school, Ville de Marie Academy, was located in Scottsdale, down the street from the ballpark and about 15 minutes from where we rented. It covered kindergarten through 10th grade and would have its first graduating class in a couple of years.

In March, 1994, Kellie began one of the greatest experiences of her young life. Everyone connected with the school— kids, administrators, parents and teachers— made her feel welcome in a way no other group ever did. When she reached school that first day, she was greeted with banners heralding her arrival. Carla and I were practically in tears at the warmth displayed by everyone.

The kids gathered around her that first day, and before we left the grounds that morning, Kellie was one of them. Now, this was not a school with nuns walking around with rulers in their hands. Of course, Principal Speier made sure there was discipline. But these children weren't living in fear. These were genuinely decent kids.

By the end of the first day, Kellie most likely knew everybody's name. She had a remarkable ability in this regard, in sharp contrast to her father, who only recognized people if they wore numbers on their shirts. Actually, this carried over to Kellie somewhat. She had a tough time accepting Chris as the principal when, to her, he was Chris Speier, No. 35, shortstop.

Each morning in Scottsdale, Kellie would dress in her school uniform (not Giants colors) of navy blue skirt and white blouse. On Fridays, when Mass was held at a nearby church, she wore a red tie. I never saw a child so eager to go to school each day. This was not an inherited trait. Kellie's abilities in school were not equal to those children her own age. This was understandable. She did, however, have an unusual ability to spell. Often when we were in the car, she'd ask us to give her words to spell .

We'd pick out anything we could think of, sometimes reading them off signs we'd pass on the road. One day, we passed a restaurant, and Doug said, "OK, Kellie, spell 'restaurant.'"

Kellie spelled out: "r-e-s-t-a-u-r-a-n-t."

Now it was my turn. Just as we passed a cafe, I said, "Cafe."

Kellie: "It's the same thing."

It's hard to argue with logic like that.

Her proudest achievement in school was the day she brought home a near-perfect score on a spelling test. Allowing for inflation, the near-perfect score has risen to 100 percent over the years, but to this day she delights in telling people about getting 100 percent on her "spelling bee test."

Kellie was a quick learner in some respects, and it wasn't long before dinner at our condo in Scottsdale was preceded by a prayer ending with: ". . .in the name of the Father, the Son and the Holy Spirit. Amen."

This never concerned us one bit. Any group of people who showed as much love for Kellie as the folks at Ville de Marie Academy were entitled to a commercial. In fact, in Kellie's second year there, the school inquired if we'd object to having her baptized. We discussed the situation and explained that while Kellie might enjoy the experience, it probably wouldn't mean as much to her as it would to the school. It also wasn't practical to think we were going to raise her Catholic. We appreciated how highly they thought of her and thanked them. They understood.

Most people who know me will laugh at this, but I consider myself a religious person. I believe in God, and I deal with Him directly. I don't need a middleman. A belief in God is something I carry inside of me. I don't need to walk into a church or synagogue to get it validated. Once I realized organized religions emphasize the things that separate people, I knew this way of life wasn't for me. The last time I was at temple was when Temple played Villanova. What other people do is their business, and it doesn't affect my relationship with them. It's a personal thing, the way religion ought to be. So much for my commercial.

In the three spring trainings Kellie spent at Ville de Marie, she had experiences she never had in San Francisco or New Jersey. She was invited to birthdays, ice skating parties and sleepovers. Kellie was usually a happy child, but we never saw her happier. Sadly, her days there were all too short, but her time there is something she'll always remember.

The most satisfying moment came one day after school when we were picking her up. A young mother of one of the students came over and introduced herself. Her youngest child, an infant girl, was sitting in her car seat.

The mother said, "My little one has Down syndrome. I can't tell you what it means to me to see your daughter and the way she conducts herself. It holds out so much hope for me. When my daughter was born I didn't know what to expect. Now I don't have to face the future with so much fear."

With all Ville de Marie Academy had given to Kellie, it was wonderful for us to know she'd given something in return.

In June of 1996, Kellie finished her high school days at Lincoln in San Francisco. While she seemed to know almost everyone there, the people she talked most about were Principal Gwen Chan and Assistant Principal Peter Yan. Perhaps it was because she spent so much time in the office. On graduation day you can bet there were two proud parents when Kellie's name was announced and she walked across the stage at Civic Auditorium. For the three years since, she's been asking, "Can you believe I'm Miss Graduate?"

In January of 1997, when Kellie was visiting us in Florida, we learned of Mr.

Yan's drowning death. It took us some time to summon the courage to break the news to her. It was imperative to do so, because Kellie still called Lincoln High to ask about him and others she knew. We couldn't let her find out that way. The three of us flew back to San Francisco together, because I had a speaking engagement on the 13th. While we were home we broke the news to Kellie. She was devastated. She ran out of our kitchen and into the family room and was sobbing. Her understanding of death was quite abstract. In some ways it may be to all of us, but this time it really hit close to home for her. We tried to explain that Mr. Yan was with God now and was happy, and wouldn't want us to be sad. We hoped we were right. Eventually she calmed down, but she still asks about him.

Several years before Kellie finished high school, Carla began talking to me about getting her situated in a group home. I didn't want to hear about it, and the thought often reduced me to tears. Although Carla was thinking of the future, Kellie was very much in the present then, and the prospect of her living elsewhere someday was not something I could deal with.

Carla kept talking about a place called The Lambs, outside Chicago. She might as well have been talking about someplace outside Bangkok. The Lambs is supposed to be a wonderful place, but it's 1,800 miles from San Francisco. I knew there had to be other places closer than that. Besides, how do you go about getting a child in Kellie's situation to make a move anywhere away from what she's used to? I couldn't imagine it ever happening, for her or for me. I knew that, at some point, Carla shouldn't have to keep finding a sitter every time the two of us wanted to go somewhere. Carla had paid her dues far more than I. She deserved some freedom.

All of this I knew, but couldn't deal with, even though it might be five years off. Fortunately, Doug provided the answer by going away to college. Boston University was about as far away as you could get from San Francisco and still be in the United States. There's always some trauma when one of your kids leaves home for the first time. Thanks to sports, Doug and I shared a lot of father-son moments. How could I watch those 10 college basketball games we got every night on our satellite system without him? How we loved those rainy winter nights, watching Middle Tennessee vs. Eastern Kentucky. There was one thing I knew when Doug went away to college. If he was having a good time there, I'd be fine. Fortunately, that's how it worked out.

During Doug's first couple of years at BU, an idea popped into my head. Mindful that younger siblings often seem to want what the older one has, I began talking to Kellie about how neat it was her brother was in college. We talked about Doug's having a roommate and about how, maybe someday, she'd be able to do the same thing. The idea seemed to appeal to her. It was perhaps more important for me to sell myself than to sell her, but I knew if she embraced the idea it would be a lot easier for me.

In October of 1993, Doug's sophomore year, we took Kellie to Boston to visit her brother. She got to see his room and meet his roommate, Alex Benson. This was big-time stuff, and I could see Kellie was eating it up. By now, Carla had joined me in encouraging Kellie to look forward to the day she could be doing the same as her brother.

My concern about Kellie's living elsewhere was that she not feel her mom and dad were abandoning her. We'd seen her through so much. We'd raised her at home when others said don't even bring her home from the hospital. We'd been through the open heart surgery, a couple of pacemaker implants, the sad days when kids made fun of her. All of that and more. If we sent her someplace to live and she felt we were getting rid of her, I'd have been a wreck. Of course, we'd call the whole thing off. We wanted her to look forward to the day she'd be in a college-like situation with roommates of her own. If it took several years to get her used to the idea, so be it. We would do it slowly and at her speed.

Carla was checking out places closer to home— much closer. We didn't know how long it would take for an opening someplace we felt was acceptable. There were places that put restrictions on how often you could see your child. We didn't want that. We had the added problem of the house in Florida and my desire to spend more time there. We'd even looked there for a place where Kellie might flourish, but found nothing.

We wanted a place that would help prepare Kellie for independent living, a place where she might go to school beyond high school, a place where she might have a job, a place where she could learn to get around on buses by herself. Naples, Florida, as wonderful as it is in other respects, has no public transportation and doesn't appear to want any.

In April, Carla got wind of a place in Corte Madera, a little town across the Golden Gate Bridge in Marin County, less than 20 miles from our house. The group home is managed by Marin Association for Retarded Citizens, or MARC. Not only were Carol Loughlin, the manager, and Phyllis Tomlinson, the assistant manager, warm and friendly, their program was what we wanted. Kellie even knew one of the girls living there, with whom she'd attended camp. The house had six girls plus staff, and was located in the heart of a residential neighborhood. It was close to shopping and buses and close to College of Marin, where Kellie would be starting in the fall. It was everything we wanted. But what about Kellie?

She was the important one. The day we went to visit, she walked in and it was like, "Hey, this is pretty cool."

She was going to college. This was going to be her dorm, and these girls would be her housemates. She was having no problem at all. The years we spent preparing her for this had paid off for her and for us.

Naturally, when the day came to move in, I was on the road with the Giants. As Carla drove Kellie to her new home, she was accompanied by our neighbor Irene Spang. It was better for Carla to have someone with her, and Irene was the perfect one. She and her husband Jack knew Kellie from the time we moved in, in 1978, when she was less than three months old. Next to us, they knew her better than anyone.

Once they got over there and got Kellie settled, it was time to leave. Carla was fighting back the tears, though comforted perhaps by the knowledge she had to come back the next day. Nevertheless, when she arrived home the tears began to flow.

When I returned to San Francisco, Carla and I made our first visit together. Kellie was doing just fine. So was I, until it was time to leave. When I got to the car and we drove off, the tears started. It was nice that Carla was driving.

At this writing, Kellie is now in her third year at Corte Madera House, and her third at College of Marin. She's been trained to take public transportation. She has a job in the summer. She has responsibilities in her house. At school, she takes computer training (she operates mine better than I do), ceramics, creative writing, swimming and tennis. Where were these subjects when I went to school? In addition to all this she now has a social life, attends dances and outings, and participates in Special Olympics.

Carla and I now spend roughly six months in California, six in Florida in each of our two homes, from June till December in San Francisco and the rest of the time in Naples. Kellie spends a month with us from mid-December to mid-January in Naples and returns around her birthday in April. We usually get back to San Francisco to visit in February or March, so we get to spend time with her then. In between, Kellie's long-distance phone bills demonstrate just how much she's her mother's daughter.

When Kellie comes to visit us in Florida, she flies by herself. Phyllis, her assistant manager, usually takes her to the airport, and someone from the airline meets her when she has to change planes in Dallas, Atlanta or Chicago. Otherwise, she's fine flying on her own. Too fine, in fact. On the day she was due to leave San Francisco to come to Florida in December, 1997, we got a phone call. I picked up the phone, and it was Kellie.

"Hi Dad."

I thought the flight must be cancelled or something similar and said, "Kellie, where are you?"

"I'm on the airplane."

"How can you be calling us? You don't have a credit card."

"The stewardess gave me hers."

Just as she conned that bartender in Fiji into giving her a drink when she was 6 years old, she had now claimed another victim. Proud as we were of her ingenuity, we took great pains to persuade her not to try that again.

In April, 1998, Kellie returned to Naples to touch off her annual month-long birthday celebration. We reminded her not to borrow any credit cards and not to call us from the plane. All went smoothly. We picked her up in Fort Myers, and she spent 10 days with us. On her return to San Francisco via Chicago, I was using my computer to track her flight from O'Hare to SFO. Just then the phone rang.

"Hi Dad."

"Kellie, where are you?"

"I'm on the airplane, but I didn't borrow a credit card."

"How did you get the phone to work?"

"I used my California I.D. card."

Sometimes it's not worth the effort trying to get an explanation or trying to figure things out. It's easier to just sit back and conclude that whatever Kellie Greenwald chooses to do, she's going to do.

*"You guys with those goddamn tape recorders
are always misquoting me."*

8

DR. NAISMITH, CALL YOUR OFFICE

In the early hours of a February morning in 1962, a bus struggled to make it up a hill outside Cortland, New York. On board were the Syracuse Nats and the Philadelphia Warriors. The teams had played each other at Philadelphia's Convention Hall the night before, and in the meantime the weather had made flying out of the question. As the bus spun its wheels once more, it was clear what had to be done. The two teams and assorted other folks, including me, got out and pushed.

These were the Warriors of Wilt Chamberlain, Paul Arizin and Tom Gola, and the Nats of Dolph Schayes, Johnny Kerr and Larry Costello. This was the NBA of 37 years ago. As primitive as that may sound, the league had been in existence 13 seasons.

My first exposure to professional basketball took place in Rochester, New York in the mid-1940s, when I followed the Rochester Royals of the old National Basketball League. The NBL included such teams as the Anderson, Indiana, Duffy Packers, the Indianapolis Kautskys, the Sheboygan Redskins, the Oshkosh All-Stars, the Buffalo Bisons, the Syracuse Nats and the Fort Wayne Zollner Pistons. If you didn't know what a Kautsky was, or a Duffy Packer, or a Zollner Piston, you were in good company. Nobody did. There was no "Kautsky" listed in the dictionary. Eventually I learned many of the teams were named after their owners, which led me to believe my hometown team was named for Mr. Royal. The Royals, to my surprise, were actually owned by Les Harrison, who also coached the team and, most likely, took tickets and sold programs. The team played its games at the Edgerton Park Sports Arena.

Calling it an arena would be like calling Muggsy Bogues a power forward. The place held fewer than 5,000 fans, and the court barely fit inside the walls. If a player was driving to the hoop and couldn't apply the brakes, he simply crashed through the doors and ended up in the lobby. This was no place to be in short pants and an undershirt in the middle of winter, and players hustled to get back inside.

The Royals' roster in those days included a baseball player, a football player and several basketball players, not all of whom looked the part. The baseball player was Del Rice, a catcher with the Rochester Red Wings who later went on to the St. Louis Cardinals and several other teams and eventually became a big league manager. The Royals' Otto Graham played football and basketball at Northwestern. Not much was ever heard from him again — unless you followed the Cleveland Browns. Graham led the Browns to four championships in the All-America Conference and three in the NFL, and entered the Pro Football Hall of Fame in 1965.

The Royals had a center named George Glamack who couldn't see very well. Like centers in those days, Glamack played the low post with his back to the basket. There was a certain spot on the floor from which Glamack was effective with his hook shot. But George, with his poor eyesight, couldn't always find it. It's been said basketball is a game of X's and O's. The Royals, taking the expression literally, had a large "X" painted on the floor near the basket so George could find his spot. It's possible that was a myth, but as I recall, when George set up in the right spot he didn't myth often.

The star of the Royals at that time was a part-time player named Bob Davies. His playing time was limited because he also coached basketball at his alma mater, Seton Hall. Even in an unusual era, this was out of the ordinary. But Bob Davies was no ordinary player. He was a guard who could have played in the NBA in any era. He had speed, he could shoot, and he had court sense. At 6 feet, he might have been smaller than many, but that's a lot bigger than Calvin Murphy, Spud Webb and Bogues, and they did quite nicely. Davies eventually gave up his coaching job, became a full-time player and began to flourish. Davies' back-court partner, Bill Holzman, also knew the game well. Better known as "Red," Holzman had learned his basketball in New York City and starred at City College of New York.

The Royals of my youth also included Arnie Johnson, whose contribution was twofold: He got the ball to the scorers, and he made us kids aware there really was a place in this country called Bemidji, Minnesota. Bobby Wanzer, from Seton Hall, joined the club. Like Davies, Wanzer became a Hall of Fame player. Fuzzy Levane, who went on to coach in the NBA, had an overhead shot known as "trolley line," which was most likely the product of gyms with low ceilings. At various times, the Royals included Cal Christensen, Andy Duncan, Frannie Curran, Richie Regan, Bill Calhoun, Arnie Risen and Alex Hannum. The latter two were inducted into the Basketball Hall of Fame in 1998.

Risen was an outstanding center in the days when 6-foot-9 was still considered big. Before joining the Royals, he had once been a Kautsky. That in itself would have put him in my hall of fame. He was instrumental in Rochester's 1951 NBA championship season.

Alex Hannum was big, strong and tough. He could pound the boards, which would serve him well in later years when he went into the construction business. Alex's talents as a player were akin to someone who's described as having "a good personality." He wasn't a pretty boy as a player, but you knew he was out there. When his playing days were over, Alex became a builder of houses. Later, as a coach, he built championship basketball teams and a reputation that earned him a place in Springfield.

The National Basketball Association was born in stages, if not stagecoaches. Its parents were the small-town NBL and the Basketball Association of America. The latter played in larger cities, such as New York, Washington, Philadelphia, Boston, St. Louis, Providence, Chicago and Baltimore. In 1948, the big boys absorbed four NBL teams: Rochester, Minneapolis, Fort Wayne and Indianapolis. In the 1949-50 season, what remained of the old NBL was absorbed by the larger league.

Now there was only the National Basketball Association. The league comprised 17 teams, about seven more than it needed. By the time the 1950-51 season ended, the league was down to 10 teams after the Washington Capitols disbanded on January 9.

By the time I was out of college in 1957, the league had shrunk to eight franchises. The Rochester Royals moved to Cincinnati, the Tri-Cities Hawks (later Milwaukee Hawks) moved to St. Louis, and the Fort Wayne Pistons were now in Detroit. The league had two divisions, East (Boston, New York, Philadelphia and Syracuse) and West (Cincinnati, Detroit, Minneapolis and St. Louis). The Minneapolis Lakers soon moved to Los Angeles.

My association with the Syracuse Nationals began in the 1960-61 season. I worked with Carl Eilenberg, broadcasting the limited schedule of Nats games on the radio. Carl and I shared the unfortunate fate of looking like each other. This was not an advantage for either of us, but we sure confused a lot of people. On one occasion, I was in New York having dinner with a friend when someone spotted us. This person, upon returning to Syracuse, began telling people he'd seen Carl having dinner with a woman who was not his wife. It made for some juicy gossip. After a while, mindful of how few dates I had, I began to believe it myself.

The following season, the Nats' last in Syracuse, I worked with Joel Fleming. It was safer. No one ever mistook us for each other. He had far more hair. The Nats were owned by Danny Biasone, who operated a bowling center in Eastwood, a Syracuse suburb. Danny, Les Harrison in Rochester, Fred Zollner in Fort Wayne, Eddie Gottlieb in Philadelphia, Ned Irish in New York, and Walter Brown in Boston were among the pioneers of pro basketball.

Biasone was not simply a man who put up money to own a team. He had a genuine love of the game and was concerned about its future. When George Mikan was scoring points at will and his Minneapolis Lakers were dominating the league, teams decided their best chance to win was to hold onto the ball as long as they could. Sometimes they'd hold it two or three minutes, hoping for a good shot, all the while keeping it away from Mikan. Watching basketball players play catch with each other was the NBA's equivalent of a pitcher's throwing over to first base 10 times before delivering a pitch. It had all the excitement of an algebra final. Some in the league were concerned about the negative effect.

Only Danny Biasone knew what to do about it. He began timing how long it took teams to shoot in games not involving the Lakers, and concluded a 24-second clock would give them a reasonable amount of time to run an offense. Eventually, Danny's invention was adopted, and, by all accounts, saved the game of professional basketball. Danny's original 24-second clock is in the Basketball Hall of Fame in Springfield, an honor that for some mysterious reason has never been accorded him. There must be a higher qualification for inclusion than merely saving pro basketball.

Danny was like a favorite uncle. If he promised you something, you knew he was good for it. No contract was as binding as his handshake. The Nats, and those associated with them, were like Biasone's family. Even I even felt Italian. This made for an easy transition years later, when I worked for Franklin Mieuli and the Warriors.

The Nats of my era played their games at the Onondaga County War Memorial, which is almost as difficult to say as it was for visiting teams to play in. (And almost as difficult as ending every sentence without using a preposition.)

Teams didn't like coming to Syracuse for a variety of reasons. Syracuse was the Green Bay of the NBA in the '60s, the smallest city in the league. A Syracuse winter was not exactly what Irving Berlin was thinking about when he wrote "White Christmas." It was more like what Admiral Peary must have been thinking about when he discovered the North Pole. In a league that included New York, Boston, Philadelphia, Chicago, Detroit, Cincinnati, St. Louis and Los Angeles, opposing players didn't come to Syracuse for the bright lights, unless you counted those on the front of snowplows. For me, nightlife in the Syracuse winter was enhanced by having a girlfriend. This not only took care of social activity but helped keep me warm.

Almost as good a method of keeping warm was going to the Nats' games— another reason visiting teams didn't like it there. The temperature inside the building didn't seem to bother the Nats. When somebody said the team was hot, they weren't kidding.

The fans who packed the 7,500-seat arena were enthusiastic. That's the politically correct way of saying they were crazy. Often it appeared they were about to descend upon the court in response to a poor call or an overly physical act by an opposing player. Often they did. One fan ended up suing Celtics coach Red Auerbach for attacking him, even though the fan went onto the floor. He didn't win, but he got his name and picture in the paper, which may have been all he wanted in the first place.

In 1960, Danny Biasone hired Alex Hannum to coach the team. Alex got his first taste of coaching while playing with the St. Louis Hawks. When Hawks owner Ben Kerner fired Red Holzman during the 1956-57 season, he named guard Slater Martin to coach. Martin hated the dual role so much he eventually persuaded Kerner to let Hannum be the coach and let Martin return full-time to the backcourt. Hannum combined playing and coaching and thus launched a new phase of his career. Alex's leadership, combined with the play of Bob Pettit, Cliff Hagan, Ed McCauley and Martin, carried the Hawks to the NBA finals, where they lost to the Boston Celtics.

The following season, with Hannum coaching full time, the Hawks evened the score with the Celtics and reigned as NBA champions. Unfortunately, the linking of Hannum and Kerner was a match made in Bosnia — they were destined never to get along. Hannum, a strong-willed and principled man, left to coach in the National Industrial Basketball League for the Wichita Vickers. His successes there made it a safe bet he'd be working in the NBA once more. Having been burned in his relationship with Kerner, Alex wasn't going to coach for just anyone. When Danny Biasone came calling, Alex knew this was just what he wanted.

The Syracuse Nats had some outstanding players. Dolph Schayes was a perennial all-star. Johnny Kerr was the best playmaking center in the league. Guards Larry Costello and Hal Greer were two of the best around. Unfortunately, the Nats found themselves in the Eastern Division at a time when the Boston Celtics dynasty was in its ascent with the likes of Bob Cousy, Bill Russell, Tom Heinsohn, and Bill Sharman. The Philadelphia Warriors had Wilt Chamberlain, Paul Arizin and Tom Gola. The New York Knicks, meanwhile, were building around the hope that other teams in the division would somehow go out of business and provide New York with its best chance of winning something. The Knicks of the early '60s were a far cry from the clubs Holzman would assemble in the latter half of the decade. In the 1961-62 season, the Knicks finished with a 29-51 record. Every other team in the division was above .500.

The NBA frowned on more than one club's flying on the same plane. The reason was obvious. The league also had a habit of scheduling double-headers. These were popular with the fans and matched two teams in one game and two more in the other.

One night, following a double-header in the Boston Garden, the Syracuse, Boston, and Philadelphia teams had no choice but to crowd onto the same plane to Philly. This was a proposition only Johnny Kerr of the Nats could put into proper perspective. "Gee," he said. "Just think, if this plane goes down, the Knicks will be in first place."

One of the plusses of those days was getting to know everybody in the league. With fewer than 100 players, most people in the NBA were on a first-name basis. Teams played each other 10 or 12 times a season, depending on playoff fortunes, and often traveled together.

It was rare that anyone below a No. 2 draft choice ever made the league. One of the great exceptions was a kid from Newark, New Jersey and North Carolina A&T named Alvin Attles. He was a fifth-round pick of the Philadelphia Warriors in 1960. That was the season I met him, unaware that years later we would end up together in San Francisco.

A special advantage of double-header nights was the chance to spend even more time with players, coaches, writers and broadcasters from other teams. We were a close-knit group.

To provide for the double-headers, each owner contributed a certain number of home games to a double-header pool. It varied, I suspect, depending how well teams drew at home. Danny Biasone felt that out of an 80-game schedule, Syracuse could not support 40 home games. In the 1961-62 season, for example, the Nats played 28 games at home, 30 on the road and 22 at neutral sites. Many of the neutral-site games were part of double-headers, and some "home" games were played elsewhere, such as the Nats' game in Utica, New York, against Philadelphia in which Chamberlain scored 62 points. While the Nats played only 28 true home games, the St. Louis Hawks had 35 and the Knicks 33.

Alex Hannum was a teacher in the days when the inmates weren't running the asylum. He had players who were willing to be taught. Hannum's influence manifested itself in the future of many of his players. Jack McMahon, Dolph Schayes, Johnny Kerr, Larry Costello, Al Bianchi, Tom Meschery, Al Attles, George Lee and Billy Cunningham all went on to become pro coaches.

Schayes was a star in the NBA long before Alex came to coach the Nats. The two were teammates in the early '50s. Dolph was a child prodigy, graduating from NYU at 18. He put his smarts to good use when it came to basketball. Though he was not blessed with quickness, he knew movement was more important. If you lacked the quickness to get open, you made up for it by going without the ball until someone got it to you. You didn't have to be quick to sustain constant motion. You had to be in great shape. Dolph Schayes knew how get open, and he knew what to do with the ball when he got it. When he retired after the 1963-64 season with 19,249 points, only Bob Pettit of St. Louis had more.

What made Schayes a great player was a stout heart that enabled him, at 6-8, to battle larger forwards and centers. When a broken right wrist sidelined him for almost a season, he spent the recuperation period perfecting a left-handed shot so smooth you couldn't tell which was his natural hand. Schayes could go to the hoop, but was equally devastating from long range. His high-arching bombs would have accounted for many more points had the three-point rule been in effect. His grasp of the game was further demonstrated by his passing ability. The Nats differed from many teams in that two of their best passers were their big men, Schayes and Kerr.

Because Alex let me sit in pre-game meetings, I acquired both a practical and fundamental knowledge of pro basketball. I learned which opposing players to overplay to their left; who never blocked out (most of them); whom to foul late in the game; who didn't want to take the last shot; who would never dive for a loose ball; who turned his head on defense, and much more. Heady players such as Schayes, Kerr, Larry Costello, Greer, Bianchi, Paul Neumann, Dave Gambee and Chet Walker all understood how to exploit a weakness. Admittedly, there were few secrets in a league where you played each other 10 or 12 times a year. Knowing how to take advantage of them was another story.

My basketball education wasn't confined to what I learned from Alex Hannum. Going into the old Madison Square Garden was an education in itself. "Old" is a relative term. The "new" Garden opened more than 30 years ago. One night the Nats were playing the Knicks in the second game of a double-header. In the opener, the Cincinnati Royals were taking on the Detroit Pistons. I was sitting at courtside, watching the closing stages of the first game. I was puzzled. Each time the Pistons got a basket, about half the Garden crowd seemed to cheer.

When the Royals scored, it evoked a similar reaction from the other half. Why did this many people in New York care whether Detroit or Cincinnati made a basket? What did I know? I was born elsewhere. Had I been born in New York I'd have known these fans didn't care who won. They were gamblers, and each basket affected the point spread. Whoever said, "Once you get out of college is when your education begins," knew what he was talking about. My new understanding about point spreads and gamblers answered some other questions about the old Garden. It explained the presence of all those characters with big cigars, and why the pay phones were so popular.

Going into New York gave me a chance to spend some time with my best friend, Sandy Heumann. We grew up together in Rochester, where we attended Brighton High School. Sandy worked for Champion, a Rochester company that made T-shirts, socks, sweat outfits, and uniforms for high school, college and professional teams. The Knicks were one of his accounts. So were the Jets, Giants, Mets, Yankees and West Point, not to mention all the high schools and colleges in New Jersey and Delaware. Whoever I didn't know in sports, Sandy did. Before games at the Garden he'd meet me at the old Manhattan Hotel, and, along with Alex, we'd go over to Jim Downey's on 8th Avenue and have an early dinner. Sandy often was my scorekeeper at the games and later served in the same capacity for Bill King.

If there was something going on in New York sports, Sandy knew about it in ways no one could have imagined. For instance, when I was doing sports shows he'd call me and say, "The Knicks have the first pick in the NBA draft this week, and I know who they're taking."

I'd ask him, "How do you know that?"

He'd reply, "They just asked me to make up a jersey with Marvin Webster's name on it." I was happy to report on the air, "Sources in New York tell me the Knicks are planning to take Marvin Webster with the first pick in the NBA draft."

Sandy even voted one year for the Most Valuable Player in the annual NBA All-Star Game. The 1968 game was played at the new Madison Square Garden, which had just opened. Alex was coaching the East team. I managed to obtain a credential for Sandy, and we sat in press row. The MVP ballots were passed out in the fourth quarter, and each of us got one. Sandy looked at me as if to say, "What do I do with this?" Moments later we cast our votes. You're welcome, Hal Greer.

In 1962 the Nats had a Christmas Night game in New York. No one likes being away from his family on Christmas, and Danny Biasone understood this. Danny decided if his players had to be away from their families, he was going to be away from his. He flew to New York with his team, which in reality was his extended family. He took all of us out for a Christmas meal at Mama Leone's.

It was an interesting day even before we left Syracuse. The club frequently used a charter plane that looked like an old DC-3 and had been reconfigured to hold about 18 people. It was comfortable. I was sitting alongside Mike Dempsey, who ran the 24-second clock at the Nats' home games. It was appropriate that Mike was flying on Christmas because he was a large and jolly man who would have been equally at home on a sleigh pulled by eight reindeer. He also had a high-pitched voice capable of bringing dogs to him from all over Onondaga County. Everybody loved Mike.

Syracuse never has to worry about having a white Christmas, and there was plenty of snow on the ground that day. At Hancock Field, the snow had been piled up into large banks lining the taxiways. As the plane was moving toward the runway (you're usually No. 1 for takeoff in Syracuse no matter when you leave) the undercarriage of one wing clipped a frozen snow bank. The pilot detected a problem with the steering and stopped the plane. We all got off to have a look. I was surprised, and not all that thrilled, to discover the underside of the wing was covered by fabric, part of which was now torn. The pilot began making repairs on the spot. That was the good news. The bad news was he was using something that looked suspiciously like masking tape. There was good reason for this. It *was* masking tape.

I reluctantly got back on board, trying to content myself with the knowledge no one else seemed to be bothered. I'd heard stories of how they held combat planes together in World War II, but by Christmas Day, 1962, the war had been over for 17 years.

Because not every Nats game was broadcast, there were nights when I was just along for the ride, although I still phoned in my sports show on WOLF. I carried a tape recorder with me at all times and got post-game comments and did interviews, which I used in later shows. I was now using a portable tape recorder, thanks to a disaster I'd had one night at the old Garden. I'd been lugging a Wollensack reel-to-reel recorder, the kind you had to plug in. That was no problem. The problem was the old Garden still had DC current in its outlets. They didn't call it the "old" Garden for nothing. I blew out the machine, and probably a week's pay right along with it.

One night in New York I was seated at the scorer's table next to the Nats' bench. Alex summoned rookie forward Lenny Chappell to go into the game. As the former Wake Forest All-America ran by me to report to the official scorer, he stopped and handed me something rolled up in a towel.

"Hold this for me, will you?" he said.

I asked what it was I was holding, and Chappell said, "My teeth."

A lot of what I did never showed up in the box score.

The night of March 2, 1962, found me at home in my third-floor walkup apartment at 733 Maryland Avenue in Syracuse. It was a Friday, and I was getting ready for our flight to Detroit the next morning. Suddenly I remembered the Philadelphia Warriors were playing the New York Knicks in Hershey, Pennsylvania, so I turned on the radio. I could pick up WCAU in Philly, which carried the Warriors' games. Bill Campbell was the announcer, and as Wilt Chamberlain scored a basket I heard Campbell say, ". . .and Wilt now has 78 points."

That got my attention. As much as I was used to Wilt having high point totals, I knew he had just tied his NBA record, which he'd reached December 8, 1961, against the Los Angeles Lakers. That took him a whole game. Tonight he'd done it in just over three quarters.

It's amazing to think how much we all took Wilt for granted in those days. I'd look at box scores and see Wilt got 52 or 61 or even higher, and would accept it as just another Chamberlain game. It was no big deal to many of us because we were used to it. We acknowledged his greatness, of course. It was almost as if a 39- or 46-point effort from

Wilt was accepted with the attitude that everyone is entitled to an off-night. In truth, he spoiled us, and we didn't realize it at the time. Sometimes it takes the perspective of 30 or 40 years, and succeeding generations of players, to realize just how great an athlete and basketball player he really was. If Michael Jordan scored 50 points in one game, it made big headlines. Wilt averaged 50 points a game for an entire season. To be accurate, he averaged 50.4 for 80 games in the 1961-62 season, a total of 4,029 points.

This was not a man who was content to stand under the basket and drop in the ball. His pride decreed he would not be remembered in that way. So he developed a fade-away shot from 15-20 feet that banked in. It was an accurate weapon and impossible for a defender to block. A defender's only hope was to try to force Wilt beyond his range. Forcing Wilt Chamberlain to do anything was never easy. Wilt was a force, the biggest in the game.

I kept my ear glued to the radio the rest of the Warriors-Knicks game. Wilt's point total continued to rise. He was now in the 80s, where no man in the NBA had gone. When it became apparent he had a chance to reach 100, the Knicks decided it wasn't going to be against them. Coach Harry Gallatin told his club to exploit Chamberlain's one weakness. Wilt was a notoriously poor free throw shooter. His career mark to that point was just over 50 per cent. Fouling him seemed like a good idea except for one thing. When the gods decide something momentous is about to take place, no one or no thing is going to stop it. So it was with Wilt Chamberlain on that night in Hershey, before only 4,124 fans.

I held the radio close to my ear. I moved near my window to get better reception. Wilt was having an out-of-body experience at the free throw line. He was making them. As much as the Knicks were trying to prevent him from reaching 100, the Warriors were feeding him the ball at every opportunity.

Just under eight minutes remained when Wilt reached 80 on a feed from Guy Rodgers — one of Guy's 20 assists. When the Knicks went to their fouling strategy, he started knocking them in. He went on to hit 28 of 32 from the line that night.

Bill Campbell on the radio was telling me a story I couldn't believe. There was still nearly 1:20 left when he reached 98. By 1962, other men had gone into outer space, but Wilt was the first to do it without leaving the ground. With 46 seconds left, he jammed down the basket that brought him to 100. The noise coming through my radio was drowning out Campbell. Fans began pouring onto the court to congratulate Wilt.

It took police several minutes to get them off the floor to complete the game. It certainly wasn't going to affect the outcome. The Warriors were en route to a 169-147 victory. When the final buzzer sounded, I felt like opening the window and letting out a joyous yell. I decided against it. The neighbors might misinterpret and think I just got lucky. I didn't want to ruin my image.

I went to sleep that night wondering if I'd been duped by another broadcast like Orson Welles' "The War of the Worlds." I knew Bill Campbell's voice, and I could hear the Warriors' public address announcer, Dave Zinkoff, in the background. One hundred points was just incredible. It wasn't sheep I was counting that night as I fell asleep.

As my involvement in the NBA grew deeper, I found myself looking forward to the nights the Nats played the Cincinnati Royals. It gave me the opportunity to watch Oscar Robertson, the best basketball player I've ever seen. I make that statement mindful of Michael Jordan, Larry Bird, Magic Johnson and anyone you can name.

I always believed if James Naismith hadn't invented basketball, Oscar would have. In the same season Wilt averaged 50.4 points a game, Robertson *averaged* a triple-double — double figures in points, rebounds and assists. Today, if someone does it in one game, writers and broadcasters make a big deal out of it.

Alex Hannum summed up Oscar one day: "Oscar Robertson has developed more skills to a higher degree than anyone in the game." Oscar developed his mind in the same manner. He was always several moves ahead of everyone else. With 24 seconds on the shot clock, Robertson's mind was already at 10, knowing exactly what he was going to do.

Oscar was not a flashy player. He was not a spectacular player. He was not a fan's player. He was a coach's player. When he came down the floor, his first option was to get the ball to someone in the best position to score. If that failed, he always knew he could get the points himself. He developed a jump shot that was almost impossible to block. His forearm bent backward, parallel to the floor. The ball, sitting in his hand, was past his head. Often he would set up low and simply back his man closer and closer to the basket, turn and shoot over him.

One night after a game, Royals coach Jack McMahon was examining the box score. He got to Oscar's line, which showed 30 points, 12 rebounds, and 11 assists. "Just another typical Oscar game," McMahon said.

He made it look so easy many of us were often surprised after games that he scored as many points as he did. Over the years, there were several players in the league who captured the fancy of the fans more than Oscar — Jerry West, Elgin Baylor, Earl Monroe, Gus Johnson, Walt Frazier and John Havlicek, to name a few. They had flair and were exciting to watch. In contrast, Robertson was a tactician.

I first saw Oscar when he played for the University of Cincinnati. I'd driven the 35 miles or so from Vineland, New Jersey, to the Palestra on the University of Pennsylvania campus, the Mecca of college basketball in the '50s. Penn, Temple, St. Joseph's, LaSalle and Villanova all played their home games there. College double-headers at the Palestra brought in the good teams from all over the country.

It was 1958, Oscar's sophomore year. Earlier that season, he'd broken the Madison Square Garden scoring record with a 56-point game in the Holiday Festival Tournament. The night I saw him at the Palestra, Cincinnati played St. Joe's, coached by Jack Ramsey. Oscar didn't disappoint, setting up his teammates and scoring some himself. Cincinnati won, and its young sensation scored 43 of the most effortless looking points I'd ever seen.

That night, he also made the only behind-the-back pass I ever saw him throw. As Oscar was taking down a defensive rebound, Connie Dierking was streaking to the other end of the floor and was all alone near the free throw line. Robertson spotted him and threw it behind his back all the way to Dierking, who was so surprised by the pass it went through his hands and out of bounds. I drove back to Vineland that night knowing I'd seen someone special. He was the best, and only Larry Bird came close.

In March, 1962, the Nats arrived at the Sheraton Hotel in Philadelphia to find, despite the fact they'd made reservations, there were no rooms. The Eastern Division play-offs were about to begin, and Alex Hannum and Danny Biasone were not amused to find the hotel had given the rooms to someone else. Just then, Warrior owner Eddie Gottlieb, whose offices were in the hotel, walked by. Eddie's appearance at that moment lent credence to the rumor this was just a Warrior trick to inconvenience the opposition. Such acts were not uncommon in the NBA. Just ask any player who ever tried to find hot water in the visitors' locker room at the Boston Garden. Gottlieb was one of the league's pioneers, and, despite various commissioners, had a lot of authority. For one thing, he was the schedule maker, a curious task for a club owner. Gottlieb, or Gotty as he was called, was a short, stocky man who owned a great many suits, all of them gray. Conventional wisdom had it that in the coat pocket of one of those suits was an envelope, on the back of which he made the schedule.

There may have been a commissioner, but it was Gottlieb who knew the innermost workings of the NBA. Frank Deford of *Sports Illustrated* wrote, "The standard response to any question in the NBA is, 'Ask Eddie.'"

As Hannum and Biasone tried to figure out where to house their ballclub on the eve of the playoffs, Gotty wandered over. He proceeded to tell the story of how he and the Warriors ran into the same difficulty in Fort Wayne years before. "We all ended up, 16 guys, staying in the same room," he said. Nobody besides Gottlieb seemed to think it was funny, mainly because there were 24 of us.

Somehow the hotel found us rooms at the Warwick. This was a step up from the hotels at which we normally stayed. This impression was conveyed to us by the sight of several women in the lobby, all wearing mink stoles.

Earlier that season the club was engaged in a three-game series with the Chicago

Zephyrs, who were new to the league. The following year they would be known as the Chicago Packers. By any name, they weren't very good. The next year they'd be known as the Baltimore Bullets.

The Chicago series opened with a game moved from the Amphitheater to the field house at DePaul University. Inasmuch as the Amphitheater was located adjacent to the Chicago stockyards, no one objected to moving the game. Fragrances aside, the contest was played at DePaul in deference to the Zephyrs' rookie guard Howie Carl, a former Blue Demon. At 5-9, Carl was probably the smallest man in the NBA. He played in only 39 games that season but had a great seat for the rest of them. Coach Jim Pollard put him in the starting lineup, and on the night of his homecoming Carl was once again a star. The same person who would average only 5.5 points a game threw in 22, and the Zephyrs got one of their 18 victories that season.

The Zephyrs figured playing the Nats two nights in a row in Chicago wasn't going to have fans knocking down the doors, so we flew the following day to Evansville, Indiana. A few years later, Jerry Sloan would come out of college at Evansville and play for a Chicago team known as the Bulls. As I recall, there was no occasion connected with playing the game there. It was becoming apparent to me that if you wanted to see the world, you could forget the Navy and join the NBA.

Both teams were on the plane that winter afternoon, and the flight was proceeding nicely until suddenly a strange voice blurted over the intercom, "All right, you guys, you better take a good look up there at heaven, especially those of you who didn't score 10 points last night, because that's the closest you're gonna get."

All the Nats recognized the voice of Joe Abajian. An Armenian with a thin mustache, Joe owned Elmwood Cleaners in Syracuse and was a close friend of Danny Biasone. He often made trips with the team. The Chicago players were ready to get off right then and there at 8,000 feet. While the Zephyrs were wondering what was happening, Abajian was just warming up. Still in control of the microphone, he said, "I don't want you guys to get worried, but I'm gonna take this plane down in a few minutes. It's the first time I've ever done it, but they say there's a first time for everything."

The uncontrollable laughter of the Syracuse players gave it away. The Nats won the game in Evansville. Hannum was not happy with their performance, however, and kept the locker room door closed as he delivered a stern post-game message. Great coaches aren't fooled by sloppy victories.

When the 1962-63 season came to an end, the Syracuse Nats were sold and moved to Philadelphia. Management held a contest to name the team, and the winning entry was "76ers." It's just as well I never saw the names that lost.

Losing the Nats was like a punch in the stomach. Playing in the smallest arena in the league had been a burden. Danny Biasone knew his team wouldn't sell out every night, and even the nights it did sell out wouldn't help him break even. There were nights Danny could have sold 10,000 or 12,000 tickets for games against the Celtics, or for double-headers. But with only 7,500 seats, he was handcuffed. Faced with declining revenues and increased expenses, Biasone was hit with another problem.

A year earlier, County Executive John Mulroy, in an effort to aid the Nats, decided to cut their rent at Onondaga County-owned War Memorial. Mulroy's announcement that the county would no longer dip into the Nats' television revenue was an empty gesture, given that the Nats had no TV contract for the coming season. Now, a year later, Mulroy announced the county wanted to raise the rent to its previous amount. Worse, the Nats would be forced to surrender their offices on the War Memorial's second floor and move to much smaller offices on the first floor. Biasone countered by moving the team to Philadelphia. No one blamed him.

After the sale of the club was officially announced, many of Danny's friends had a party for him at Tubbert's Restaurant, owned by boxing promoter Norm Rothschild. Things stayed upbeat for most of the evening until someone got the idea to sing "Danny Boy." Anyone who hadn't already been depressed now qualified.

Although the Nats became the Philadelphia 76ers, not all of them went. Alex Hannum accepted an offer to coach the San Francisco Warriors. A native Californian, Alex didn't have to think long. He knew, of course, he'd have Wilt Chamberlain as his center, but he also knew the club had drafted 6-11 Nate Thurmond from Bowling Green. Many months later, when the next season got underway, Alex told me, "I now have the guy who can play Bob Pettit when we face the St. Louis Hawks."

With the Nats gone, I no longer had games to broadcast, limited as the schedule was. But I did have NBA teams to follow. I did a nightly radio sports show for the Maley Tire Company in Syracuse. I also had a wonderful arrangement with my station, WOLF. The station traded out advertising with both Mohawk Airlines and Sheraton Hotels. Mohawk was a regional airline covering mainly the northeast, but flew as far west as Detroit. In exchange for advertising, Mohawk provided the station with books of flight tickets, while Sheraton gave us coupons we could use to pay for our rooms at their hotels. Mohawk flew to several NBA towns and close enough to others. Sheraton Hotels were everywhere.

Often I would fly Mohawk as far as Detroit, then pay my own way to Cincinnati or St. Louis to see Alex and the Warriors. Just as often, I would go to Philadelphia to cover the former Nats, who were now coached by Dolph Schayes. While traveling, I was able to do my show by telephone and also feed taped comments from players after games. When I was back in Syracuse, I used longer pieces I'd recorded when I could sit down with a coach or player.

Thanks to the advertising tradeout, I was able to get material the listeners seemed to enjoy. One night in Philadelphia, however, I ran into a roadblock named Red Auerbach. I was in the Celtics' locker room at Convention Hall after Boston played the 76ers. There was a group of reporters around the Celtics' coach, and I was among them with my small tape recorder. Suddenly Auerbach pointed at me and cried, "You! You get outta here. You guys with those goddamn tape recorders are always misquoting me."

You might say I was having trouble understanding Red's logic, but I knew he meant business. I turned to leave, and as I was making my way out someone called to me. It was Bill Russell. He was sitting by himself in front of his locker. Having overheard what Auerbach said, Russell tried to make me feel better.

"Listen, kid," Russell said. "Don't take what Red said personally. He's always saying things when he doesn't know what he's talking about."

Based on what I'd heard from Auerbach, I concluded Bill Russell was a smart man. I also knew he didn't have to take the time to make me feel better, but I was grateful he did.

In addition to my shows on WOLF, I was doing pre-game and halftime features on the New York Giants Football Network throughout the Northeast. Woody Erdman, who owned my station, also owned the rights to the Giants' network. My features were taped during the week, and I attended a lot of the games in person.

One weekend in 1963, I flew to Philadelphia, planning to catch the 76ers on Friday night, the Knicks in New York Saturday, then the Giants-St. Louis Cardinals football game at Yankee Stadium on Sunday. Sandy Heumann happened to be in South Jersey on Friday and planned to meet me at the Sheraton. We would drive to New York after the game.

Friday afternoon, I had some time to wander around. I stopped at a bookstore on Walnut Street. As I was glancing at various books, I could hear a voice on a radio in the background: "It has now been confirmed that President Kennedy is dead. The president died of wounds from bullets fired by a sniper during a visit to Dallas."

I couldn't say a word. All the breath had gone out of me. I was almost 10 when President Franklin D. Roosevelt died. My mother was crying when I came home from school that day. She must have felt then as I did now, standing in that bookstore not knowing what to do next. When some semblance of rationality returned to me, I concluded there was no way the 76ers' game was going to be played that night. I walked around in a daze, trying to grasp the implications of what I'd heard.

Lyndon Johnson was now the president, and some guy named Lee Harvey Oswald had been arrested in connection with the killing. I made my way back to the Sheraton to meet Sandy. We decided we would eat there and then drive to his place in Fort Lee,

New Jersey. Everywhere we looked, television sets were on, covering the assassination. We stood and watched. There was the reassuring face of former President Eisenhower. The sight of him made me feel better, at least momentarily.

Sandy and I finally tore ourselves away long enough to eat. Later, we made the drive to his place. We spent Saturday reading all the newspaper accounts while following the events on television.

It was a relief to walk into Madison Square Garden, where, for a couple of hours, Sandy and I could get our minds on something else. The Knicks beat the Detroit Pistons, 108-99, one of their few victories in a 22-58 season.

By Sunday, Commissioner Pete Rozelle had declared NFL games would be played. Not unexpectedly, this brought a torrent of criticism from those who felt he should have respected the fallen president by not playing at all. For my part, I'd felt enough grief already, and knew there would be a lot more the next day when I watched the funeral on television. I was right.

Meanwhile, the games were on for Sunday, and I had to be there. I was flying back to Syracuse afterward. I arrived at Yankee Stadium early enough to spend time in the press room. Media people milled around, talking and eating. The door opened, and Red Smith, the famed *New York Herald Tribune* columnist, walked in. Red announced to all within earshot, "Oswald has just been shot and killed." Many thought it was a joke, and not a very good one. Obviously it couldn't be true. But Jack Ruby's pistol made sure it was. The prevailing thought at that moment was: What else could possibly happen?

The NBA season moved on. In February, the San Francisco Warriors traveled to St. Louis for a two-game series that opened on a Saturday night. I arrived that morning from Cincinnati and called Alex Hannum. We made plans to watch the Bradley-Wichita State game on TV. He was interested in Wichita's Dave Stallworth, as were many other NBA coaches.

While we were watching the game, the telephone rang. This was not uncommon. Coaches are often pestered by reporters or people purporting to be old friends or alums from college days who are looking for a couple of tickets. This time, though, it was different. Just when you think you've heard them all, there's always one that tops everything. The call was from a woman from Peoria who was in St. Louis with her two sons. She was on the house phone in the lobby. As only a mother with two sons could, she asked Alex if he could bring the team down to the lobby so her boys could meet them. Hannum explained that during the day the players were on their own and that many of them were either out of the hotel or up in their rooms resting before the game. He told her the best bet was to catch some of them when they were walking through the lobby on their way to eat. This satisfied the woman, or so it appeared.

About an hour later, the phone rang again. Once again it was mama. She and the boys hadn't seen any of the players walk through, so she thought she had a better idea: "How about if I brought the boys into the dressing room before the game?"

Now, Alex Hannum wasn't exactly what you'd call a prude, but there was something about mama and her boys, especially mama, coming into the Warriors' dressing room that struck him as unorthodox, even for a group from San Francisco.

Later that evening, Hannum averted another headache. On my way to the game I jumped in a cab with Guy Rodgers, Nate Thurmond and Wayne Hightower. The cabbie asked, "Where to?"

"Kiel Auditorium," Rodgers said. In most cases that wouldn't have been a bad reply, except that night's game was being played at the St. Louis Arena, several miles away. Luckily, the rest of us were better informed. Inasmuch as Rodgers went on to score 25 points in a 103-97 victory, it was fortunate we were with him when he got into the cab. Afterward I decided not to mention the incident to Alex, funny as it was. There's only so much you can take in one day.

In April, at playoff time, the Celtics were playing host to the Cincinnati Royals. I decided to try my luck with Auerbach once more. After his team knocked off the Royals, 103-87, I figured he might be in a better mood than he was the last time I tried catching his comments on tape. I approached him, and he said, "You'd better clear it with Howie."

Howie McHugh, the Celtics' publicity director and one of the truly nice guys in the business, said, "That's what Red's like when we win. You should see him when we lose." Unable to recall the last time the Celtics had lost, we made our way back into the dressing room, where McHugh assured Auerbach it was all right to talk to me. Or, as Howie put it, "It's okay, Red, he's one of Adolph's boys from Syracuse," referring to Dolph Schayes, who was loved throughout the league. Thus assured, Auerbach was willing to risk the possibility my tape recorder would misquote him.

From Boston, I moved on to the Warriors-Hawks playoff series in St. Louis. St. Louis led two games to one. Kiel Auditorium was sold out. I wasn't exactly covering the game in the traditional sense, and as we went through the players' entrance, Alex said, "You can sit on the bench with the rest of us."

The NBA of 35 years ago was a casual experience in many ways. It was a common practice for coaches to smoke during the games. Non-combatants such as Syracuse owner Danny Biasone often sat on the bench. While sitting on the bench provided a great vantage point, it also left you fair game for Hawks fans who believed the back of a bench-sitter's neck was for tweaking with a thumb and middle finger. Sitting there also made you a target for thrown objects that failed to reach the floor.

I was sitting toward the end of the bench, next to Kenny Sears and George Lee. Lee was a happy-go-lucky individual who didn't overly concern himself with situations at hand. With the rabid St. Louis fans hurling both sharp words and objects in the direction of the Warriors' bench, he managed to remain cool.

But as one of the missiles grazed his shoulder and bounced out onto the court, George's even disposition suddenly took a sour turn. He calmly turned to the crowd and addressed them in such a manner that, had he been Lenny Bruce, and had Kiel been a nightclub, he'd have been arrested. It was colorful, to say the least. I didn't keep count, but I'm relatively certain that with the exception of one, none of his words exceeded four letters. Perhaps fearing for his player's life, and trying to prevent a full-scale riot, Alex called George over to sit next to him for the rest of the game.

The riot nearly came later, but for different reasons. With nine seconds left in the game, the Warriors led by two points. St. Louis had the ball. This, of course, was before the three-point rule. The ball went to Cliff Hagan, who took a left-handed hook shot. The ball hit the rim and bounced off. But before anyone on the Warriors' bench could breathe a sigh of relief, Richie Guerin got the rebound and threw it back up. Guerin's shot missed, but once more the ball bounced into the hands of the Hawks' Zelmo Beaty. But before Beaty could get a shot off, the buzzer sounded, and the longest nine seconds of the season had come to an end.

Hawk fans were incensed that neither of the referees, Richie Powers and Norm Drucker, had called a foul in the waning moments. Several decided they would foul Drucker and see if anyone would call it. Powers wisely left the court for the safety of the officials' dressing room, leaving Drucker, teeth clenched, mouth tightened, ready to take on the fans. Ushers and police moved in, and Drucker lived another day to incite another crowd. The Warriors' experience in St. Louis that night was only the forerunner of what they and I would experience at Kiel Auditorium a few years later.

As I followed the 1963-64 Warriors, both Alex and Bill King, the team's broadcaster, encouraged me to move to San Francisco. The team went to the NBA Finals that year and lost to the Celtics, but had enjoyed a great season. During the playoffs, I met Warriors owner Franklin Mieuli. Over the years, I'd met many owners around the league, and it was obvious Franklin wasn't cut from the same cloth as Gottlieb, New York's Ned Irish, Boston's Walter Brown, St. Louis' Ben Kerner or Detroit's Fred Zollner. Franklin did wear a coat and tie on occasion, but the occasion was usually the sighting of Halley's Comet.

I began to think I'd gone as far as I was going to go in Syracuse. I loved the place and still do. When people ask me where I'm from, I often say Syracuse because I had such a wonderful time there. In truth, I was born in Detroit and also lived in Rochester, a truly beautiful city. Despite my feeling for Syracuse, I realized it was time to go.

Eddie Hancock, my landlord and old friend, dropped me at the Syracuse airport. A great sadness came over me as the plane took off and one phase of my life came to a close. I touched down in San Francisco on the afternoon of Saturday, December 5, 1964. Alex had found a studio apartment for me in the building where he lived in downtown San Francisco. It had a bathroom and a small refrigerator. That was it. I had no job, and the place rented for something like $85 dollars a month. Besides, where else could you find a decibel level like you could at the corner of Geary and Jones streets? Years later, a fellow broadcaster, Gil Haar, once lived near the same corner. "When you lived at Geary and Jones streets," Haar said, "every night was Saturday night and every Saturday night was New Year's Eve."

From my window, I was an eyewitness to life in the big city. I couldn't see the Golden Gate Bridge, but I could see fights, prostitutes, arrests, police cars and ambulances, and I heard wailing sirens at all hours of the night.

The NBA season was well under way, and in terms of finding a job, I hadn't picked the best time to come to San Francisco. I'd been broadcasting Syracuse University football games, and their season hadn't ended until late November. In deciding to come west, I'd passed up a chance to go to the Sugar Bowl in New Orleans.

My first break came three weeks later when John Vick, who'd been the Warriors public address announcer, left. Franklin Mieuli asked me to replace him. It didn't pay much, but I didn't care. Like the guy who walked behind the elephants at the circus, I was back in show business. During the day, I was also helping out in the Warriors' offices in the basement of the old Bellevue Hotel, a block from where I lived.

There were two ways to get to the team's headquarters. You could enter the hotel from Geary Street and walk downstairs, or through the garage on Taylor Street, via a long corridor that led directly to the offices. Franklin Mieuli usually took an even more direct approach, entering through the garage on his motorcycle, then driving it the length the corridor and right to the front door. It wasn't at all difficult for those of us inside the office to know when he was coming.

Most of my office work consisted of stuffing reams of envelopes for the team's mass mailings. If even half the people who got them came to the games, we'd have had some decent crowds. Instead, about the only time the Warriors drew a sizable crowd was when the Celtics were in town. The fact that Bill Russell and K.C. Jones had won back-to-back NCAA championships at the University of San Francisco was believed to have something to do with it. It also explained why most of the crowd rooted for the Celtics.

The Warriors clearly needed to develop a fan base of their own. In contrast to the success of the 1963-64 season, the club was not doing well the year I arrived. Although

Nate Thurmond played well at the forward spot, his career was being stifled at that position. Other clubs were making offers for him and saw him as their center. The Warriors didn't want to trade him. They wanted him to be their center of the future. A big chunk of their payroll was going to their center of the present, Wilt Chamberlain.

On January 15, 1965, the Warriors traded Wilt to the Philadelphia 76ers for Lee Shaffer, Paul Neumann, Connie Dierking and cash. The trade freed Thurmond to play the position that suited him best, but otherwise it didn't pan out. Neumann, who had gone to nearby Stanford, played well. Dierking had stayed in the league because of his willingness to battle when he got on the court. A former member of the Nats, Dierking had a strong fear of flying and once quit the league because of it. His former teammate Johnny Kerr once said to him, "You know, Connie, taking the train isn't any safer than flying. Why, just the other day there was a terrible train accident and 120 people were killed."

Dierking asked, "How did it happen?"

Kerr answered, "An airplane crashed into it."

Connie failed to see the humor.

What made the trade so disappointing was the failure of Lee Shaffer to report. He had been bothered by a knee injury, and following the previous season decided to quit the game. Because Alex had coached him in Syracuse and knew he was an excellent shooter, the Warrior coach accepted the deal with the idea of convincing Shaffer to play in San Francisco. It was no dice.

The trade was also a blow to Chamberlain. The big guy liked San Francisco and Hannum. It was tough to leave, even if it meant going back to his home town. Wilt decided to take his time getting back there. By airplane it was only five hours. Wilt decided to drive. He was a careful driver. It took him two weeks.

One night before he left, Wilt attended a Warrior game at Civic Auditorium, one of the team's many home arenas. He put on dark glasses and sat in the balcony. When someone spotted him and asked why he was wearing dark glasses, Wilt said, "I wanted to come incognito."

The Warriors went on to finish with a record of 17-63, one of the worst in league history. I was faced with the prospect of an equally dismal summer, not knowing where I'd be working next and wondering if leaving Syracuse had been the right move.

I got a phone call that both rescued me and led to something truly wonderful. The man on the phone introduced himself, "I'm Joe Herold. I'm the General Manager of KGMB in Honolulu. Don Klein at (San Francisco radio station) KCBS tells me you've had experience re-creating baseball games. My announcer, Harry Kalas, is leaving to go to Houston. How would you like to work in Hawaii?"

Sitting in San Francisco with a dwindling supply of money and no prospects for the summer, and never having been to Hawaii, I decided to play it cagey. I responded, "How many seconds do I have to answer that?"

The Pacific Coast League began play in April, so I was off to the Islands less than four months after coming to San Francisco. I liked the idea of having a job, but I was concerned about the direction of my career. What was I going to do next season on Guam? As apprehensive as I was, I had the greatest summer of my life. It was 1965, I was about to turn 30, I was single, and I had a terrific apartment right across from the beach. There were more girls than I'd ever seen in my life. Though I was single, I was also single-minded. The girls never distracted me, except for seven or eight of them.

Even more important, my stay in Hawaii brought me in contact with Ferd Borsch, the baseball writer for the Honolulu Advertiser. Shortly after I began broadcasting the games, Ferd passed on to me the most important baseball adage I'd ever heard.

"Let me tell you something about this great game of baseball," he said. "You come out here every night and you see something you've never seen before."

Ferd Borsch's words sustained me through all my years in baseball.

The pace of life in Hawaii was much different from what I was used to. I had a tough time adjusting at first. Perhaps my habit of wearing sport coats and ties had something to do with it. After a couple of months, I allowed myself to be seduced by the lifestyle and began wearing sport shirts and shorts.

The best part of my job was not having to travel. Why would you want to go on the road? I re-created the away games from the KGMB studios and made sure they never went more than two hours. It was the only time I ever had control over what happened on the field.

All too soon, the baseball season came to an end, and I was heading back to San Francisco. There's an old saying in the Islands that when you sail away you're supposed to throw your flower lei into the sea. If it drifts back toward the shore, that means some-day you'll return to Hawaii. I was glad I was flying, for fear that if I tossed my lei into the sea it would start drifting toward Guam.

Upon my return to San Francisco, I was surprised to find I'd acquired some status. The folks in the Warrior office seemed impressed with what I'd done in Hawaii. I'd broadcast minor league baseball before in Syracuse and didn't think it was such a big deal. One thing I knew for sure: I owed a debt of gratitude to Don Klein at KCBS. You meet a lot of people in the broadcasting business who will tell you, "We don't have any-thing at this time, but we'll keep you in mind." When Joe Herold called him looking for someone who could do re-creates, Don Klein kept me in mind. You never forget people like that.

My timing was better this time around. When I returned to San Francisco, Franklin Mieuli said, "I've got a contract for television this season and I want you to do the games. When a game isn't on TV, you'll sit in with Bill King on the radio for the home games."

Because the Warriors and the New York Knicks had finished last in their respective divisions, each was allowed two of the first four picks in the NBA draft. The Warriors took Rick Barry and Fred Hetzel, and the Knicks drafted Cazzie Russell and Bill Bradley. Bradley, a Rhodes Scholar, studied at Oxford and wouldn't join the Knicks for two seasons. The New Yorkers didn't do poorly, however. They also managed to draft Dave Stallworth.

It was obvious Barry was something special, a fact not unknown to Barry himself. Hannum was not about to let the rookie's opinion of his own ability get out of hand. Even Rick understood Alex's approach. He said to me one day after practice, "Boy, Alex was really on me today. But I know the reason he's doing that is because he knows I can play."

Indeed, Barry could play, and with Thurmond's development, big things were expected. It was obvious there weren't enough basketballs for Barry and Guy Rodgers. It was also obvious Barry was a rising star. Thurmond was establishing himself as one of the premier centers, but something was missing. The Warriors were struggling, and their playoff hopes were in serious doubt as the season swung into its final month.

On March 15, the Warriors played St. Louis at the old San Jose Auditorium. The place held fewer than 3,000, but Franklin was a San Jose native, and the building was just large enough to accommodate his family and friends. In the third quarter, Thurmond and the Hawks' Zelmo Beaty got into a heated elbowing match. Neither player had the ball. The officials called a double foul and awarded each a free throw. Beaty made his. Thurmond missed.

Hannum argued with the officials, claiming no free throws should have been given. The rule book stated that on a double foul off the ball (when neither player is in possession), no free throws are awarded. The officials didn't seem interested in what the rule book had to say. They'd already screwed up and didn't want to hear about it.

Now Richie Guerin, the Hawks' player-coach, came over to the scorer's table, where the argument was raging and where I was working the public-address mike. The referees saw him approaching and waved him away, as if to say, "This doesn't concern you." As they were waving him off, a couple of us began doing the same thing. He spotted me and, full of fury signifying something, grabbed my tie and started choking me, yelling, "You little shit! Mind your own business!"

With my life passing before me, it was difficult to mind anything at that moment. Finally, Guerin let go, at which point I managed to blurt out, "Everyone else is going for a win and you're going for a tie." My friends at the scorer's table thought what happened to me was pretty funny. As I recall, most of them weren't wearing ties.

The game finally resumed, and the Hawks won 110-109. Beaty's one point in the third quarter made the difference. The Warriors protested on the only grounds allowable, a violation of the rules.

The NBA commissioner at the time was J. Walter Kennedy, whose chief qualification for the job was having been Mayor of Stamford, Connecticut. There seems to be a standard procedure in professional sports to disallow all protests, no matter how valid, then to put some kind of spin on it. In the NBA, a commissioner didn't dare incur the wrath of powerful owners, in whose hands rested his job. Ben Kerner was a powerful owner; Franklin Mieuli was a guy who drove a motorcycle and wore funny clothes. To no one's surprise, the protest was turned down on the grounds that even though the officials misinterpreted the rule, it happened in the third quarter and both teams still had a chance to win. From that, we concluded anything that happens in the third quarter really doesn't matter. Perhaps it was true all NBA games really were decided in the last two minutes.

The Warriors had a disappointing season, and their record of 35-45 left them one game behind St. Louis for the last playoff spot. You didn't have to look far to find that game.

Franklin fired Alex Hannum shortly after the season ended. This created a problem for both Bill King and me. Bill had grown as close to Alex as I had, and Franklin knew that. We kept our feelings to ourselves and were delighted when Hannum was named coach of the 76ers. This would reunite him with some of the old Syracuse Nats and his big man from San Francisco, Chamberlain.

To replace Alex, Franklin hired former Celtics star Bill Sharman. Bill was a big name throughout basketball, but especially in California, where he starred at USC. Since leaving the NBA, he'd been coach and Athletic Director at Los Angeles State. He appeared to be a personable enough guy, but had some rigid ideas about coaching that would cost the Warriors dearly in the next two seasons.

The 1966-67 season was the Chicago Bulls' first in the NBA. They were coached by one of Alex's disciples, Johnny Kerr. Expanding the league to include the Bulls allowed Sharman to dispose of Guy Rodgers, whom Sharman had quickly determined didn't fit his plans. Rodgers was traded for guards Jimmy King and Jeff Mullins in a rare deal that actually helped both teams.

Trading Rodgers was something Hannum had pressed for a year earlier, recognizing that Guy controlled the ball but Rick Barry was the star of the future. Mieuli hadn't bought it, claiming Rodgers was an attraction. That might have been true if the Warriors played their home games at Temple University, Rodgers' alma mater — about the only place they didn't play.

Thurmond and Barry were just reaching their peak. Starting alongside them were veterans such as Tom Meschery, Al Attles and Paul Neumann. Fred Hetzel was entering his second season, and newcomers Mullins and King, along with rookies Clyde Lee and Joe Ellis, gave Sharman a lot to work with.

Meanwhile in Philadelphia, Hannum was putting together one of the greatest teams, if not the greatest, in NBA history. With offensive support like he'd never had before, Chamberlain found out how it felt to be Bill Russell. For years, the Celtics' center had the luxury of knowing he could get 15 points and his team would still win. If Wilt scored 15, his team wouldn't have a chance. He needed to score at least twice that many. Now, for the first time in his career, Wilt was surrounded by people such as Hal Greer, Chet Walker, Billy Cunningham, Luke Jackson and Wali Jones. His scoring average of 24.1 was only fifth-best in the league, but, for the first time ever, he led his team in assists. As Russell had been able to do for years, Chamberlain could now concentrate on rebounding, getting the ball to teammates, and stopping the opposition. You couldn't blame the "Big Dipper," as Wilt was known, for wondering, "Where has this been all my life?"

The Boston Celtics were NBA champions for eight consecutive years. No one could question their right to those titles. They ran better, passed better and played better defense than any team in the league. With Russell clogging the middle, the Celtics could play a hands-on defense out front. If a defender got beat, the man with the ball was lulled into a false sense of accomplishment as he headed to the basket, only to find Russell in his way. It was not a pleasant sight. Russell also learned to block shots directly to his teammates and get the Celtics' fast break under way. Boston teams always seemed more alert. They seemed to get every loose ball, every good bounce, every break, and Red Auerbach seemed to get away with more than any other coach. For every time Red was thrown out of a game for complaining to officials, there were 10 more times he should have.

The Celtics were the class of the league. Outside Boston, it was easy to hate them while grudgingly admiring their style of play. Auerbach's genius was in drafting players who fit the Celtics' pattern and have them ready to step in when their time came. To replace Bob Cousy and Bill Sharman, he had the Jones boys, Sam and K.C. When Frank Ramsey stepped aside, John Havlicek was ready. Auerbach drafted forward Satch Sanders, who became the perfect complement to Russell. No one in my time had a nose for an offensive rebound like Sanders. A Celtic would shoot and sometimes miss at a critical moment. Sanders would come up with the rebound and break your heart. What made it even harder was that Sanders was such a likable guy. Auerbach drafted Larry Siegfried and later Mel Counts, a 7-footer who could fill a lane on a fast break. If he needed veterans, Auerbach went out and got Carl Braun, Arnie Risen, Andy Phillip, Clyde

Lovellette, Willie Naulls, Don Nelson, Wayne Embry and Bailey Howell. All seemed to fit right in.

The Celtics won their first title in 1957. The only team to keep Auerbach's team from 10 straight championships was the 1957-58 St. Louis Hawks. The coach of that team was Alex Hannum. In 1967, he was about to stand in Red's way again.

There seemed to be hardly any middle class to the NBA in the 1966-67 season. Only three teams finished above .500, and Sharman's Warriors topped it by only seven games, a record good enough for first in the Western Division.

By the time the regular season ended, Hannum's 76ers had set a new record for victories with 68, and for fewest losses with 13. The Bulls of a later era would break it. The Philly club finished eight games ahead of Boston, whose 60-21 mark would have been good enough to win almost any other year.

For Bill King and me, our cups were running over. The Warriors won the West, and Alex's team won the East. Wouldn't it be something if those two teams met for the title? They did, but it wasn't that easy.

With the Warriors in the playoffs, I was doing a lot of television and working with Bill on road games, as well. Mieuli had given me an opportunity in San Francisco, and the Warriors' success was giving me a lot of exposure. For the first time, people in the Bay Area knew my name. To many it was Hank Greenberg. That never really bothered me because Hank Greenberg was my idol when I was a little kid living in Detroit. I took my first name from him. When people said "Greenberg," I simply said, "Close enough!" I still do.

I got a lot of satisfaction when the Warriors swept the Lakers in three games in the opening round of the playoffs. It had little to do with the Lakers personally, but they were owned by the boorish and pompous Jack Kent Cooke. A year earlier, I'd done my first TV game for the Warriors from the Los Angeles Sports Arena. Cooke had just purchased the Lakers from former owner Bob Short, and someone decided he'd be a good halftime guest. He might have been — for Jerry Springer.

I was standing at the end of the court as Cooke approached. We introduced ourselves, and went on the air. I began by saying something really profound, like "Welcome to the NBA."

Cooke said, "Well, let me tell you something, young man. The Dodgers always beat the Giants in baseball, the Rams always beat the 49ers in football and now I just bought the Lakers and we're going to beat you in basketball."

I was having a rough welcome to halftime shows.

Despite the Warriors' success in knocking off the Lakers, all was not well with the club internally. Nate Thurmond hurt his wrist and missed 16 games. Barry carried the team on his back with his prolific scoring and increased effort on the boards. At 6-7 and 200 pounds, Rick was not a monster among NBA forwards. His brilliant play, especially with Nate on the sidelines, was taking its toll on him physically. Bill Sharman was taking his toll on Rick mentally. Sharman instituted the practice of a morning shoot-around on the day of the game. For Sharman, the reasoning was simple enough. He always did it as a player, so why shouldn't everybody else? Sharman is often remembered as a good shooter. In truth, he was a great free-throw shooter with a lifetime mark of 88.3 percent. From the field, however, his 42.3 was average, especially for someone who worked at it so hard. As a coach, Sharman preached the theory of muscle memory. It was a fine concept, but not everyone's muscles could remember at morning shoot-arounds.

The Warriors knew that with Nate sidelined, Barry was their ticket to the playoffs and beyond. One day, guard Jimmy King said, "Rick, you sleep in tomorrow morning. We'll pay your fine."

Unlike Hannum, Sharman had difficulty understanding you don't have to treat all players the same way. Alex seemed to know what worked with some players and what didn't. Bill was unbending in his approach, but as long as the club was winning, he felt justified.

Sharman had other ways of annoying his team. He was especially image-conscious and coached from the viewpoint of "don't embarrass me." Whenever we did a telecast from the road, Sharman would always stress to the team that the game was going back to San Francisco on TV, so let's really play hard. I suppose the corollary to that is, when the game isn't going back home on TV it doesn't matter.

A Rick Barry-Bill Sharman battle was brewing, and it would surface before the playoffs were over. At the same time, the American Basketball Association had formed. Rick's father-in-law and former college coach, Bruce Hale, was one of the ABA's coaches. This did not go unnoticed by Barry.

Barry was no angel. He was brash and argumentative, and he rubbed a lot of people the wrong way. None of this bothered me. We got along fine. I was one of the first to get to know Rick and his wife, Pam, when they moved to San Francisco. When they arrived, one of my duties was to drive them around town for various radio, TV and newspaper interviews. Later on, he would call me "Hanker," and he knew who the real Hank Greenberg was. He followed every sport.

In the second round of the playoffs, the Warriors faced their old nemesis, the St. Louis Hawks. These two teams did not like each other, and things would not improve in the playoffs. Bill King further charged the rivalry on the air by referring to St. Louis as the country's only organized slum. The remark was heavily publicized by Hawk broadcaster Jerry Gross. The Warriors had a grace period in this regard, as the series opened at home. They made the most of it, winning the first two games, 117-115 and

143-136. In the more highly charged atmosphere of St. Louis, the Hawks took two, 115-109 and 109-105. St. Louis fans had lost none of their ferocity in the three years since that wild Warrior victory in 1964. The proximity of the fans to the players' bench hadn't changed, either. This was especially unfortunate for Jeff Mullins, who had once played for the Hawks. As before, fans routinely walked behind the bench and tweaked the players' ears. Jeff's ears, which bore a resemblance to small satellite dishes, made him an easy target. Perhaps they received signals that enabled him to become one of the deadliest shooters in the league.

Abusive fans at Kiel Auditorium were a serious problem for the visiting Warriors, and Hawk owner Ben Kerner showed no inclination to provide security near the bench. Bill King continued to harangue the fans, Kerner, the city of St. Louis, and maybe even Charles Lindbergh's plane.

The Warriors won game five in San Francisco, 123-102, giving them a 3-2 edge and sending us back to Kiel. Our return to St. Louis coincided with the start of the 1966 baseball season. The Cardinals opened against the Giants, and several of us took in Juan Marichal's victory over Bob Gibson. Not only was it the sort of pitching match-up you rarely see anymore, it was a good omen.

Franklin Mieuli accompanied the Warriors to St. Louis, and he was determined his team's bench would be better protected. If Ben Kerner wouldn't provide security, Franklin would hire his own. On the morning of game 6, Mieuli, along with me, Art Santo Domingo of the Giants and Harry Jupiter of the *San Francisco Examiner*, went to the Burns Detective Agency to hire a couple of guards. This was out of the ordinary, but the same could be said of Franklin himself. More than once, we'd walk through the players' entrance of some arena before a game, and the guard would look at this bearded man in his deer-stalker cap and Haight-Ashbury vest and ask, "Who's this guy trying to sneak in with you?"

Someone would answer, "He's okay. He's the owner of the Warriors."

To which the guard would reply, "Yeah, right, and I'm Robert Redford."

Mieuli completed arrangements with the Burns people, who dispatched the two guards. When we got to Kiel that night, there they were, decked out in their uniforms. One looked like Wally Cox, the diminutive star of the "Mr. Peepers" TV sitcom. The other looked old enough to be Wally Cox's grandfather. As one Hawk fan said before the game, "These guys don't look so tough. They're not even carrying a gun."

Ben Kerner, meanwhile, was not amused. He came over and started yelling at Mieuli. Franklin defended his right to protect his players. Kerner, who had once been punched in the mouth by Red Auerbach, settled for calling Mieuli a "fink" and took his seat. The St. Louis crowd had come armed with a variety of objects, including eggs, pennies, and Snickers bars. Barry had done a commercial for Snickers.

*He was Big Mac before McDonald's
and McGwire.*

With Tommy Hutton at Yankee Stadium, 1987. We were smiling, we hadn't met Fred Weinhaus yet.

At Cooperstown, 1991, with Mel Allen, the ONLY "Voice of the Yankees."

With Ron Fairly in Arizona. He always knew what was going to happen in a game before it did.

Commissioner Fay Vincent with "Secret Service" man (left) at Giants-Cubs NLCS, 1989. Vincent made the mistake of caring about the fans. It cost him his job.

I could always get excited about baseball just looking at my office at home.

In Jasper, Alberta, crossing Canada by train, 1991.

On the Eastern and Oriental Express, Bangkok to Singapore, 1993.

With Carla, Doug and Kellie at the Alfred Dunhill store in San Francisco at a party marking my 2,500th consecutive broadcast, 1995.

Franklin Mieuli, who, outside of Northern California, no one believed owned the Warriors. He gave me my start in San Francisco.

A face only a radio could love.

From left: Dick Dolinsky, Don LaVine and Dick Abend, the "Little Coalition" back at Syracuse 40 years later. Amazing that we hadn't changed a bit.

All Hank Greenwalds look alike.

Mike Krukow called me "The Captain" and presented me with this hat at my retirement ceremony at Candlestick, 1996.

A pat on the back from Kellie, the world's best daughter, at my retirement ceremony, 1996.

Meanwhile, the Warriors were more concerned about whether Rick could play at all. He was bothered by a bad ankle and required several shots before he could go out and try it. Rick never doubted he would play. The only question was how effective he would be. Before the night was over, the Hawks would find out.

I was doing TV that night, and Bill was across the way on radio. Because the Giants had a night off, Art Santo Domingo kept score for me. Bob Stevens, the Hall of Fame baseball writer from the *San Francisco Chronicle*, sat next to Art. All of us were in the line of fire, and it didn't take long for it to begin. No sooner did the ball go up than eggs came flying out of the stands and onto the floor. Fortunately for those of us at courtside, Hawk fans had strong arms.

Referees Mendy Rudolph and Norm Drucker were not amused, most likely because they were in the line of fire. Rudolph was a fastidious man, and the thought of a hair out of place, not to mention egg on his face, was unthinkable. Soon after the eggs came the Snickers bars. Barry seemed unfazed by it all, and I recall his picking them up as if to say to the fans, "Hey, thanks." Once, he even made as if he was going to eat one.

The Hawks were fighting through the barrage and seemed ready to run the Warriors off the court. By the end of the first quarter, they led by 18. It appeared a seventh game would be necessary. The Warriors regrouped, adjusted to the hail of foreign objects, and between eggs managed to get a few baskets, cutting the Hawks' lead to nine at the half.

Now the fans had taken to throwing pennies, but not before they heated them by holding the edge to a match or cigarette lighter. Not all the pennies reached the floor. Some hit the press table, and later in the game someone threw a lighter that grazed Warrior guard Al Attles.

In the third quarter, the Hawks' lead was dwindling, as was the fans' supply of eggs. The fans appeared to be calming down, but the Warriors were warming up. With a minute to play in the game, the visitors pulled to within two points. Attles was fouled and had two free throws.

In those days, the limit for team fouls in a quarter was five. Any foul after that automatically brought two free throws. There was one restriction. A team could not save its fouls for the last two minutes of the period. If it didn't reach its quota in the first 10 minutes of the quarter, a team could only use one without penalty in the last two. The PA announcer would signal that two minutes remained. If a team had fouls to spare and used one, he would announce, "That's the first foul in the last two minutes."

So here's the scene. The hostile environment of Kiel Auditorium. If the Warriors win, they go on to the NBA Finals. A loss for the Hawks ends their season, but a victory sends the teams back to San Francisco for a seventh game. The Burns guards are at their posts, "protecting" the Warriors' bench. There's Franklin Mieuli, urging his team on.

There's Ben Kerner, slumping deeper in his seat as each point brings the Warriors closer. Attles goes to the free-throw line.

It was so quiet you'd have thought Ben Hogan was on the 18th green at Augusta. Suddenly an egg came flying out of the crowd and landed near the foul circle where Attles was getting ready to shoot. Just then, Art Santo Domingo leaned over to me and whispered, "That's the first egg in the last two minutes."

Now I couldn't talk. With the big ball game on the line, I was doubled up laughing, all the while trying to cover my microphone. Mendy Rudolph, seething, halted play. He ordered the egg wiped off the court. I let the TV picture tell the story, and was able to regroup but unable to look at Art.

Attles regrouped, too, and was ready to shoot. This was a chancy proposition. Al was not a great free-throw shooter, which was borne out by his regular season mark of .583. For the playoffs, he would make only six out of 16. At the line, he decided he'd waited long enough. They were either going in or they weren't. He was handed the ball, and he fired. I'm not sure he even looked. It went in. The Warriors were down by one.

Attles took the ball again. No sooner was it in his hands than it was gone. He made the second. Tie game.

Rudolph was still seething. The Hawks came down the court, and he called Zelmo Beaty for charging. I'm not saying Zelmo never charged. All I'm saying is Mendy chose that moment to call it. Zelmo didn't throw that egg. Elbows were his specialty. But Rudolph was going to show those Hawk fans a thing or two. The call turned the game in the Warriors' favor. They went on to win, 112-107, and were forced to admit that, on occasion, Mendy Rudolph was a good egg.

While Attles' two foul shots were the key moments, there was no mistaking this was Rick Barry's game. He took seven injections in his painful ankle before the game, and six more at halftime, then went out and scored 41 points, one for every Snickers bar. He scored 47 in game two and averaged 32 points a game for the six-game series. Nate Thurmond averaged 20 rebounds a game over the same stretch.

There are few greater feelings in sports than winning a championship series on your opponent's court. The San Francisco Warriors were now Western Division Champions. Those of us associated with the club celebrated well into the night at a restaurant in the Hill section of St. Louis. The Warriors had earned the right to meet Alex Hannum's Philadelphia 76ers for the NBA Championship.

The 76ers had done something no team had accomplished for the last eight years. They dethroned the Boston Celtics. They not only beat them, but they did it in five games. Because the two cities are so near each other, the schedule called for the teams to alternate games. The 76ers had the home court advantage, and were hosts for Games One, Three, Five and Seven. It didn't matter where the Philadelphia 76ers of 1966-67 played. They won the first game at home. They won the second game in Boston. They split Games 3 and 4 before burying the Celtics in Game Five, 140-116. To the fans at Convention Hall, that was like winning the league title.

Many had never known a time that Boston failed to hold the crown. Only the Warriors, the franchise that once represented Philadelphia, stood in the way. There wasn't much concern about the Warriors. All that mattered was the Celtics were dead, at least for a year. Alex Hannum must have felt someone had scripted the season; he ended up coaching in the NBA finals against the team that fired him.

For me it would have been a strange feeling going to the NBA Finals no matter whom the Warriors played. You can't be around a group of players all season long, especially a group as small as a basketball team, and not want to see them do well. But I had mixed feelings because of Bill Sharman. I didn't dislike him personally. I didn't like what he was doing to the Warriors, and I felt they were successful despite his coaching. On the other hand, could I honestly say I knew more than he? The truthful answer was no, but it was close. One thing was for sure. I knew there was trouble brewing that would seriously affect the franchise, and I didn't think he had a clue that he was the cause.

The Championship series got under way on a Friday night in Philadelphia. Philly won in overtime, 141-135. San Francisco had a chance to win when Chamberlain fouled Thurmond at the buzzer in regulation, but the officials swallowed their whistles. As the two centers lined up for the jump ball to begin overtime, Wilt said to Nate in front of the officials, "I fouled the shit out of you, babe."

The Sixers made easy work of Game Two, winning by 31 points. The teams flew to San Francisco, where the next two games were scheduled for the Cow Palace. Led by Barry's 55 points, the Warriors won Game Three, 130-124, and despite Barry's 43 points in Game Four, the 76ers won, 122-108. Philly was now poised to finish it off at home in Game Five.

Rick Barry was not the only player on the verge of rebellion. A faction had developed, but the guys were playing through it. It was only a matter of time.

With the 76ers and their fans ready to celebrate, the atmosphere at Convention Hall was charged but orderly. Owner Irv Kosloff had promised the 76ers a trip to the Caribbean for winning the title. They came with bags packed for the islands.

Game Five was close for the first three quarters. Barry was on the bench when the final quarter began. Things began to fall apart for the Warriors. They fell further and further behind, and Sharman made no move to put in Barry. Rick was fuming. Finally, as his club fell 14 points back with roughly seven minutes to play, Sharman called time out.

The game was nationally televised, so Bill King and I were working together on the radio. Our broadcast location was next to the Warriors' bench. We could hear everything. As the team huddled, we could hear shouting. Barry was yelling at Sharman, wondering why the league's leading scorer was on the bench when the team needed points, time was running out, and elimination was staring them in the face. Several of his teammates joined in support of Rick. Assistant Coach George Lee, who knew Rick was right, dutifully tried to keep order.

Sharman looked at Barry and said, "Gee, Rick, don't you want any of the other guys to play?" Bill and I couldn't believe what we were witnessing.

The timeout period ended, and Sharman put Barry back in the game. With Rick and Tom Meschery leading the charge, the Warriors staged an unlikely comeback. Meschery summoned every ounce of energy in his battered body. Barry, meanwhile, was hitting from everywhere west of the Ben Franklin Bridge. He capped the Warrior charge with a drive on Chamberlain that carried him around and seemingly over the big man to put one home. When it was over, the Warriors, despite their coach, had extended the series one more game. They forced the 76ers back to San Francisco and far from the Caribbean. Losing to the Warriors both incensed and embarrassed the team from Philadelphia. Now they were headed back to the big barn known as the Cow Palace, home of the Grand National Rodeo and Livestock Show — something a couple of deep breaths never let you forget.

Game Six was not unlike the opener. It came down to the final seconds, with the Warriors trailing by a point and the ball in their possession. The situation clearly called for the pick and roll, which Barry and Thurmond had executed so successfully all season. Nate would come out and pick Barry's defender. If Wilt stepped out to pick up Barry, Nate would roll to the basket, now covered by the smaller man who'd been guarding Rick. If Barry could get off the shot before Wilt stepped out, he'd take it. Otherwise he would dump the pass to Thurmond. It had worked countless times. But not this time.

The best Rick could get was an off-balance shot that never had a chance. Philadelphia came up with the ball. The Warriors had no choice but to foul, which only increased the 76ers' winning margin to three, 125-122. Barry's 36 points would not be enough. Did I mention that one of the greatest feelings in sports is winning a championship on your opponent's floor? Imagine, then, how this must have thrilled Alex Hannum.

It was also a beautiful time for Wilton Norman Chamberlain, who could finally shed a tag put on him by those whose ignorance had no limits. If there was one thing Wilt never was, it was a loser. When his teams needed him to score points, he scored points. When they needed him to rebound, he rebounded — and blocked shots. His biggest crime, apparently, was not playing for the Boston Celtics. It's hard to imagine Bill

Russell, great as he was, playing for the Detroit Pistons of the early '60s, or the New York Knicks, and leading them to NBA titles.

When Chamberlain finally had a team with talent comparable to the players who surrounded Russell, he won a championship. Had the two great centers traded places, the results would have been the same. Just think what Wilt would have done defensively playing in Boston and only having to score 15 points a game for his team to win. There's no question Russell revolutionized the concept of defense in the NBA, but he was the right man in the right place.

Bill King and I had bittersweet feelings when the season ended on the Cow Palace floor. We'd wanted the Warriors to win, but at the same time we were happy for Alex.

Nate Thurmond owned a club in downtown San Francisco. You'd have to go a long way to find a gentleman like the Warriors' center. He was a man about town, and the town loved him. The 76ers weren't flying home until the next morning. Nate opened his place to the victors for a celebration. He provided the champagne. Bill King, his partner Nancy Stephens and I were invited to join the celebration. I had no problem doing so. I felt good at that moment. I proved to myself that season, despite my feeling for Alex and my shock and dismay at his firing, I could remain loyal to the Warriors emotionally while sharing in the joy of his success. I'm sure Bill felt the same way. We'd given it everything we had, and Franklin Mieuli knew he could count on us.

The celebration started at Nate's club, and after closing time shifted to Nate's apartment atop Twin Peaks. I recalled Alex saying to me at dinner one night, not long after I moved west, "If you're going to live in San Francisco, you've got to learn to drink wine." What did I know? The only wine I drank in Syracuse came in jugs with handles on them. At Nate's apartment I was putting everything Alex taught me into practice.

Twin Peaks overlooks the city, and the view of San Francisco was spectacular. We'd been watching it by night, and now we were beginning to see it by day. People had come and gone throughout the evening. Among those remaining were Bill and Nancy, Alex, Nate, Hal Greer, Dave Gambee and I. The celebration was taking its toll. Some of us were speechless. The rest couldn't talk.

The morning sun was on its way from the East Bay to join the party. Fingers of light were gently erasing the darkness, and soon a city would come to life. There was a feeling of reverie. There was a feeling of euphoria. There was a feeling some of us were going to have one hell of a headache. No one seemed capable of caring.

We looked up and shared a poignant moment. Alex Hannum was standing on the balcony at the dawn of a new day, the city of San Francisco at his feet. All too soon, he would experience a similar feeling in Philadelphia. I wondered what Charles Dickens would have done with this tale.

It was 5 in the morning, and the 76ers' plane left at 8. It was time to go. We squeaked out goodbyes and thanks to our host and went our separate ways.

Bill and Nancy got in their car and drove off. Bill has the same attitude about cars as I do about clothes. When they wear out, you just leave them somewhere and buy something else. Bill and Nancy lived in Sausalito, across the Golden Gate Bridge. About all Bill knew at this point was that the bridge crossed water, so he headed west for the Pacific Ocean and Hawaii. Chances are he'd have given it a shot, had Nancy not realized there was no bridge in that direction. She was eager to get home, especially in one piece, and directed Bill through the city's Richmond district.

Bill made a turn. Nancy made a comment. An all too familiar dispute ensued. It ended with Bill's stopping the car, handing the keys to Nancy and saying, "If you think you can do better, then you drive." With that, he got out of the car and started walking. Nancy, needing no further encouragement, drove off.

At close to 6 in the morning, Bill King was now going to walk all the way to Sausalito. There was one problem. Standing between him and the bridge was the quarter-mile-long Presidio Boulevard tunnel. He'd have to approach the bridge from another direction.

He trudged though the Presidio, the headquarters of the Sixth Army. By now, fatigue was setting in, and Bill decided a little sleep would do him good. He was about to become a forerunner to the hundreds, if not thousands, of homeless in later years who would sleep out any place they could. A couple of hours later Bill King, voice of the Warriors and the Oakland Raiders, was awakened by the voice of an MP.

Military Police are not noted for their sense of humor. To find some guy with a beard sleeping in their domain might have suggested the Russians were coming. Bill was asked to leave in a tone not altogether friendly. Having dueled with NBA referees over the years, Bill understood the mentality that often engulfs a person when he puts on a uniform. Bill got up and proceeded to walk across the Golden Gate Bridge and home to Sausalito. Thirty-two years later, Bill and Nancy still drive together. They continue to argue now and then, and they continue to love each other.

It was my responsibility to get Alex Hannum back to the Jack Tar Hotel, where, if he was lucky, he might get an hour of sleep. I negotiated the curves leading down from Twin Peaks and ultimately to upper Market Street and to the hotel on Van Ness Avenue. After several attempts, we shook hands and called it a day, a night, a morning, a season — all of which we'd long remember.

There were so many things to recall about that year in the NBA. The Warriors played their home games in many places — the Cow Palace, Civic Auditorium, the University of San Francisco, Oakland, San Jose. On March 4, 1967, they also played a home game in Fresno. It was the first of back-to-back games against the New York Knicks. The next day, the teams would meet again at Civic Auditorium. Dave Stallworth had developed into a front-line performer for the New Yorkers. Shortly after the Fresno game began, Dave came over to Coach Dick McGuire and complained about pressure in his chest. Trainer Danny Whelan summoned Dr. Jim Raggio, the Warriors' physician, and off they went to the visitors' dressing room. Raggio's advice was to keep Stallworth in a Fresno hospital overnight for observation. Raggio felt that if Stallworth was having a heart problem, it was not wise to let him fly with the team to San Francisco.

After the game, the Warriors and Knicks headed to the airport, where they'd take the same plane. I climbed aboard, and who was sitting there but Dave Stallworth. Doc Raggio was left to comment, "I'd hate to be in the Knicks' shoes if something happens to that kid."

Upon landing, the Knicks went to their hotel, convinced Stallworth would be fine after a night's sleep. The next evening he was in the starting lineup when the teams took the floor at Civic Auditorium. Not long after the tipoff, Stallworth pulled up with a charley horse and had to leave the game. It may have saved his life.

After returning to New York, the Knicks sent him to their doctor. An examination showed there was heart damage, and that Dave had suffered an attack. He was out of basketball the next two years. I'm sure, wherever Dave is today, he must think back to those two days in California and realize how lucky he was.

Later that month, the Warriors had a game in Chicago. It was St. Patrick's Day, and there was a huge parade on State Street. I'd been out for a walk through the Loop area and decided to head back to the hotel. As I approached State Street, I heard the bands and saw the crowd congregated to watch the parade, which stretched for what appeared to be miles. I suddenly realized I was on the wrong side of the street. I had these awful thoughts:

1. I would freeze to death standing there.
2. I was single, and no one would miss me.
3. I would miss the game.

It struck me that the only way I was going to get across State Street was to march in the parade and gradually angle myself from one row to another until I reached the other side. In the age-old riddle, I had now replaced the chicken. I could see it now in every children's book: "Why did the basketball announcer cross the road?"

I waited until one of the 42,712 marching bands passed and spotted five lines of men marching in business suits, each of whom seemed to look like Mayor Daley. Their eyes were frozen straight ahead, and none appeared to notice me. I began to march. It didn't matter if I was in step. No one else was. Marching forward, I began to slide gradually to my left and into another column. I felt invisible. Finally I made it to the other side, appreciating, for the first time since childhood, how the chicken felt. The difference was I was now five blocks out of my way.

Alex Hannum once said, "The inherent weakness of the game of basketball is that it must be officiated." During the course of a season, Bill King and I were often critical of referees during our broadcasts. It was an easy thing to do. They were often wrong. We understood basketball was a tough game to officiate, and we understood the need for a third official long before the owners were willing to spend the much-needed money to hire them. Still, some of the calls officials made were flat-out awful, and their attitudes even worse. Bill and I loved the game, and it didn't matter which team was on the receiving end of a poor call. We'd speak our minds.

About this time, broadcasts from around the league were being taped, either by the NBA office or other sources, so Commissioner J. Walter Kennedy could hear what various announcers were saying about the referees. After Kennedy's decision on the Warriors' protest of that wild game with the Hawks the year before, Bill and I had begun referring to him as "J. Walter Calamity." Bill also used the word "invertebrate" in connection with the esteemed Commissioner. I probably would have used that term, too, if I'd known what it meant.

Our gripe with the officials centered on a few specific areas. We thought it wrong when a referee near mid-court, with his view obstructed by several large bodies, called a foul under the basket he couldn't possibly have seen. What troubled us even more was that the official under the basket would stand looking as if he were simply glad to be there. There were many times when we knew a referee was guessing, and we said so. We decried the way referees so often let Red Auerbach stomp his feet and do a war dance protesting a call, then slapped a technical foul on another coach for doing less.

Once in a while an official would summon the nerve to toss Red from a game, but it didn't happen nearly enough. Sometimes, if his team was playing poorly, Auerbach would deliberately get himself thrown out just to fire them up.

There was no question in our minds a class system existed and teams with more influential owners, or coaches, got more breaks. Did this speak to the integrity of officials? You bet it did. Some have already answered to it and have faced possible jail sentences and fines for evasion of taxes. Do officials carry grudges? Of course they do. What makes anyone think a man is any less human just because he officiates in the NBA?

The league office didn't always help the situation. In 1961, an NBA referee named Jim Duffy was also an American League umpire. Duffy couldn't move well in either league. The playoffs were underway, and the Lakers and Hawks were engaged in a best-of-seven-game series. I don't know where Jim Duffy was from, perhaps St. Louis, but for some reason the fans in that town held a Jim Duffy night. According to reports, they showered him with gifts whose value totaled $1,000. Guess who refereed the first six games of that series. How could a league that called itself "major" allow such a thing? How, too, could the NBA have allowed its referees to be seen gambling in the casinos in Las Vegas? It was a common practice for some of them to flock there coming or going to the West Coast.

Few have as much control of the outcome of a basketball game as referees. Whether such gambling was legal was not the point. It aroused suspicion in a league that could ill afford it. No one ever said officiating is easy, especially in basketball. No player ever commits a foul on defense and fails to get fouled on offense. Every coach is battling for an edge. Those are givens. But no fan ever buys a ticket to see a referee. It would have been nice if some referees understood that.

Another thing that spoke to the integrity of the game was the class system that separated rookies and veterans. If a veteran or a star took steps going to the basket, it usually was overlooked. If a rookie did it, it was a violation. The attitude was, and may still be, that the rookie hadn't earned his stripes. The same thing exists in baseball with balls and strikes. I have a B.S. degree from Syracuse University. I know what B.S. is. So don't try to sell me that.

While Bill and I voiced our criticisms on the air, J. Walter Calamity, who apparently had nothing better to do, was monitoring our broadcasts. One day Franklin Mieuli received a notice from the commissioner informing him he'd been fined $500 for certain remarks we'd made about officials during a specific broadcast. Bill and I were relieved because:

1. We'd said much worse on other broadcasts.

2. It was Franklin who got fined, not us.

We went over the remarks with Franklin. He didn't think some of them were so bad. Others he felt didn't need to be said. Then he looked at us and said, "I'll pay the fine because I believe in having a strong commissioner. But if he does this again, I'll be damned if he'll get another cent out of me."

It was obvious what the Commissioner had in mind. If he fined Franklin enough times for our "indiscretions," Franklin would have no choice but to get rid of us. Franklin Mieuli was a broadcaster's friend. He'd been in advertising, and he'd been a producer. He even had a radio studio in the Warriors' offices. When I came to San Francisco, he was the producer of the 49ers' radio broadcasts. J. Walter Calamity wasn't going to bamboozle him.

The Commissioner himself came to San Francisco and appeared at a Warriors-Celtics game on January 5, 1969. Casually striding up to us as if nothing had happened, he extended his hand to Bill and said, "Happy New Year." Bill ignored him. Kennedy then turned to me and extended his hand. I hesitated for a moment and said, "I'll shake your hand, Walter, but I want you to know we're very upset."

There followed a conversation the likes of which I've never heard, let alone joined. We said to the Commissioner, "You seem to want to stifle radio broadcasters. What are you going to do about newspaper guys who write about poor officiating as strongly, or more strongly, than the things we say?"

Kennedy: "I refuse to discuss that."

Greenwald: "Why won't you talk about this with us?"

Kennedy: "I refuse to discuss that."

King: "Walter, if we're such a problem for the league, let's talk about it."

Kennedy: "I refuse to discuss it."

Greenwald: "Why do you avoid the subject?"

Kennedy: "I'm not avoiding anything. I just refuse to discuss it."

We gathered from this he didn't want to discuss it. But for some reason he felt compelled to add, "Do you guys think you are talking to an idiot?"

At this moment, Bill King exercised the greatest restraint I've ever seen in my life. I have no doubt his silence was not to be mistaken for a "no."

Kennedy departed and headed in the direction of Franklin Mieuli. Perhaps he wanted to complain to the Warriors' owner about our reluctance to shake hands with him. Looking back on it, I never said I wouldn't shake hands with him. I just refused to discuss it.

It was a shame Kennedy acted the way he did. I'd had other dealings with him in years past, and he seemed like a decent guy. I never understood why so many top executives in sports seem beset by paranoia.

Despite the on-court success of the 1966-67 Warriors, the season was a disaster. Bill Sharman had done his damage, and Rick Barry had an alternative. The upstart American Basketball Association placed a franchise across the Bay in Oakland. Coincidence had little to do with the Oaks' hiring Bruce Hale, Rick's father-in-law, as their coach.

Bill Sharman lived a lot like the way he played for the Celtics. He was relentless. He seemed never to know when he'd made his point, especially with the players. He continued to beat it into the ground until he drove them up the wall. In the end, he drove Rick Barry to move to Oakland. Paul Neumann retired at age 29 with several good seasons ahead of him. And Tom Meschery was not at all unhappy to be drafted by the expansion Seattle SuperSonics.

Barry's decision to go to the ABA resulted in a landmark court case. The Warriors sued, claiming every player's contract contained a clause for an option year. In other words, if you signed a two-year contract, it was for two years plus an option the club could exercise for one more. Barry's contract was up, per se, but the Warriors still held the option for another season. This didn't mean they could force him to play, but he was prevented from playing elsewhere. Rather than play another year for Sharman, he made a simple choice. It was made easier by the ABA's paying him to sit out.

I was among several people called as witnesses in the lawsuit. The case was heard after the season Barry sat out. The Warriors were suing for damages suffered by Barry's absence, induced by the rival league. Of course, they couldn't acknowledge how much inducement was provided by their own coach.

One of the witnesses Warrior attorneys considered putting on the stand was Eddie Gottlieb. The old war horse flew out from Philadelphia. Before the case was heard, attorney Luther Avery was discussing the NBA contract with Gottlieb, who, for all anyone knew, might have written the first one himself. Luther was asking Gotty his interpretation of the contract. In essence, what did it mean? Gotty replied, "It means when a player signs one of these contracts, we've got him by the balls." Luther didn't need to deliberate long to decide Eddie would need some coaching.

Without Barry, the Warriors finished third in the Western Division. With former Laker Rudy LaRusso added to the club, San Francisco managed to eliminate St. Louis in the opening round of the playoffs. That was as far as the Warriors got, however, as the Lakers swept them in the second round.

In addition to working on Warrior broadcasts, I was also doing a radio sports show on KNBR. I'd got wind from Merv Harris, a former *L.A. Examiner* sportswriter, and from Pidge Burack, whose L.A. motel housed many sports teams and who knew everything that was going on, that Bill Sharman had been making inquiries about going to the ABA. I reported this on my show one night. Franklin Mieuli was in negotiation with Sharman on a new contract. He couldn't believe it was true and questioned my decision to mention it on the air. When I told him where I'd heard the information, he looked sick. He confronted Sharman, who acknowledged it. Franklin set out to find a new coach.

The Lakers, having made it to the finals, waited for the outcome of the Eastern Division semifinals between the 76ers and the Celtics. Thirty years ago, playoff games weren't telecast nationally unless they were on a weekend. Once again, Philadelphia had finished eight games ahead of Boston to win the Eastern Division. Wilt Chamberlain not only led his team in assists, he led the league — the only time a center has done it. He also led the club in scoring with 24.3 points a game, and led in rebounding as well. In December, a newspaper article suggested Wilt was no longer capable of those big games offensively, and might be slowing down. Wilt apparently was among those who read the article. He promptly scored 68 points against the Chicago Bulls on December 16.

The 76ers-Celtics series went to a seventh game in Philadelphia. Mieuli knew it would be telecast in Los Angeles. He wanted to see the game and invited me to fly with him to L.A. Though I didn't know it at the time, Franklin had more on his mind than just watching the game.

We landed at Los Angeles International Airport and got a room in a nearby hotel. It was then that Franklin told me what he had up his sleeve. He wanted Alex Hannum back as his coach. If nothing else, Franklin had a flair for the dramatic. He knew Alex's contract was up in Philadelphia. If the 76ers lost to Boston that night, Philly's season would be over. He'd wait an hour or two after the game, then call Alex at home. If Philadelphia won, he'd forget the call, and we'd return to San Francisco.

As much as Franklin liked me, he hadn't invited me to watch the game in Los Angeles just because I was good company. He knew if he called Alex himself, the coach would probably hang up on him. In 1968 they were not exactly the best of friends. He also knew Alex and I were very close. He asked me to make the call. I would commiserate with him about the game and the season and tell him I had someone there who wanted to speak to him. After the 76ers lost to the Celtics, that's exactly what I did.

Franklin, on the extension, swallowed hard and spoke.

"Hi, Alex, this is Franklin."

There was a pause while this sank in.

"Hi, Franklin."

"Alex, I want you to know that I'm letting Bill Sharman go and I'd like you to come back to coach the Warriors."

"Franklin, it's a little difficult for me to grasp all of that at this moment," Alex said. "It's been a very emotional and disappointing night for me. I'm sure you can understand I can't possibly give you an answer right now."

"I understand," Mieuli said. "Just take some time and let me know."

Alex took some time and decided that returning to the Bay Area sounded good to him. The next thing Franklin knew, Alex Hannum signed to coach the Oakland Oaks of the ABA, starring Rick Barry. Fire me once, that's your mistake. Fire me twice, it's mine. Alex's Oakland team went on to win the ABA championship, making him the only coach to win titles in both leagues.

Mieuli named George Lee to succeed Sharman as the Warriors' head coach. George in turn selected Al Attles as his assistant. In 1975, Attles would coach the Warriors to an NBA Championship.

By now Franklin had moved some of the Warriors' home games to the Oakland Coliseum Arena. The people who ran the arena at that time were very protective of their floor. Before and after games, uniformed guards practically surrounded it to make sure fans didn't step on it in their street shoes. God forbid someone should put a foot on their precious floor. You had the feeling you might end up in some secret room, never to be heard from again.

One night during a heated game, George Lee called a timeout. The players came over and sat down. George turned to face them and crouched down, his back to the court. The coach was now addressing his team in the latter stages of the game, and plotting strategy. Just then, one of the Coliseum's guards, in his official looking uniform, came over. In the middle of George's remarks, the guard tapped him on the shoulder and said, "You can't be on the floor in your street shoes."

The coach had one of his heels over the sideline. He and the players rose as one and told the guard not only where to go but how to get there. The uniformed guard didn't need to be told twice and left. After all, the guys doing the talking also were wearing uniforms.

December 6, 1968, is a date that will live in infamy in the annals of the San Francisco Warriors. The team flew to Seattle without Jeff Mullins, Nate Thurmond, Joe Ellis and Jimmy King, all of whom had the flu. King arrived later, and although he couldn't play, suited up so the team would conform with the league rule that specified a minimum of eight players had to be in uniform for each game. Clyde Lee was sitting in the dressing room with his top coat over his uniform and a towel around his head. He had a 102-degree temperature and was shivering. George Lee's decision was a simple one: Get him dressed, and send him home on the next plane.

Without Lee, Mullins, Thurmond, Ellis and King, the club faced a difficult task. The starting lineup that night consisted of Billy Turner and Rudy LaRusso at the forwards, Dale Schleuter at center, and Al Attles and Fritz Williams at the guards. It was evident early that this would be a rough game. The referees, Ed Rush and Paul Ruddy, seemed content to let almost everything go. This was not a good sign for the beleaguered Warriors, who somehow managed to lead at the half, 45-43. It was unreasonable to expect they could sustain that effort for another 24 minutes. The Sonics built up a six-point lead in the third quarter, but the Warriors managed to recapture their two-point margin at the end of the quarter, 69-67. The task that seemed so impossible before the game suddenly held all sorts of possibilities, and George Lee told his team, "This game is ours to take."

I was doing a telecast that night and was seated at the press table several seats up from Bill King, who was on the radio. Bill and engineer John Cameron were next to the Warriors' bench. On the nights I worked on TV, John placed a crowd mike on the table, where I would normally sit.

With 51 seconds left, the Warriors led 91-89 and had the ball. Eleven seconds later,

Rudy LaRusso drove across the lane. Seattle's Bob Rule struck him in the eye with an elbow. The blow knocked LaRusso several feet, and he fell to the floor in pain. Referees Rush and Ruddy blew their whistles.

They called LaRusso for traveling. No foul, just traveling. Despite this, they granted the Warrior forward a 20-second injury timeout to shake off the effects of Rule's elbow. How, I wondered, did Ed Rush and Paul Ruddy think LaRusso got hurt? Finally, he got up on one knee and asked his coach what the call was.

"Traveling," George Lee said.

"Oh no!" LaRusso said, and began bellowing at Ruddy about the elbow in his eye. Ruddy must have consulted his referee's manual, containing the 10 most often used replies. "Whaddaya want me to do about it?" he said.

Seattle got the ball, and Joe Kennedy tied the game with a 20-foot jumper. The Warriors had one last chance. Fritz Williams put up a shot from the baseline and was whacked by Lenny Wilkens. There was no whistle. Dale Schleuter tried to follow in the rebound and was shoved. Still no whistle. There was no way Rush and Ruddy were going to call a foul on the home team in the final seconds. The buzzer sounded, and the game went into overtime. George Lee went into a rage. Overtime wasn't exactly what he needed. No Thurmond, Mullins, Lee, Ellis and King. Fritz Williams was playing with a bad ankle. All this and another game the next night.

Overtime began, and the teams traded baskets. The Sonics ran off six points in a row to lead, 99-93.

Then it happened.

LaRusso had the ball and was bumped by Tom Meschery. This time the whistle blew. Meschery jumped up and down in protest, convinced the call was against him. He should have saved his energy. Ed Rush called an offensive foul on LaRusso. It was his sixth, and he was out of the game. George Lee would join him in a minute. He'd had enough, and walked onto the floor to express his feelings to Rush. The Seattle Center Coliseum also had uniformed guards, but apparently they understood basketball. Lee directed a few choice words at Rush, who proceeded to hit George with a technical foul. Moments later George drew a second technical and was gone.

That was enough for Bill King. He jumped from his seat, gave a signal to Cameron to cut his mike, slammed his mike harness on the table and screamed at Rush, "You mother#%&*er!"

Somehow, it seemed everyone in the Bay Area must have heard it. Among them was a man driving on the winding roads of the Santa Cruz Mountains. It was Franklin Mieuli. Immediately his mind went into action. Ever the announcer's friend, Franklin decided it must have been some enraged Warrior fan in Seattle who came down near the bench and yelled. His voice must have been picked up by Bill's mike. I suspect

Mieuli was upset enough and wasn't going to let his announcer take the rap for this one. He knew, of course, who'd screamed at Rush.

Nor was there any doubt in the minds of listeners. Some called KNBR to protest. They should have known any basketball-related protest is never upheld. The next day, back home, everyone I ran into asked the same question: "Did you hear what Bill King said on the radio last night?"

Actually, I didn't hear it. I saw him jump out of his seat and slam his mike harness down, and I knew he yelled something. With all the noise, it was hard to hear. But George Lee had actually been closer to Rush out there on the floor when he was blasting him. After the game, I was on the phone to San Francisco. Bucky Walter of the *Examiner* asked me, "Did he really say that?"

"Did he say what?" I said.

"Mother#%&*er."

Thinking Bucky meant George Lee, I said, "I guess George must have. He was pretty mad."

On the way to the Seattle Airport I was in the car with George, Bill and John Cameron. I mentioned the phone call and how George's description of Rush must have gone out over the air. Suddenly Bill looked up and said, "Wait a minute! That was me. I was the one who yelled that."

Then, looking at Cameron, Bill said, "But John, didn't I signal you to cut my mike?"

John said, "I did cut your mike, but it was picked up on the crowd mike where Hank usually sits."

The next day Franklin Mieuli was quoted in the San Francisco papers: "I was listening to the game myself. It must have been some enraged Warrior fan up there for the game."

From that night on, December 6 became known to us as "Mother's Day." Some time later, Bill and Ed Rush made up over the incident, and one year Ed even sent Bill a Mother's Day card.

It was Franklin, however, who created enough doubt over who said what to take the heat off Bill. We agreed it was nice to have a boss who was willing to put his money where his announcers' mouths were.

It doesn't matter how often you give the score; if someone's not paying attention he'll complain you never give the score at all.

9

FOUR SCORES AND MANY YEARS AGO

When I was a college student at Syracuse back in the '50s (the 1950s) one of the radio stations in town played a jingle whenever it was about to do the sports. The jingle went:

> *What's the score*
> *and what is the inning?*
> *What's the score,*
> *is the home team winning?*
> *. . . Here are the scores.*

It was a corny little thing, but whenever you heard it you knew you were going to get the scores of whatever sport was in season. As the years passed, I gave a lot of scores on a lot of radio stations, including WOLF, the one that played that corny jingle. And even before I began to make a living at this game, I was giving scores on WAER, the campus station. The thing was, some of those scores weren't always real.

I realized early in my broadcast days that if you're giving scores on the radio, or TV, for that matter, someone on the next station is giving the same scores. Why, therefore, should anyone listen to you?

During the college football season, the most complete source of scores from Saturday's games is the Sunday sports section. The listings resemble a page from the telephone directory. Almost 60 years ago in New York, there was great competition between The Sunday *New York Times* and The *Herald Tribune* to see which paper had the most college scores listed. Eventually, someone began to wonder if anyone at those papers ever paid attention to the teams involved, or if they simply printed scores as they were reported. The papers obviously couldn't send a reporter to every game. Scores from other parts of the country came in over the news wires, while the big local games were covered by the staff.

In the New York metropolitan area, however, there were many smaller colleges playing football on Saturdays, and the papers counted on the schools' publicists to phone in the results. A desk man would take them down, and they'd be added to the list.

One year, someone decided to see if anyone was paying attention. When football season started, he called The *Herald Tribune* and said, "I'm the sports information director from Plainfield State Teachers College and I've got a final score."

The desk man said "Okay, I'll take it."

The next day, there it was in The Sunday *Trib*:

Plainfield State 21, Millville 7

Our devious friend now had proof that no one was paying attention. Each Saturday thereafter, he continued to phone in the Plainfield State scores. Each week, he talked to the same man on the desk, who dutifully took down the score and ran it with the rest of the results. Only now the "SID" began to provide some details on the games.

It was becoming obvious to the man on the desk that Plainfield State was having a hell of a season, and this halfback named Johnny Chung was becoming a real star. Well into the season, Plainfield State was still undefeated, and Chung was scoring two and three touchdowns a week. One day, the desk man suggested it might be a good idea to send someone out to Plainfield State to do a story on this guy Chung. Indeed, it was a good idea, except there was no Plainfield State Teachers College, and there sure as hell was no running back named Johnny Chung. It was one of the great pranks in newspaper history, though The *Herald Tribune* could be excused for failing to share the amusement.

The *Tribune*, despite its desire to run more scores than The *Times*, hadn't intended they be fictitious. On the other hand, when I was giving scores on the radio, I had every intention of slipping in a couple every now and then. It wasn't going to hurt anyone, and if I got someone to say, "What was that score he just gave?" I knew listeners would start paying closer attention. In college, about the only listeners I had on WAER were friends. Knowing this, I would always slip in a special score for them whenever I was doing my sports show.

"Here are today's college football results: Army 41, Pittsburgh 14...Harvard 17, Princeton 14...West Virginia 13, Boston College 7...Colgate 21, Pepsodent 14...Michigan 35, Iowa 10…Holy Cross 28, Red Cross 21...Notre Dame 42, Purdue 20...and Penn 7, Ink 6."

It trained me to try to make something different out of the ordinary. It was fun. It was harmless. The only people who might have seriously questioned it were the gamblers, who probably didn't remember seeing a line on the Colgate-Pepsodent game or a couple of the others.

Over the years, I began collecting scores suitable for slipping in among the legitimate. To fellow broadcasters, I say: Don't try this unless you're really confident about yourself, or have a long, guaranteed contract.

Vicks 44, WD 40
Pope John XXIII, Pope Pius XII
Boeing 747, DC 10
Roe 9, Wade 8
Beverly Hills 90210, Hawaii 5-0
Chapter 11, Verse 4
Zantac 75, Phillips 66
Jackson 5, Brothers 4
John 3:16, Marsha 2:14
Partagas 10, Montecristo 3
Route 66, Interstate 10
Monistat 7, Rocky 3
Henry VIII, George III
Duke 26, Duchess 21
Heinz 57, Seagram's 7
Dave Clark 5, Fiddlers 3
MI 5, Et tu
Philadelphia 76ers, San Francisco 49ers
Big 12, PAC-10
Back 9, Front 4
G-2, Mach 1
Pennsylvania Avenue 1600, Downing Street 10
Black Jack 21, Craps 7
Apollo 13, Mercury 7
Magna Carta 1215, Norman Invasion 1066
Ocean's Eleven, Home Alone Two
Love Potion No. 9, Chanel No. 5
Apostles 12, Commandments 10

Mercedes 500, Olds 88
Humidity 85, Barometer 29.91
AK-47, M-16
Sun Block 15, Cell Block 10
Pi 3.14, H20
Half 50, Quarter 25
Magellan 1521, Columbus 1492
K-9, Blind Mice 3
Mile 5280, Space Odyssey 2001
Gross 144, Baker's Dozen 13
Maids a Milking 7, Golden Rings 5
Speed Limit 65, Term Limits 2
Starting Rotation 5, Wise Men 3
V 8, A 1
Lower 48, North Dallas 40
Science 120, English 101
Stalag 17, Motel 6
Jack Benny 39, Bo Derek 10
Sunset Strip 77, Surfside 6
And this just in. . .
Catch-22, Mila 18

These final results are not available in stores, but only through this special offer. Order now, and you'll also receive my buyer's guide to halftime scores.

An Alou-Sedating Moment

In the early 1980s a man named Bob Aurigemma came up to me on Market Street in San Francisco and asked if I could name the eight Alou brothers. Without benefit of a Dominican Republic phone directory, I knew I was stumped, so I conceded defeat.

Aurigemma proceeded to reel off the names: Felipe Alou, Matty Alou, Jesus Alou, Toot Alou, Bob Alou, Skip Alou, Bebop Alou and Boog Alou. I jotted them down and mentioned the names during the Giants broadcast that night.

Almost immediately I received requests to repeat the names, and I began to do so at least once or twice a season. Later on Aurigemma somehow managed to locate the Alou brothers' long lost sister, Hullub. The Alous began to assume a popularity among fans they'd never before experienced. Many Alou wannabes started to come out of the woodwork. Foremost among them was Walleeb Alou, but he was never able to prove a relationship to the others.

"Of course he had a big ego. Would you rather send your son into battle with a general who expected to lose?"

10

A GENERAL YOU COULD NAME YOUR SON AFTER

My parents Ray and Bea Greenwald and I sat in the living room of our flat at 3238 Calvert Street in Detroit, waiting for a voice to come through the radio. It wasn't easy to hear short wave transmissions in September of 1945, but on this day that wasn't going to stop anyone from listening.

I was 10. The formal signing of the Japanese surrender had just taken place on the battleship Missouri, and General Douglas MacArthur was about to address his countrymen.

"Today the guns are silent," he said. "A great tragedy has ended. A great victory has been won . . ."

There were tears of joy and sadness in my household that day. I'm sure it was the same in homes throughout the country. The war was over, yet when the General said, "I speak for the thousands of silent lips forever stilled among the jungles and the beaches and in the deep waters of the Pacific . . ." I couldn't help thinking of our neighbor's son, one of those who had lost his life there.

MacArthur spoke of his hopes for the nation he had helped to defeat. "If the talents of the (Japanese) race are turned into constructive channels, the country can lift itself from its present deplorable state into a position of dignity." He concluded his address,

"And so, my fellow countrymen, today I report to you that your sons and daughters have served you well and faithfully . . . Their spiritual strength and power has brought us through to victory. They are homeward bound — take care of them."

This was the first time I'd heard Douglas MacArthur speak. Of course I was familiar with his famous words, "I shall return." I didn't hear him say it. My ears weren't quite that good. But on that Sunday in Detroit my ears were good enough to know this man who knew how to win a war also knew how to make a speech. When you grew up in the pre-television era you were much more conscious of what people were saying on the radio, as well as the sounds of their voices. I can't say General MacArthur influenced my career in the way Tiger broadcaster Harry Heilmann did, but even at 10 I knew a great speaker when I heard one.

Six years later I sat in an assembly at Brighton High School in Rochester, New York. The General had been relieved of his command in Korea by President Harry Truman and was addressing a joint meeting of Congress. This was MacArthur's "Old Soldiers Never Die" speech. What a marvelous exit line for a career unparalleled in American military history. But it was something else he said that had a greater impact on me. In discussing the stalemated hostilities in Korea in which soldiers were dying every day, MacArthur said, "War's very object is victory, not prolonged indecision." How prophetic those words would become.

I had always admired Harry Truman. I was thrilled by his improbable victory over Thomas Dewey in 1948. There was no question he had every right to relieve MacArthur. He had every right to make a wrong decision. If you have no intention of fighting for a purpose, then negotiate a "peace" with the enemy and get out. Don't ask people to die for nothing. MacArthur could no longer ask his soldiers to do that. I was intrigued by this man and I remain so.

Douglas MacArthur was a man people either loved or hated. Such people make the best studies. I was never a great student. The only time I ever saw 100 percent, it was the humidity reading in Manila in May, 1972. Carla and I arrived in the Philippine capital, each of us on a mission. Mine was to further my study of MacArthur's career. Carla's was to get out of there as quickly as possible. I couldn't blame her. It was disheartening to check into the Manila Hotel and find a sign on the desk that read, "Delegates to the convention are kindly requested to check all firearms at the front desk."

The country was holding a constitutional convention, the outcome of which would be many years of martial law. Carla's uneasiness was further abetted by a toilet seat that fell off and a light bulb that exploded. Who said white women can't jump? After a search of our room showed no traces of land mines, we decided to gut it out. That is, one of us decided.

As we were unpacking, the telephone rang. It was Ray McGowan. He was the former husband of our friend Ann, who worked for a travel agency in San Francisco. They'd met while serving in the Peace Corps, and she contacted him to say we were coming. Ray said he'd pick us up and take us out to dinner. Carla needed to hear a friendly voice.

The Manila Hotel was where General MacArthur lived during his days as head of the Philippine Army. He'd taken that position after retiring as Chief of Staff of the U.S. Army. The hotel was located along picturesque Roxas Boulevard and looked out on Manila Bay. But this wasn't 1937. It was 1972, and the hotel had seen better days. There were more modern and comfortable places to stay, but MacArthur hadn't lived in them. It wouldn't have been the same.

We were standing in front of the hotel when Ray McGowan's chauffeur-driven car pulled up. It was a Mustang. If I hadn't previously believed there was a first time for everything, I was now a convert. We climbed in the back while Ray sat in front with the driver. We tried not to laugh. Later, after riding in Manila's taxis, we came to appreciate Ray's driver a lot more. Taxis in that city apparently don't come with brakes. The only time the drivers stopped for anything was when they ran out of gas. My wife still gets nervous in cabs. I have scars from her fingernails.

Ray took us to a place called Gloria's on A. Mabini Street, where some of his friends were waiting. The food was good, and there was music and dancing. We were starting to relax. Ray asked if there was anything I especially wanted to do during my stay. I told him of my interest in MacArthur and our plans to fly to the island of Leyte. I had to see the landing beach where the General waded ashore, fulfilling his pledge to "return."

He looked at me the way people do when they think you've been in the sun too long. Carla now had a kindred spirit.

I also mentioned my hope of meeting Philippine Foreign Secretary Carlos Romulo, the former Secretary General of the United Nations who had been an aide de camp to MacArthur during the war. McGowan said he knew Romulo's sons and could probably arrange a tour of the family compound, where the Secretary kept his memorabilia. Meeting the man himself would be more difficult.

Not counting the day we arrived, we had scheduled five full days in the Philippines. Husbands and wives don't always share the same views. The only thing we shared about the five days being long enough were differing points of view. I had to make the most of my time.

The plane for Leyte left at 4:45 a.m. We were surprised to find we weren't the only people on board. We were, however, the only ones who didn't live or have family there. We made an intermediate stop in Cebu City. (The last nonstop flight to Leyte took off from an aircraft carrier in 1944.) It was 6:30 a.m. when we touched down at Tacloban, the island's capital. It was here that the government was handed back to the Filipinos following MacArthur's return. It was also in Tacloban that the General established his headquarters after the invasion. Our landing was not greeted with quite as much fanfare, although we were looked upon with great curiosity. It was the kind of look that said, "These people must have got on the wrong plane."

We took a taxi to the center of town. It was not a long ride. We faced a difficult task to get to the beach where the General waded ashore. We were told to take a bus from the marketplace to the village of San Jose, then find a ride to the beach at Palo.

Our return flight to Manila didn't leave until 5:30 p.m. I had the feeling Carla didn't want to miss it. We spotted a vehicle of uncertain origin. It had wheels and a driver who assured us it was headed for San Jose. It was apparent our fellow passengers had done their marketing for the day, as men, women, children and live chickens got on board. It wasn't difficult to spot us. We had no children or chickens, only straw hats we purchased in the market. The "bus" had no roof. It might have at one time, but it was probably better not to ask.

Shortly after we began our ride down the road toward San Jose, Carla's straw hat headed back to Tacloban. That she didn't jump off and run after it showed how little I knew about my wife of two years. I suppose we should have known better. That bus had "hold on to your hat" written all over it.

The sight of Carla's "sombrero" rolling along the road provided the passengers with a hearty laugh and seemed to make us a lot of friends. The young girls, both on the bus and earlier in the marketplace, had been intrigued by Carla's watch. It had a black band and a big, round face that showed a black-and-white wedding photo of the two of us. It was apparent the girls had never seen anything like it. They kept looking at the picture, then at Carla and me, making sure it was really us. So I'd put on a few pounds since then. What was the big deal? The watch was a great conversation piece, and we had no problem meeting people because of it. Carla still has the watch, but, like her aging husband, it no longer runs.

Somehow the bus made it to San Jose, but we still had more than two miles to the beach. Fortunately, there was a young man who had a motorbike with a side car, called a trishaw. We climbed in, and several minutes later he deposited us at the beach. MacArthur had beaten me by only 28 years.

We made our way onto the sand fronting that most hallowed coastline. We examined the monuments placed there years earlier to commemorate the landing. One explained the significance of the event itself. Another was dedicated to the unknown Filipino and American soldiers who died there. There was also a set of MacArthur's footprints cast in cement when he last visited Leyte, in 1961, three years before his death. Today there are statues of the General and his landing party as they appeared in the famous picture showing them as they waded ashore. We read all the inscriptions, then sat down on the beach. It was 8:30 in the morning, seven hours before our return flight to Manila. Carla turned to me and said, "This is it?"

I explained this wasn't simply something you saw, it was something you felt. "The largest naval armada ever assembled was right out there in that gulf laying down a barrage of gunfire never seen before," I said. "All these beautiful palm trees you're looking at had been blown away. Two hundred thousand men landed all along this coastline. Then came MacArthur with Philippine President Sergio Osmena at his side. After two and a half long years, he stepped ashore, redeeming his pledge of 'I shall return.' What drama! What history!"

By now I must have sounded as if I was narrating an episode of "Victory at Sea." If I'd had an M-1 rifle I'd probably have been charging up the beach and heading for the jungle. I was pumped. What a dichotomy. Here on this idyllic beach in the early morning sun, surrounded by palm trees, my wife beside me, I was ready to fight the war all over again. The feeling passed quickly, and we walked down to the water and took pictures of each other wading ashore.

I also had brought a small tape recorder to gather in the sound of Leyte Gulf. It was a good thing no one else could see what I was doing. The sight of a grown man crouching down in the water, recording splashes, is not one to suggest an abundance of mental competence. Unlike General MacArthur, I didn't know if I'd ever be returning. I was soaking up everything I could. We sat on the beach for about two hours. By this time there was nothing left to see or feel. We got up and headed back toward the road. On the other side stood what looked like a farm with a small store in front. The sign on it proclaimed: "Red Beach Store."

If we hadn't known it earlier, we now had confirmation we'd come to the right beach. The lady in the store sold us that most famous of Filipino beverages, Coca-Cola. We were told how fortunate we were to have come there on this day because they were inoculating the pigs. We were invited to stay and watch. Invitations such as this don't come along every day. Naturally, we accepted.

It didn't seem as if the pigs were enjoying it a lot; those weren't squeals of joy I was hearing. Nevertheless, it was comforting to know the pigs were now immune from things such as measles, pig pox and anything to which those animals are susceptible.

An hour later we decided to return to San Jose to catch the bus back to Tacloban. It was obvious we couldn't just step out on the road and hail a taxi. In fact, there wasn't anyone to be seen. We started walking. It was now getting on toward noon. It was May. It was hot. There were no trees to stand under.

Carla and I shared the one hat we had. Whoever said "two heads are better than one" would have a tough time explaining it to us. We continued to trudge along. I feared my marriage was in jeopardy. I told my bride I had merely intended to show her the landing beach. I wasn't trying to reenact the Death March. We continued walking. I told her, "Someday you'll laugh about this." She had more modest goals. Seeing tomorrow was one of them, and laughing about this wasn't likely.

Just when things were really looking bleak, along came another young man and his trishaw to save my marriage. He delivered us to the bus, and we headed back to town. By now, Tacloban looked like one of the major cities of the world. The streets were paved, and there was a hotel where we could eat. We climbed the steps to the dining room and had lunch. I declined the pork adobo. I'd seen enough pigs for one day.

Lunch took the better part of an hour, leaving us plenty of time to explore the city. We had another four hours before our plane left. Exploring Tacloban was not likely to take that long. We began our tour, and again Carla was besieged by young girls wanting to see her watch. Many people asked why we had come to visit their island. I explained I wanted to see the landing beach. More than a few asked if I was there in 1944 with MacArthur. Though I had been only 9 at the time, by now I was looking old enough to have participated.

It wasn't any cooler in the city than it had been walking up that road from the beach. We stopped in front of a little travel office with a large map of Leyte in the window. I was showing Carla where we were in relation to the beach when the door opened and a man stepped out. He introduced himself and invited us inside, pointing out he had air conditioning. He didn't have to ask twice. We sat in his office for the next couple of hours, during which time he served us Coca-Cola and cookies made from caribou milk. I thought caribou were water buffalo and didn't know they gave milk. It was a continuing education for me.

Our host was apparently a prominent man. We should have figured that from the air conditioner. He had been a legislator at one time and was now running a travel agency. We discussed the political situation in the Philippines, which he didn't think was going to change much in spite of the constitutional convention.

We talked about Carlos Romulo, whom I was still hoping to see, and whom he described as better known around the world than he was at home. He said Romulo was one of the few honest men in the government. Sitting in the comfort of that office made our day. Carla, though still a long way from that "someday" when she'd look back on all this and laugh, was still talking to me. She was a great sport and still is. She also proofread this chapter.

We thanked our host and got a ride back to the airport. It was after 7 p.m. when we returned to Manila. It had been a long day, but I'd accomplished what I set out to do. To have walked in MacArthur's footsteps was an exhilarating experience, but I was tired. The General was 64 when he came ashore. I was 36. No doubt he felt better at the end of his day than I did.

Each day we attempted to see Carlos Romulo. The foreign secretary's secretary was most polite but noncommittal. She held out hope something could be arranged toward the end of the week. I was hoping to get over to Corregidor, which, along with Bataan, symbolized the courageous stand made by American and Filipino forces in the dark days of the war. A hydrofoil ferried passengers the 25 miles out into Manila Bay to reach the island. I was hesitant to sign up in case an appointment with Romulo came through.

By now we'd seen much of the city. Parts of it looked as if it had just been bombed; others were modern, beautiful and world-class. You didn't have to be a genius to figure out there were rich and poor and not much in between. Within a year of our 1972 visit, Ferdinand Marcos declared martial law. He would have in his hands the power to do wonderful things. He did. For himself. It was hard to believe such wealth and poverty could exist in such close proximity to each other. It made you realize the walls guarding the big estates were there to blind the "haves" from the needs of the "have-nots." Several years later we would see the same thing in Rio de Janeiro.

Everywhere we went in Manila, people engaged us in conversation. Each time I mentioned the name MacArthur, the response came in reverential tones. While America was no longer as respected there as it once was, Douglas MacArthur remained a hero. He transcended geographic boundaries. To the Filipinos, "He was one of us."

The General spent much of his life in the Philippines. His first assignment there was after graduation from West Point in 1903. His father, General Arthur MacArthur, was Military Governor of the Islands. Young Douglas was assigned to the Army Corps of Engineers, where he did surveys of Leyte, Corregidor, and the Bataan Peninsula. Forty years later those names would become synonymous with his career. In 1905 he served as an aide to his father while the senior MacArthur was an observer at the Russo-Japanese War.

It was there the future general took note of the fighting capabilities of the Japanese soldier. Spending time with the Japanese commanders gave him an insight that would serve him well. He noted their singleness of purpose and willingness to sacrifice their lives for their emperor.

Years later he fought for retention of the imperial system in Japan when almost everyone in Washington wanted to hang Hirohito. MacArthur knew directives issued through the emperor would be the key to a successful occupation. Douglas MacArthur was, after all, a student long before he became a general. By 1905 he had been out of West Point for two years, but his education was just beginning. He hadn't forgotten how to study.

While waiting for word from Romulo's office, Carla and I got a call from Ray McGowan. We had permission to tour the Foreign Secretary's home and observe his memorabilia. On display were personal letters from MacArthur, many ribbons, campaign flags and other decorations. Romulo had attained the rank of brigadier general during the war. He was the last man off Corregidor before the Japanese took the island.

I realized viewing this collection was not something most people had a chance to do. In Romulo's home, we saw a staircase draped with his many flags. I was getting there. I'd been to his home. Now I had to see the man himself.

During our stay in Manila, Carla and I celebrated our second anniversary. The fact we were celebrating was testimony to Carla's commitment to marriage. After dragging her to Leyte, I suspected future goodwill would be in short supply. We were still talking. We dined that night in the rooftop restaurant at one of the city's newer hotels.

The view was lovely — my wife, as well as the city. There was music. There was romance in the air. I knew I owed her big time. I waited till the band played something slow. I asked her to dance. She knew why. In addition to our anniversary we had something else to celebrate. Earlier that day we got a call from Romulo's secretary. We would be able to meet with him at 8 a.m.in his office for about 30 minutes.

Romulo was on a tight schedule and was expecting the Danish Ambassador after he finished with us. This meant our appointment would fall on the morning of our last day, and we still hadn't been to Corregidor. We immediately went to the tour office in the hotel to book the hydrofoil. There was one a day. It departed at 10:30. It was full. I was crushed. As a joke, I said to Carla, "Well, maybe we could charter a plane."

The tour lady heard this. Thinking I was serious, she said, "You want to charter a plane? Let me check for you." By now I was too embarrassed to say anything, as her fingers were flying through the Yellow Pages in search of a plane. "Okay," she said, "There's one right here. We'll arrange for it to fly you to Corregidor and time the arrival to meet the hydrofoil. That way you can join up with the tour."

With visions of five or six hundred dollars in my head I sheepishly asked her how much. She said, "For the two of you it will cost $37." I tried to make it seem as if chartering aircraft was an everyday occurrence for the Greenwalds and, disguising my glee, said, "That will be fine."

The next morning we arrived at the Foreign Ministry well before the appointed hour. There was no way we were going to be late. We looked around the impressive building and made our way up to Romulo's office.

His secretary met us, and we thanked her for her efforts. She ushered us in to meet him. He greeted us with a typically warm Filipino smile. Carlos Romulo stood about

5 feet 2 inches. It was hard to believe he'd survived all he'd been through during the war.

On the other hand, he was one of the few who could have stood up in a foxhole and still be safe. It was hard to believe we were with this man who had been part of so much history and who, along with President Osmena and Sergeant Francisco Salveron, were the Filipinos who accompanied MacArthur ashore at Leyte.

The Foreign Secretary extended his hand and said, "I understand you're interested in Douglas MacArthur. I'm sure I have some stories to share with you." Then he called for the official photographer, who entered the room and took a picture of the three of us. He said he would sign it and asked us to leave our address with his secretary so she could mail it to our home.

Romulo apologized for what he felt was a chaotic atmosphere around the office that morning. "The Ambassador from Denmark is due to arrive shortly," he said, "and I've got people looking all over for a Danish flag to fly out front." I didn't imagine Danish flags were in great supply in Manila.

I'd read several books Romulo had written about his days during the war, and I was eager to talk about his experiences, as well. In a paragraph about a battle scene on Bataan, he describes standing next to another soldier when artillery fire struck the man and blew his head off.

Romulo was so stunned he could only think to call out, "Corpsman, please help. This man's been hurt." He wrote, "I couldn't comprehend what had happened to him. One second we were talking and the next, he had no head." The title of one of Romulo's books, "I Walked With Heroes," might well have been phrased the other way around.

He talked about his many visits to San Francisco, reminding us the United Nations Charter had been signed there. He discussed his days as Secretary General of the UN. Naturally we talked about General MacArthur and how his pledge to "return" gave Filipinos hope during the Japanese occupation of the islands.

He told us, "MacArthur was not understood as well in his own country as he was here. Washington resented his saying 'I' instead of 'We shall return.' They didn't realize it was MacArthur we believed in, not the United States. Roosevelt had written us off. Europe would come first."

Romulo told us that when his term was up at the United Nations he decided to make a leisurely journey across the United States before coming back to the Philippines.

He said, "One of the places I stopped was Independence, Missouri, to visit former President Harry Truman. He was showing me around the house and commenting on the many pictures he had on his wall. I was rather surprised to see he had a picture of General MacArthur." Romulo saw the surprise on my face as well and continued,

"President Truman pointed to the picture and said, 'There's a man who thought he was God.'

"'I replied, Mr. President, in my country he was.'"

There was no better note on which to end our visit. Carla and I were exhilarated as we left the Foreign Ministry and headed to the airport to catch our charter. When we arrived at the hangar we were encouraged to find they were expecting us. We were even more encouraged to see the pilot was wearing a shirt with epaulets. At least he looked like a pilot.

I was comforted by this thought until I remembered drum majors wear them as well. What the hell. For $37 we were going, no matter what. If we'd been able to board the hydrofoil it would have cost us $26. For 11 bucks we were big spenders. As we were flying over Manila Bay, we spotted the hydrofoil up ahead. It didn't take long to cover the 25 miles, even in a plane small enough to give your little nephew for Christmas. We swooped down over the "foil" as we began our descent to a bumpy grass landing strip on Corregidor. We were on the bus waiting when the rest of our fellow tour members climbed aboard. At some point, someone asked if we were the ones who came in on the airplane. They must have thought we were big shots, and I certainly wasn't about to spoil it by telling them it only cost $37.

We toured the island and saw the gun batteries as well as the famous Malinta Tunnel, which inspired MacArthur's detractors to pin on him the name "Dugout Doug." There were those who felt he had holed up inside the tunnel, where he had his headquarters, and never came out.

They blamed him for sagging morale on Bataan. They blamed him for lack of supplies. They blamed him for lack of food. They might have blamed him for the hot weather while they were at it. History shows the General gave the enemy plenty of chances to kill him during the war. Those who disliked him, and there were many, probably blamed him for the Japanese failure to shoot or bomb straight enough to finish him off.

Let's face it: With his dark glasses and corncob pipe, he wasn't exactly traveling across the Pacific incognito. Often he traveled recklessly ahead of his local commanders to view the situation at the front.

While MacArthur's judgment in such cases might have been questionable, it would be difficult to doubt his personal courage. For many, he was not easy to like. He often came across as haughty or arrogant. Many years after the war, Colonel Roger Egeberg, MacArthur's aide and physician at that time, told me, "Of course he had a big ego. Would you rather send your son into battle with a general who expected to lose?"

The Southwest Pacific was the farthest theater of operations under U.S. control. It was the end of the supply line in a war in which the bulk of supplies were going to Europe. There are many things that combine to make one an unpopular commander. Such considerations aside, the fact is he was a brilliant general and his campaigns repeatedly brought fewer American casualties than those elsewhere. Perhaps someone should have asked the parents of those who returned safely under his command what they thought of him.

There appears to be no end to the number of books written about MacArthur. Carla was convinced I had all of them. For some time I'd promised to help straighten up the house once I retired. When that time finally came, I decided straightening things up was going to be too much like work, so I took the easy way out and donated my collection to the MacArthur Memorial Library in Norfolk, Virginia. I saw walls in my house I didn't know I had.

Over a 25-year period I'd read all the books. Besides me, no one was impressed that I had them. They could be put to better use in their new home. I won't go into an analysis of all those studies of the General. It was obvious they fell into three categories: the love letters, the hatchet jobs and the few that attempted to be serious studies. Naturally, some were written during the war, when the country needed heroes.

Others were laced with hearsay and myths that were later debunked. Some books contained moments in his life he might have wished he could undo. There were books written after Korea. The authors' feelings weren't any more difficult to ascertain than the ones in this chapter.

There were things I read about MacArthur that made me embarrassed. Embarrassed! Hell, I didn't even know the man. How could I be embarrassed? I continued to read everything I could. I talked to people who fought under him. I talked to people who'd been on his staff. I talked to people in Japan who'd lived under the occupation he administered. I talked to many Americans, each of whom seemed to have a different point of view.

One, in fact, blamed MacArthur for a decline in the steel industry in the United States because he helped make Japan so successful after the war. It's the diversity of opinion that makes him a worthwhile study. I was fascinated by the fact he was nearly 61 when the war with Japan began, and 65 when he accepted Japan's surrender.

He was 70 when he conducted what many consider his most brilliant campaign, the Inchon landing in Korea. Many have been generals. Who but MacArthur had a career like his? I'm reminded of a remark by another World War II fighter, Admiral William F. Halsey, who said, "There are no great men, only great challenges that ordinary men are forced by circumstances to meet." No one was born great, but certainly those who are thought of in that light met Halsey's criterion.

After MacArthur closed his military career, surviving members of his staff would gather each year on January 26 at the Waldorf Astoria Hotel in New York, where the General lived, to help celebrate his birthday.

Following his death in 1964, the custom continued, though the scene shifted to Norfolk, where he is buried. Norfolk was the ancestral home of his mother, and the city offered to provide a memorial to house his memorabilia and to serve as a final resting place. Jean MacArthur, the General's widow, would come to Norfolk each January to join the birthday observance.

One night in November 1979, I was sitting at home in San Francisco when it occurred to me that the following year would mark the 100th anniversary of the General's birth. It's likely none of my friends or acquaintances were struck with the same thought. I'd just finished my first season broadcasting the Giants' games and had time off until spring training in March.

I said to Carla, "I wonder if they're going to do something big in Norfolk to mark the occasion. If they are, I'd like to go."

Having paid her dues in the Philippines in 1972, Carla said, "This time, you're on your own."

I got the number of the MacArthur Memorial and spoke with the Director, Colonel Lyman Hammond, Jr. I explained my longtime interest in the General's life and asked if they had special plans to mark what would have been his 100th birthday. Colonel Hammond said, "As a matter of fact we do. There will be ceremonies during the day, and the U.S. Army Association is sponsoring a banquet that evening and General Mark Clark is going to be the speaker."

I asked whether the event was open to the public, and when he replied in the affirmative, I said, "Count me in."

Colonel Hammond said, "You mean you would come all the way from San Francisco just for this?" Convinced I was serious, he said, "I'll be glad to hold a ticket for you and make whatever other arrangements you'd like."

He must have wondered why anyone who didn't know the General or was otherwise required to be there would make this trip. Of course he couldn't have known that someone who'd gone all the way to Leyte Gulf wouldn't bat an eyelash at making a journey to Norfolk. Actually, this would be my third time in the Virginia seaport. I was there in 1959 when Syracuse beat Navy at the Oyster Bowl. My old college roommate Tom Lotz and I were spotters at that game. Tom was then an Army Lieutenant. In 1971, I visited the MacArthur Memorial when I was on a basketball trip with the Warriors.

I arrived in Norfolk late Friday afternoon the day before the big event. My plan was to attend the memorial the next day and try not to get in anyone's way. The memorial itself was actually the old city hall, which the late Mayor Fred Duckworth made available. I spent a quiet Friday evening in anticipation. At a respectable hour the following morning, I entered the building, which stood behind an impressive statue of the General. Like a good tourist, I'd remembered to bring my camera. Before the day was over, I put it to good use.

Douglas MacArthur is buried beneath the rotunda of the memorial. A place beside him was set aside for Mrs. MacArthur, who reached the age of 100 on December 28, 1998, and as of this writing still lives in the Waldorf Towers in New York. I spent a couple of hours taking in the exhibits and trying to absorb the history behind them. To look at Medals of Honor won by both the General and his father is impressive.

A considerable number of people were touring along with me, as this was a busier day than usual. Afterward I decided it was time to find Colonel Hammond and say hello. With all the activity going on, I was surprised to find him alone in his office. I stuck my head in and identified myself. "I'm the man who came from San Francisco," I said. "I know this is a big day so I don't want to bother you. I just wanted to thank you for your assistance."

The director of the memorial invited me to come in and take a seat. We talked for a while, and I explained why I'd come to Norfolk. Once he asked me what I did for a living, we spent quite some time talking baseball. Graciously, the Colonel arranged for me to sit at dinner that night with him and his wife Sarah Ann. He also invited me to a reception later in the day for General Clark and handed me a press kit with a copy of Clark's speech. I was stunned he was doing all this for some crazy guy from San Francisco. He may have been retired as an officer, but he was still very much a gentleman.

After leaving Colonel Hammond's office I walked over to the gift shop. Inside were biographies of the General, tapes of his speeches, and many other items no MacArthurphile should be without. Unfortunately for me, the one item inside the shop I wanted most to take home was not for sale. It was Mrs. MacArthur. Small of stature and large of life, she was standing there chatting with the lady who ran the shop. I couldn't believe my good fortune. I'd met a lot of famous people in my life — it comes with the territory when you work in sports — but this was different.

Mrs. MacArthur and I had corresponded briefly several years before, and I'd received a lovely letter from her after our son Douglas was born. I waited until she noticed me. How could she not? My knees were playing the Army fight song.

She smiled and I introduced myself, hoping I'd got the name right. Mine, not hers. I realized at that moment I was talking to the most powerful person I'd ever met. She was the only one who ever gave orders to General MacArthur. Who could have imagined this little lady from Murfreesboro, Tennessee, whose grandfather's regiment fought against Douglas MacArthur's father in the Civil War, would help unite those two families?

Here was a woman who endured the daily bombing of Corregidor, refusing opportunities to return to the safety of the United States. It was Mrs. MacArthur who, with their 4-year-old son Arthur, joined the General on the PT boats that successfully ran a Japanese blockade to reach the island of Mindanao. From there they flew to Australia.

Mrs. MacArthur remained with her husband all the way to Tokyo. So little is known about this remarkable lady by anyone other than those who knew her personally or have studied the life of her husband. She has turned down many book offers. There are taped interviews with her in the archives of the MacArthur Memorial Library, and they will be released after her passing.

Mrs. MacArthur and I chatted for several minutes. We discussed the movie "MacArthur," which had come out a couple of years earlier. She admired the job Gregory Peck had done in portraying her husband but felt his life couldn't be told within the short format of a movie. She had a point. When you think about it, his exploits in World War I alone would have constituted a career for most military figures. If they'd really made a movie of his life it might have run longer than the wars themselves.

Mrs. MacArthur was pleased so many old military friends were on hand for the occasion in Norfolk and told me Carlos Romulo was unable to make it but promised to visit her in New York. I told her of the stories Romulo related to Carla and me in his office eight years earlier. When I reminded her we'd named our son after her husband, she asked if I had a picture, which she was delighted to see. By now others in the shop were coming over to her, so I thanked her for her time and moved on. This would have been enough for me for one day, but my day was only beginning.

Later, I attended a ceremony at the site where Douglas MacArthur is buried. Major General William C. Chase, whom MacArthur once described as "a brilliant front-line fighter," presented a salute to his former commander. General Chase must have been close to 80 at that time, but I recall thinking how impressive and fit he looked in his World War II uniform. It was the famed flying column of Chase's First Cavalry Division that liberated the prisoners at Manila's Santo Tomas and Bilidid prisons in 1945. These were many of the same men MacArthur had to leave behind in the Philippines more than three years earlier.

The reception for General Mark Clark began at 17:30. Whoops, let's not get carried away here. It was around 5:30 p.m. A lot of important-looking people seemed to be there, underscoring the fact that I had no business being in the room. But Colonel Hammond had provided me with the invitation, and there was no way I was going to let it go unused. I didn't see anyone I recognized milling around, so I tried to make myself look as official as anyone talking to himself could. Not far from where I was standing, I saw General Clark talking with two other men. He was no longer as tall as he appeared in World War II photographs, but at 83 he was every bit as handsome, decked out in his tuxedo. He finished his conversation and walked toward me.

"Hi. I'm Mark Clark," he said reaching out his hand.

I thought, "This is all backward. I know who you are."

A similar incident happened to me in the summer of 1968 in Reno's bar on Post Street in San Francisco. Reno's was one of the few places Joe DiMaggio had been known to hang out. Reno Barsochini, the owner, was Joe's buddy. I walked in, and, sure enough, Joe was sitting at the end of the bar near the front door. Respecting his privacy, I walked to the other end and sat down. I ordered a drink and was intent on minding my own business. Reno was standing on a stool, trying to get the Oakland A's game on TV. It was being carried on a UHF station, and this was before cable. I could see he was struggling, so I said, "If you move those two wires from where it says 'VHF' to 'UHF' it might help."

Reno moved the wires, and suddenly a recognizable picture appeared. He looked at me and said, "How do you know so much about this?"

I said, "I've done some work for that station."

"What did you do?"

"I did the telecasts of the Warriors' games."

Reno studied me a little harder, and there was a sign of recognition.

"Wait a minute. You're Greenberg, right?"

As usual, I responded, "Close enough."

Reno climbed down from the stool and yelled to the other end of the bar, where DiMaggio was sitting.

"Hey Clipper! Ya know who this is?"

I was ready to bury my head at this point. DiMaggio got up, walked over and held out his hand.

"I'm Joe DiMaggio. It's nice to meet you."

Everything seemed turned around to me at that moment. The man with the most recognizable face in San Francisco was telling me his name. So it was that night in Norfolk when Mark Clark introduced himself. I told General Clark my name and said, "I'm a friend of Al Davis." I knew Davis admired Mark Clark the same way I admired MacArthur. Years earlier, when Clark had been president of the Citadel, Davis was an assistant football coach there. Clark's face lit up at the sound of Davis' name, and he immediately asked about the condition of Al's wife Carol, who'd been seriously ill and was recovering.

We talked for a while. Then he said, "You know, Al Davis coached for me at the Citadel. He kept bringing in these guys 7 feet 4 and 350 pounds. Finally I said to him,

'Al, we're just a small military school in South Carolina.' If he'd have stayed with me much longer we'd have been on probation for 20 years."

I smiled and said, "I guess there was one man who believed there's no substitute for victory."

The General looked at me and said, "That's MacArthur's line. I'm using it in my speech tonight."

I said, "I know. I've read your speech."

Mark Clark put his arm around my shoulder, leaned over and whispered, "Whaddaya think? Too much bullshit?"

I remember thinking at that moment, "I don't believe this is happening and who the hell can I ever tell this story to?"

Clark said, "You know, I don't usually do these things anymore, but Mrs. MacArthur called and asked me. When she asks you, you just can't say no to her."

It was fortunate General Clark didn't say no. He turned out to be an engaging speaker. He told of the days when he was a young boy in West Texas. Douglas MacArthur was a student then at the West Texas Military Academy. One night MacArthur came to the Clark home to call on Mark Clark's older sister. "He came to our door in his uniform," Clark said. "He was the handsomest man I'd ever seen."

Colonel Hammond introduced me to the rest of the party at his table. Among them was General LeGrande Diller. He had been one of the "Bataan Gang," the group of officers who served with MacArthur during the fall of the Philippines. He was among those who got out of Corregidor in the PT boats.

In the course of our conversation I discovered Diller had attended Syracuse University in the 1920s, proving that someone had actually gone there before I did. We talked about Vic Hanson and Roy Simmons, two great Syracuse athletes of that time. Diller had been MacArthur's public relations officer, which may have been an oxymoron.

History suggests he didn't do much to help the General's popularity. Still, he was loyal and downright defensive about his old boss. When one of the lesser speakers at the dinner made reference to General MacArthur's "escape" from Corregidor, Diller mumbled loudly enough for some of us to hear, "Escape! It was no damn escape. He was ordered out of there by the president."

The man who engineered the daring and successful run of the Japanese blockade was also at the dinner. John Bulkeley was a young Navy Lieutenant whose fleet of four PT boats enabled MacArthur and his party to reach Mindanao under cover of darkness. Given Bulkeley's precious cargo, it was one of the most important operations of World War II.

I was delighted to be sitting next to Bill Dunn, who had been a war correspondent with CBS. In those days you didn't have to say "CBS Radio" because radio was the only electronic journalism. Bill Dunn was a familiar name to me, as were many CBS correspondents of that era. People who listened to the war news each day knew what a powerful reporting lineup CBS had. Edward R. Murrow was the most famous, but there was Eric Severeid, Howard K. Smith, William L. Shirer, Charles Collingwood, Winston Burdette, Richard C. Hottelett and Robert Trout. Most of them covered the war in Europe. Among those who reported from the Pacific were Dunn and Webley Edwards of the old Hawaii Calls radio show.

Dunn was the pool correspondent assigned to MacArthur's party as they waded ashore at Leyte. You see him in the famous picture of that historic moment. He's the one without a hat. Earlier in the day I had seen Dunn and Sergeant Francisco Salveron posing for photographers. There's a huge mural of the landing party at Leyte on one of the walls of the MacArthur Memorial. The two of them were standing in front of where they were depicted in the mural.

Colonel Roger Egeberg had been with General MacArthur throughout much of the war as his physician. I recalled the pictures I'd seen of him. He was tall and seemed to tower over MacArthur. In January 1980 he was still tall and looked like he might have appeared in one of those "Man of Distinction" ads holding a highball in his hand. Egeberg feared for MacArthur's safety as the General walked the streets of Manila, unfazed by the prospect of Japanese sniper fire. Egeberg recalled, "The General told me, 'Doc, those are second-line troops the enemy has left behind here. They're more likely to hit you while they're aiming for me.'"

All evening I kept thinking, "These people must be wondering, 'What is this guy doing sitting at our table?'" I finally realized I was the one doing the wondering. I had no relationship to Douglas MacArthur. I had no relationship to the Army. The closest I'd come was the three hours I spent in an induction center in Buffalo in 1957 until a doctor decided I had a bad back and sent me home. I was embarrassed about it because people held going-away parties for me and had given me gifts. My mother was crying at the front door when I left to report. I was probably the only person who received a hero's welcome when I returned from the "front" in Buffalo.

The one thing my dinner companions knew about me that night in Norfolk was I cared enough about General MacArthur to be there. That was good enough for them.

Occasionally I think about the places I've been in my quest to get a feel for this man and what he meant. I think about the time in 1969 when I walked into the old Lennons Hotel in Brisbane in Queensland, Australia. It was there the General established his headquarters after leaving Melbourne. He and his family lived in the hotel, as well. I entered the hotel bar and ordered a drink. A group of men and women were sitting at a table near the bar and detected my American accent.

"You're a Yank, are you?" one of them said. When I confirmed this they invited me to join them. One of them asked me what I was doing in Brisbane.

When I told them I'd come to see the hotel where General MacArthur had his headquarters, one of them said, "Bloody good thing for us he was here, wouldn't ya say?" Before MacArthur arrived in 1942, the Australian high command seemed convinced the Japanese would invade their country. There was talk of a "Brisbane Line." The Aussies would concede everything north of the line from Brisbane to the west, and fight to the death to defend the southern half of the country. MacArthur had other ideas. He told them, "The fight for Australia will not take place in Australia. It will take place in New Guinea." He wasn't going to wait for the Japanese to come to him; he was going to them.

Lennons Hotel was no longer standing when I returned 15 years later. In its place was a large office building, but the General had not been neglected. I visited what is called "MacArthur's Quarters," a suite of rooms at the approximate spot where he had his headquarters. The Aussies hadn't forgotten the man who changed the course of the war for them so many years ago.

I suppose my school years might have gone much easier if I'd had as much interest in history then as I seem to have now. If my parents were alive today, they'd no longer have to ask, "Is sports the only interest you have?"

I think they began to suspect otherwise when I got married. By now, they'd know for sure. I make no pretense at being a historian. I'm a person who has an interest in a man and his place in history — the Philippines, Australia, Japan and South Korea. Few men have been as prominent and respected in the history of so many countries outside their own as Douglas MacArthur.

I didn't know much about Australia at first. I thought the Melbourne Cup was something Lord Melbourne wore when he played Aussie rules football.

11

CAPTAIN COOK MISSED SYDNEY HARBOUR

U ntil I was 34, I had never been anywhere that I had needed a passport. I applied for one years before but hadn't realized it was no longer a requirement for getting into Texas.

All my friends had been to exotic places such as Paris, Hong Kong or Chernobyl. It's not that I wasn't well-traveled. I'd been to Worcester, Massachusetts, and Lawrence, Kansas, and even Morgantown, West Virginia, but it was time to expand my horizons. Where could I go that no one I knew had visited?

It was 1969. Neil Armstrong had just been to the moon, so that was out. Somewhere in the back of my mind I recalled hearing about a place on the underside of the Earth, where people stood upside down and water went down the drain in a direction opposite the way it goes down here. This mystical place was called Australia. I was intrigued. It's not that I needed to prove to myself which direction water went down the drain, but . . . I guess you could say I just did not grasp the gravity of the situation.

In the late '60s I had been working with Bill King on Warriors broadcasts. Bill had a sailboat and used to talk about his plan to sail off someday to the South Seas. I had a brief experience with islands in 1965 when I broadcast baseball in Hawaii. While there, I used to hear these oddly riveting radio commercials for QANTAS, the Australian airline. The man who did them (Bill thought it was Martin Gable) had a voice deep and resonant.

Radio is a wonderful medium. It allows you to conjure up images that transport you anywhere. Listening to those commercials I could "see" the sprawling metropolis called Sydney and picture those "eight lanes of traffic pouring across the Harbour Bridge."

I still wanted to go. No one I knew had ever been. Most people I knew thought there was no such place. It must have been mythical, like the Kingdom Beneath the Sea. The consensus seemed to be: "You can't get there from here." The people at QANTAS in San Francisco felt differently.

Erika Dougherty, a ticket agent, said she was Danish, but she saw to it that I met my first Australian, himself a ticket agent. He was from Darwin. Deep intrigue was setting in.

The more I read about Australia, the more eager I was to make the trip. I'd always admired those who traveled to far-off places. I marveled at what Neil Armstrong had done in going to the moon. Australia was farther. Erika recommended I not fly all the way through.

The QANTAS flight from San Francisco made stops in Honolulu and Fiji before touching down in Sydney 18 hours later. Her suggestion made sense. I would spend a few days in Fiji. I'd read a little about this tropical paradise in a publication called *Pacific Islands Monthly*. Bill King subscribed to it. Over the years I'd learned a lot from Bill. Had it not been for him I never would have known how much I loathed the combination of peanut butter and onions.

QANTAS made all my arrangements. I'd be gone three and a half weeks, spending a few days in Hawaii on the way back. Now I was ready to see the world, or at least the part of it covered by water. I packed my golf clubs and my suitcase and took off on a Sunday night. I was prepared for a long flight, but when I landed in Fiji it was Tuesday morning. I had been warned that this would happen, but losing a whole day for the first time is not something you are ever really prepared for.

The international airport on Fiji is located in a town pronounced "Nan-dee" but spelled Nadi. After 13 hours and a lost day, they could call it anything they wanted. I was staying at the Fiji Mocambo Hotel, which was close to transportation. *Air* transportation. Something your ears never let you forget.

Fortunately, I was still young enough that all my nerves hadn't frayed yet. I was excited just to have my passport stamped. It didn't take long to realize Fiji was not a place to be without female companionship. As much as I loved my golf clubs, even my fertile imagination had limits. I slept late that first day — whatever day that was. Later I sat out by the pool and concluded that the guests were either honeymooners from New Zealand or airline pilots. Neither group seemed particularly interested in me.

I had my first meal of Australian beef and wine. This offered encouragement for the remaining two days.

I spent those two days at the Nadi Airport Golf Course. Its proximity to the airport made it difficult at times to separate fairways from the runways. I didn't see a lot of Fiji in the short time I was there. Most of what I saw was wherever my golf ball took me. But you're never far from the blue Pacific, and what I saw was beautiful. Next time, I vowed, I was not coming alone.

Kingsford-Smith Airport in Sydney was considerably different from Nadi. In Fiji, at least, I could understand the language. How was I supposed to know that "audimight" was a greeting? "Eggjelly," I didn't care. I was excited. I was in Australia. Down Under. And I wasn't upside down and in apparent danger of falling off the earth. I could see the danger lay elsewhere. I'd never been anywhere where people intentionally drove on the left, with the exception of a few times in college. As the cab made its way through early morning commute traffic, cars seemed to be coming at us from all directions. Just as I was convinced there was going to be a collision, other drivers seemed to turn away in a manner familiar only to New Yorkers. I arrived at the Wentworth Hotel in downtown Sydney and called the one contact I'd been given in Australia.

He was Tom Crow, the International Marketing Director for Precision Golf Forging, a golf club manufacturer. Later that day I went out to the factory and Tom showed me around. In his office, he introduced me to a friend who was being fitted for a new set of clubs. He was Kerry Packer, a media mogul whose family owned the half of Australia not already owned by the Murdochs. That night I had dinner with Tom and his wife Cally, and a long friendship had begun.

Tom was a former Australian Amateur Golf Champion and an Eisenhower Cup teammate of Bruce Crampton and Bruce Devlin. He took me to his club, Royal Sydney, and we played 18 holes. That was my first mistake in Australia. I should have caddied for him instead. Later on we sat in the clubhouse and ordered a drink. Upon hearing my voice, the waiter immediately knew to bring ice. Australians seemed to know a lot more about Americans than we did about them.

There was much to learn. I thought the Melbourne Cup was something Lord Melbourne wore when he played Aussie rules football. I found people like to think of our two countries as cousins, sharing common roots. The bond grew considerably closer during World War II, when England couldn't come to Australia's aid because Australia's best soldiers were fighting to save England. It was left to the Americans to step in and keep the Japanese from invading.

The first settlers sent over by England were convicts. This was the British way of keeping the jails from getting overcrowded. The First Fleet under Captain Arthur Phillip arrived in 1788. It's interesting to look back and see just how our two countries have developed over the years. Given the ever-increasing prison population in the United States, one could probably make the comparison this way: Australia is a nation settled by convicts who worked hard and raised families who became nice people. America is a nation settled by nice people who worked hard and raised families who became convicts.

After several days in Sydney I traveled up the east coast to the state of Queensland, the vacation capital of the country. I visited Brisbane and later spent time on the beautiful beaches of the Gold Coast at Surfer's Paradise. As I was nearing the end of my first visit to Australia it appeared the only crime this nation of convict heritage had committed was to steal my heart.

I returned to Sydney for a few last days with the Crows and their friends. When the time came to depart, Tom took me to the airport. As we shook hands, I said to him I'd be coming back next year.

On January 27, 1970, I decided to cross another large body of water. This one was called the Sea of Matrimony. I'd gone to Seattle a couple days ahead of a Warriors-Sonics game. My apprehension at popping the question had been eased to a considerable extent by Carla's proclamation three weeks earlier. While visiting me in San Francisco over New Year's she said, "I'm going to marry you." It was hard to respond to that, as I wasn't used to being addressed in that manner. I remember thinking, "You poor girl," something I'm sure she often thought after we were married. Buoyed with the confidence that comes with what appears to be a sure thing, I casually, but with a rapidly beating heart, asked her, "How would you like to go to Australia on your honeymoon?"

If I had known her as well then as I do now, I might have expected her to say, "I'd love to. I hope someone asks me." Instead, she responded in a style unique to the great romances of all-time: "Goddammit, don't say that unless you're serious." I insisted I was. She screamed. I took that as a "yes."

Four months later we headed for lands Down Under. While Australia was the centerpiece of our honeymoon, we also stopped in Fiji, New Caledonia and Tahiti. The year before I'd determined South Sea islands were no place to be without female companionship. Getting married may have been a drastic way to resolve that dilemma, but I was now 35, and I was ready.

I'd had a good time being single but I was tired of being thought of as a sex object. I was told getting married would take care of that. I was sorry it was Carla who told me. By the time our honeymoon officially ended (Carla still thinks it's going on) I was becoming more enchanted with the Southern Hemisphere. If someone asked me how I would describe myself, it would be as a dreamer or a hopeless romantic. I never wanted to go through life regretting things I hadn't tried, with the possible exception of vegetables. From our apartment in San Francisco I could watch ships heading out through the Golden Gate bound for the far-off Pacific. I said to Carla, "Someday we're going to be on one of those ships and just sail off."

By now I was reading everything I could about Australia. I was a quick study. I could name all six states. The more I read and thought about that part of the world, the more wanderlust was taking hold. In 1972 we decided to visit Asia and stop in Australia on the way back to feel out the job situation.

The only reason we could afford to make such a trip was that things were a lot less expensive then. We were gone more than six weeks and visited Japan, the Philippines, Hong Kong, Thailand, Penang, Singapore, Australia, New Zealand and American Samoa. We stayed in good hotels and didn't spend more than $25 a night. Remember, that was 27 years ago, when people could still afford tickets to professional sports events.

When our flight from Singapore touched down in Sydney I had a definite purpose. Tom Crow arranged for me to meet with Kerry Packer at his office at Channel 9. I was told that "colour television" was coming to Australia in a couple of years. If I was interested in finding work there it would be good to come out a year ahead of time when a lot of hiring would be done. I didn't need much more encouragement. Carla wasn't nearly as enthusiastic about the thought of moving halfway around the world, and probably thought it was just a stage I was going though.

Just for fun (mine, mostly) we did look at a couple of apartments. This might have discouraged a less stalwart person. We left Sydney and stopped to visit our friends, Maggie and Fred Szydlik in Wellington, New Zealand. Maggie and I had worked together at KNBR. She was originally from England. Fred was in the Navy when Maggie met him one St. Patrick's Day at Harrington's Bar in San Francisco. They were now making a life together Down Under. I wasn't the only dreamer. I was encouraged by what they'd done. But New Zealand was not Australia, a point New Zealanders take with pride.

We returned to San Francisco, and that fall I began my final season with the Warriors. Carla still wasn't keen on the idea of pulling up stakes. Reluctantly, she said she'd go along if I agreed to start a family — with her. A person can't really have wanderlust and want to sail off on a cruise ship. It had to be a freighter. This seemed like a far more romantic scenario, and considerably less expensive. We had to make our reservations well in advance.

We booked for mid-June 1973. Even an NBA season has to end sometime. In the fall of '72 I was deemed by the Australian authorities to be employable and applied for their Assisted Passage program. This meant they would pay your way over, but you had to agree to stay for two years. My plan was to approach it as if we were going for good. If you went with the idea of going for a specific length of time, you might never let yourself get involved in the life of the country. I wasn't sure what I was going to do when I got there, but life wasn't meant to be organized. I had no job when I came to San Francisco in 1964, and somehow I had managed.

We arranged our passage through the Knutsen Lines and would sail on June 13 on a freighter called the Gudrun Bakke. There was no turning back now. For the last two years, my friends had heard me talk about wanting to do this. It was time to do it or shut up. I hadn't made my living by shutting up. Besides, people were starting to give us going-away parties. When that happens you'd better be serious.

The ship's itinerary called for a 43-day voyage terminating in Fremantle, Australia. Other ports of call included Hong Kong, Manila, Penang, Port Klang (the port city for Kuala Lumpur, Singapore) and Darwin. It sounded so exotic, and we'd been to some of the places before, so we'd know our way around.

One of the things I liked best about the schedule was getting to see Western Australia. Fremantle was just a few miles south of Perth and was the major port on the west coast. Many U.S. Naval vessels were there during the Pacific war. Our plan was to spend a week in Perth and then take the train across the continent to Sydney, where we planned to settle. I was an inveterate train lover, and the thought of capping off our journey in this manner seemed perfect. I was counting the days until we left. Carla was counting the seconds. We each had our reasons.

When we became engaged I told my bride-to-be, "The only thing I can promise you is that it will never be dull." I don't think she expected me to go this far to prove it. Carla was a good sport. She still is, but drew the line at thoughts of retiring to Singapore. "Get Dorothy Lamour to go with you this time," she told me. I gave up hope.

Eventually June 13 arrived. I expected thousands at the pier in San Francisco to make sure we didn't change our minds. Instead we had a small bon voyage party in our cabin with friends Shirle and Ed Schaffnit, Pat Kidd, David Bush and Carla's uncle Sol Silverman. Freighters were limited to 12 passengers and had eight cabins — four singles and four doubles. When you're thrown together for that length of time, it's a good idea to have a compatible group. Carla and I decided to give ourselves the ultimate compatibility test and share the same cabin. Such tests worked before we were married. Why not now?

The ship was still taking on cargo, and we had some time before our 6 p.m. departure. We began meeting the other passengers. There was a couple from Washington, D.C., three people from the Monterey area, a lady from Toronto, a man from San Leandro (just south of Oakland), a young girl from Switzerland, and a couple from Australia. The ship's officers were from Norway, and the crew was Chinese. Despite containers on board, there was plenty of deck space. There was a small pool, a combination game room and library and a dining room. We would eat with the captain and chief engineer.

Captain Leervik was my kind of guy. I knew he wouldn't get lost on the way to Australia. One look at him told me he crossed the Equator every day when he bent down to tie his shoes. We got underway a little later than scheduled, something you get used to on freighters. We passed under the Golden Gate Bridge, and everyone was on deck to mark the occasion. We were outbound, but I couldn't help wondering if the bridge people made you pay a toll when you came into the city.

Finally we sat down to dinner. The passengers gave toasts to a successful journey while taking stock of one another. One of our shipmates, the 20-year-old girl from Switzerland, seemed to be taking stock of the crew. We didn't see a lot of her in the next few weeks. I don't recall what was served for dinner that first night, but if the next two months were any indication, it was pork. It didn't matter how they disguised it, or what they told me, it was always pork, or as our Chinese steward put it, "pawk."

In time it became a standing joke. "What are we having for dinner tonight, Stephen?" He'd reply. "We having veal."

Somehow, I knew it was *pawk*.

Our first port would be Hong Kong, and we were scheduled to be at sea for 16 days en route. You'd know everything you wanted to know about each other by then. Warren and Ruth Hunsburger were an interesting couple. He was a professor of Asian Economics at American University in Washington, D.C. He was taking a six-month sabbatical and was going to teach in Rangoon, Burma, as it was known then. Ruth told us when she was a young woman during World War II, she worked in the War Department. One of her assignments involved her in the planning for Operation Torch, the invasion of North Africa.

Warren was a young naval officer at the time, and she couldn't even tell him what she was doing. Their daughter is Ellen Hume, a writer with the *Los Angeles Times*. The Hunsburgers would be leaving the ship in Hong Kong and heading on to Burma from there. Ron and Vera Young were the Australians. They were from Gaynda, a small town in Queensland. There's a good chance they knew everybody there. I remember talking with Ron one day. He asked me why I thought America seemed so much more advanced than other countries.

It really wasn't something I'd thought about much because when you live here you tend to take a lot of things for granted. The only explanation I could offer was we had so many people here, compared to his country, where they only had 17 million. Ron countered by saying, "On that basis China should be more advanced than all of us." I don't think he bought my further theory that it had something to do with the water.

One of most intriguing passengers was the gentleman from San Leandro. He appeared to be in his 60s and was traveling alone. I wasn't sure why he was making the trip, but then Carla was probably wondering the same thing about herself. His name was Jay, and he liked to drink. Perhaps that explained why he was on board. He had plenty of time to do it. I liked him, and I think he needed someone to make him feel important. I spent a fair amount of time with him, although I didn't always understand everything he was saying.

As we were heading due west toward Hong Kong, the sun came up each morning over the stern of the ship. You can imagine our surprise one morning upon awakening to discover the sun rising in the west. There it was, coming up over the bow. I wondered if Captain Leervik had been sharing a pop or two the night before with my friend Jay. I began to suspect there was something different when I woke up. When you travel on a freighter you become acutely aware of the sound made by the engine. There wasn't any that morning.

During the night the engine was shut down for repair work, and the Gudrun Bakke was adrift. We were somewhere west of Hawaii and south of Midway Island. When the engine work was completed we would make two less knots, and it would add two more days to our first landfall at Hong Kong. That meant a total of 18 days from the time we left San Francisco. I don't know if anyone ever checked the ship's log when the Pilgrims landed, but I suspect the Mayflower made better time.

Fortunately I'd brought plenty of reading material and had my short-wave radio. Carla was a whiz at Scrabble and found a couple of the ladies to join her. About two weeks into our odyssey I marked my 38th birthday. The cook was kind enough to make a cake. It had candles and frosting. I was reluctant to cut into it for fear it was pork. Carla and I brought some California wine on board with us. At dinner that night we also ordered some Australian wine. I poured some from each bottle into a glass in a ceremonial toast to the marriage of our American background with our new life in Australia.

The ship, which seemed so large when we boarded, was getting a little smaller each day. I was almost ready to climb to the crow's nest and see if I could spot land. The words, "Are we there yet?" were never far from my lips. Each day the purser would update the map showing the progress of the freighter. Inch by inch, we were getting there.

The other signs of progress were the frequent advisories to change our watches each time we entered a new time zone. Crossing the International Date Line, we turned them ahead a full 24 hours. Still, it didn't seem to bring Hong Kong any closer. At long last, on the night of July 3, 1973 we sighted the outlying islands and eventually made our way into Hong Kong Harbour. Captain Leervik was no Captain Bligh, but I was beginning to understand how Fletcher Christian and the boys felt when they jumped ship in Tahiti.

We hit the streets running, or more likely wobbling. After 18 days at sea I wouldn't have wanted anyone to ask me to walk a straight line. Carla and I had been to Hong Kong before and knew our way around the main districts. The Gudrun Bakke was supposed to be in port three days, during which time work on the engine, which began at sea, was to be completed. Guess again.

Generally speaking, there isn't anything you can't find in Hong Kong — with one exception, the part needed to complete work on the engine. Plan B was to contact Singapore and have it flown in. It was Plan C that was ultimately adopted. This one called for having the part flown in from Norway, where the ship was built. After day three we were told to check each day upon leaving the dockyard to see if the good old Gudrun would be sailing that evening.

Our three-day stay stretched all the way to nine before we sailed. I loved it. It was one of the few times in my life when it didn't matter when I got to where I was going. We had a place to sleep and we still got three meals a day on board. Carla and I couldn't imagine being in this exciting city and running back to the ship just to have lunch and dinner. Some people did.

The joys of Hong Kong are the sights, sounds and smells. Some of them. One of the most memorable moments occurred as we wandered through the Monko district of Kowloon. There was an old man sitting in a stall so narrow it might have easily been bypassed. With great concentration and precision, he was hand painting mahjong tiles. You didn't have to walk very far in the former British Crown Colony without hearing the familiar clicking of mahjong tiles. It was usually coming from behind a drawn curtain. The huge shopping terminals were clean, modern and a shopper's paradise, but this was the real thing.

The repair work was finally completed, and we were told, the morning of our ninth day in port, the ship would be sailing for Manila that evening. I made sure I had one last dinner in Hong Kong to avoid being welcomed back with another serving of pork. Our friends the Hunsburgers had disembarked and were working their way across the continent to Rangoon. Now there were ten of us.

We hadn't seen much of our fellow passengers while in port except for breakfast, the only meal we ate on board. I took the opportunity to take on provisions of my own, laying in a supply of Cadbury's various candy bars. This was my hedge against monotonous dinners. There's nothing quite like breaking up a chocolate bar into small pieces and mixing them into a bowl of rice. This is a particularly tasty meal, and when taken in with the use of chopsticks makes one feel authentic. The most fun of all was when other passengers asked what I was eating. The explanation tended to make them wonder if the captain had the legal right to declare a passenger insane. It did, however, gain me new respect with the kitchen staff, who knew I'd found an alternative to "pawk."

We reached the capital of the Philippines in a few days, and our stay was only a day and a half. It was too short for me and too long for Carla, for whom the sight of armed soldiers on street corners was unnerving. The Islands were under martial law, and I tried to explain that unlike our previous visit there, it was now the good guys who had the guns. I was left with the impression she wasn't buying it.

We made a brief stop at Butterworth, a small town in Malaysia.

We took the ferry across to Penang and paid our sentimental visit to the Eastern and Oriental Hotel, better known as the E&O. In hotel terms it was one of the grand old ladies of the Pacific Rim. The Peninsula in Hong Kong, the Oriental in Bangkok, The Manila Hotel, The Grand Pacific in Suva, Fiji, and Raffles in Singapore all fit that description. One of our favorite pastimes visiting other countries was to see the great hotels. We couldn't always afford to stay there, but we could always get a good meal. The E&O had been the scene of one of our dinners the year before.

Down the Straits of Malacca we sailed on to Port Klang. This serves as the jumping off point for Kuala Lumpur, or KL, as it's widely known. The pilot boat pulled alongside, and the pilot climbed aboard to guide the Gudrun Bakke safely into port. Each pilot is a local man who has knowledge of that particular harbour. I was standing on the bridge with Captain Leervik while the pilot was directing the operation. In close proximity to us was another freighter making a wide turn. Its captain or pilot didn't appear overly concerned that it seemed about to hit us. Neither was our pilot. The same, however, could not be said for Captain Leervik. Generally speaking, one doesn't retain the rank of ship's captain by allowing his vessel to be rammed by another ship. The good captain was unloading a few choice expressions in his best Norwegian, for which there was no need of translation. Somehow the other ship managed to avoid hitting us, but it was close enough that on fourth down you'd have gone for it. The near-miss provided me with a clue as to how Port Klang got its name. The port itself was about 20 miles from KL, which is the capital of Malaysia. We would be there four days. Each day Carla and I boarded a bus and made the trip into town. We were sitting in the lobby of the Hilton reading the newspaper and spotted a small item in the *International Herald-Tribune*: DON TO SPEAK

"Professor Warren Hunsburger of American University in Washington, D.C. will speak tonight at the United States Information Service office at 8."

We decided to surprise him and take in the lecture. We explained to the person at the door the reason for our visit, and he arranged for us to remain in the studio where the lecture was being recorded. Afterward, while Professor Hunsburger was standing around with some local students answering questions, we stood at the back of the group. Finally I spoke and asked something like how he would compare sailing on the Gudrun Bakke to ships operated by the U.S. Navy. He quickly zeroed in on these two touristy-looking Americans and couldn't believe it was us.

That evened things up because we couldn't believe we'd be in Kuala Lumpur on the same day. Warren still had a couple more weeks before he was due in Rangoon. He called Ruth at their hotel, and we sat and talked until just before the last bus left for the trip back to Port Klang. Once again we said goodbye to the Hunsburgers. Port Klang quickly gave way to Singapore, which remains my favorite city in Asia. We came alongside at Keppel Harbour. Freighters don't usually dock at glamorous terminals. In fact, there's nothing glamorous about freighter travel at all, which, for many, is one of its attractions. The romance one associates with cruise ships is not the romance one associates with freighters. Freighter romance is watching cargo nets swinging onto the deck and unloading its goods. It's the sight of huge container cranes. It's dry docks and painters. It's climbing off your ship and walking across the deck of an adjacent vessel in order to climb down the other side to reach the dock. It's recognizing another line's ship you saw two stops ago outside Kuala Lumpur. I won't get involved describing cruise ship romance. Danielle Steel does it better.

Thanks to Tom Crow we had a contact. His name was John Kirkham, Precision Golf Forging's representative in Singapore. We met for lunch at the rooftop restaurant of the Hilton Hotel on Orchard Road. It was the first time I'd been to a place where they served Rijshttaphel. It was also one of the last. It seemed the main reason to order it was to watch the parade of young ladies who serve it. It's made up of several different Indonesian dishes carried in by a line of women each a little taller than the one in front. I was happy to watch them serving but most likely settled for a cheeseburger. We spent three days in Singapore and, as we did the year before, made sure we got to the famous outdoor food stalls. By day these were parking lots, but at night they sprung to life with all sorts of little stands selling wonderful food.

Compared to our meals on the freighter, skewered beef or chicken with a teriyaki or peanut sauce was a four-star entree. Unfortunately, in today's more antiseptic world the outdoor food stalls are no longer legal. Because Singapore is also a shopper's paradise, comparisons with Hong Kong are inevitable. You can find anything you want in both places; the difference is Singapore has greenery. There are actually parks and trees. It's a livable city.

Many Americans think Singapore is a repressive society. I suppose compared to America, most societies are. Somehow it never bothered me to be in a place that enforces laws against littering and graffiti. I never found it difficult to put something in a trash can, especially when they're readily available. Nor does it bother me to be in a country that deals harshly with selling drugs. I understand that living in the United States is different. You can't enforce such laws here because someone will sue for infringing on their constitutional right to litter. Heck, marking up walls is your God-given right of self-expression as outlined in the First Amendment.

Americans love to tell other countries how to live. Singapore has high employment, a low crime rate, good health and prosperity, and it hasn't gone to war with anyone. What do these people know about running a country?

In the five weeks since we'd left San Francisco, personalities had taken hold among our fellow passengers. Our friend Jay had established by this time that an unemptied bottle was a crime against nature. I enjoyed his company. He was a nice man. He was quiet, and he never bothered anybody. It didn't matter to me if I couldn't understand much of what he was saying. Hell, if understanding what people were saying was that important, I wouldn't have had a career.

When we were in port, Carla and I usually went off on our own. Having been to many of these cities before, we had some favorite spots we wanted to revisit. We may have compared notes with others while on board, but otherwise we minded our own business. The fact that our friend Jay didn't return to the Gudrun Bakke for two nights while in Singapore didn't really bother us. Our feeling was he's a big boy, it's his vacation, let him have a good time.

Such a philosophy must have been foreign to a couple of the ladies on the freighter. They were indignant about his failure to return and were sure he must be lying dead in an alley somewhere in Singapore. The two of us did not set out specifically to find him, but find him we did. As we walked into Raffles Hotel, there he was. He was sitting by himself at a table in the bar having a drink. He was wearing a coat and tie and a big smile. Though we suspected all along he'd be fine, we were relieved to see him. He knew what time the ship was sailing and was prepared to be on board at the proper time.

When we told him of the ladies' "concern" for his whereabouts, we had no trouble understanding his response. "They've got too much time on their hands," he said. For Jay the reason for not returning each night was simple. If he was going to tie one on, he'd find himself a hotel room instead of going all the way back to the ship. Made sense to me.

We got underway and headed for Darwin, our first stop in Australia. Our five days at sea took us through the Java Sea as we passed such exotic-sounding places as Bali, Lombok, Sumbawa and Sumba. I couldn't believe we were doing this. Here we were in some far-off corner of the world sailing by places I'd only heard of in old war movies. I was loving every minute of it because I knew this was probably the only time I'd be doing something this crazy. Although we'd only been married three years I suspected I'd pushed Carla to the limit on this one. In future years we made many more trips to distant places, but we always had round-trip tickets.

Carla took great comfort in that.

When we reached Darwin we accomplished something most Australians hadn't. On the other hand, Australians have been to Yosemite and Mount Rushmore, which is more than I can say. Darwin is the capital of what is known as The Northern Territory. Australia has six states and two territories. The other is The Australian Capital Territory, where Canberra is located. It's like the District of Columbia. It was drawn up to appease the states of New South Wales and Victoria, both of which wanted to include the nation's capital. The Northern Territory is large. When you're in Darwin, the nearest "major" city is Alice Springs, 930 miles south.

It didn't take us long to realize Darwin is in the tropics. It's about 12 degrees south of the Equator and about 110 degrees north of zero Fahrenheit. Our ship would be in port for four days, which was three days, twenty-three hours and 45 minutes longer than it would take to see the city.

We decided to see if we could do something more extensive, and stopped at a local travel office. No sooner had we walked in than a man working there said to me, "You look familiar." In and around Darwin there are Aboriginals, Australians, Chinese, New Zealanders, Timorese, Greeks, Italians and water buffalo, none of whom resemble me or Carl Eilenberg, my double from Syracuse. The man continued, "You were in the QANTAS office in San Francisco. I used to work with Erika Dougherty."

It all came back to me, and with wisdom far beyond my years I replied: "I remember now. You're the guy from Darwin." Sometimes it's amazing how I can put two and two together. If nothing else, I'd be able to confirm to Erika there really was a Darwin.

We booked an excursion into the bush country outside of town. It was the most fortunate decision we made in our whole Australian experience. Ten people crowded into the van for our late afternoon excursion. Among them was the couple who would become our guardian angels throughout our time down under.

When we reached our destination, several miles outside of Darwin, we partook in a ritual commonly practiced in warmer climates. We sprayed ourselves with mosquito repellent. Right there on the can it said, "Use for mosquitoes." It worked. They loved it.

Our small group was joined by some water buffalo, who seemed to wonder what kind of people would come all the way out here just to sit around and have a drink. Apparently they decided they could do better elsewhere and moved on. We introduced ourselves, and, right there in Crocodile Dundee territory, the social hour began. Among the people we met was a couple from the Sydney suburb of Killara, Judy and Julian Lee. I think they were the only Australians in the group. We told them of our plans to locate in Sydney, and they made the mistake of saying, "You must ring us when you arrive." Never say that to the Greenwalds. We have long memories.

We spent the bulk of the evening visiting with the Lees. When our little safari into the wilds was over, we returned to Darwin and brought them aboard to see the Gudrun Bakke. Julian Lee was a physician and regularly attended medical conferences in the United States. Judy had been a student at the University of Kansas and spent a fair amount of time in Washington, D.C. Most likely, they knew more about my country than I did. On the other hand, Carla and I knew the best fish and chips shop in Gosford, on the Hawksbury River north of Sydney.

Call it a draw. We wrote down the Lee's phone number and promised to call. It was a promise we fully intended to keep. Our long voyage was nearing its end. We set sail for Fremantle, which we would reach in another four days. It would be exactly 60 days from the time we left San Francisco, or 17 days longer than scheduled. I learned a lot in those two months.

1. Don't take a freighter if you're in a hurry

2. Don't take a freighter unless you can get along with other people. It's a long trip and a small dining room.

3. Learn Norwegian. You'll understand swear words in a whole new language.

4. Don't judge the captain by his looks. A fat captain knows the best restaurants in every port.

5. Don't panic if a fellow passenger disappears for a couple days while in port. He's probably having a better time than you are.

6. Don't take a freighter unless you love "pawk."

When we reached Fremantle we bid farewells to all our shipmates, with one exception. We said hello to the young girl from Switzerland. It was one of the few times we'd seen her since we left San Francisco. While we didn't really get to know her, we felt confident the crew had. I'm sure her book will be a lot more interesting than mine.

We stayed in Fremantle only long enough to arrange transportation to Perth, a few miles north along the Swan River. This beautiful city is the capital of Western Australia, a state about the size of the western one-third of the United States. At the time of our visit there were roughly a million people in all of Western Australia, about three quarters of whom lived in Perth. It was easy to see why. On the other hand, if you don't care for beautiful beaches, a healthy climate, friendly people, good restaurants, a picturesque river and an unhurried lifestyle, you might not like it.

We spent a week in this paradise near the Indian Ocean regaining our land legs. We still had a whole continent to cross to reach Sydney and would do so by train. We planned the routing of this journey so we could end up on the west coast. This enabled us to book reservations on the famed Indian-Pacific, the train named because it spanned those two great oceans.

Our stay in Perth was made even more hospitable by another of Tom Crow's contacts. Bruce McEwen was Precision Golf Forging's representative in that part of the country. The bulk of the terrain of Western Australia suggests the sand wedge was the company's best-selling club. Bruce drove us all around the city and surrounding area. He probably saw places he rarely got to, just as I do when people come to San Francisco. We had dinner with Bruce and his wife, and it was a nice feeling to be welcomed in a city so far from home. Later, friends in Sydney told us if they were to live anywhere else in Australia it would be Perth. The Indian-Pacific departed on schedule at 9:30 in the evening. It takes almost three full days to cover the 2,461 miles, roughly the same as crossing the United States. It didn't take long to determine there was a lively group on board. We entered the bar car to the sound of piano music and singing. Australians refer to their country as Oz, and while much of it looks like Kansas, even without Toto we knew we weren't on the Gudrun Bakke anymore.

The train quickly became a rolling pub, and although the train hadn't left until the middle of the evening, it seemed as if many of our fellow passengers had been in the bar car since the middle of the afternoon. Unlike the freighter, there were far more than 12 passengers on board. In fact, as the train made its way across the country it seemed there were more people inside than outside. In 1973 there were some 16 million people in Australia, none of whom were visible as we looked out our window.

The train itself was modern and clean, and we had a comfortable bedroom, complete with our own shower. There was a fully equipped dining car, and we could actually order off a menu. "Pawk" was no longer the specialty of the house. We slept most of the first 408 miles, awakening the next morning at 6:15 in the Western Australian town of Kalgoorlie. There was a 45-minute stopover, which allowed about one minute to visit with each of the folks who lived there. The place reminded me of an old western ghost town, although, in fairness, at 6:15 in the morning a lot of places look that way. In the 1890s, Kalgoorlie was a big gold mining center where many made their fortunes. Now, it seemed, the only fortune to be made was by the people running the local pub.

You wouldn't be too far off base to suggest that beer was one of the country's greatest natural resources. It may not come out of the ground, but a lot of it ends up there after filtering through the human system. Australians also make excellent wines, and they've made strong inroads in the U.S.

Upon leaving Kalgoorlie we began to see what the Aborigines must have seen 40 million years earlier. Don't hold me to that figure, it might have been 39 million. Your actual mileage may vary. There wasn't a whole lot to see for the next 38 hours. If there's one place you won't find an Outback Steakhouse, it's in the outback. For a sizable segment of it you won't even find a tree. That's why it's known as the Nullabor Plain. Without a tree to be found, it's easy to understand how the track on which the Indian-Pacific rode was dead straight for 300 miles.

Some may have found this part of the trip boring, but I thought it was phenomenal. So much of the folklore of Australia derives from the nothingness of the plains and the deserts — what the Aborigines refer to as The Back of Beyond or The Never Never. I was awed by this, but also knew if I looked away for a minute or two I wasn't going to miss anything. In fact, there were little outposts alongside the tracks, a few shacks here and there that housed track maintenance workers and their families. It's a lonely existence, and supplies were dropped off by train. Communication with more inhabited areas was by radio.

We traveled through such remote places as Narthea, Loongana, Mungala, Malbooma, Wirraminna and Bookaloo before reaching the more populous Port Augusta. By now we had turned our watches ahead an hour and a half. Before reaching Sydney in another 946 miles, we would add yet another half-hour to our clocks. It was only a short hop to Port Pirie, where the Indian-Pacific stopped for an hour and 15 minutes.

It was lunchtime, and we decided to hit one of the local eateries, not far from the train. Generally speaking, it's not a good idea to let the train get out of your sight. Most likely I had fish and chips. That, and meat pie, would become two of my basic food groups for the next year and a half.

We departed Port Pirie and sped through Ucolta, Paratoo, Yunta, Cutana, Mingary and Thackaringa before pulling into the mining town of Broken Hill. This was the ultimate company town. Everyone there worked for Broken Hill Propriety Limited. The ore deposits mined there are some of the richest in the world. We had some time to walk around and, like many Australians, stopped in at one of the RSLs, or Returned Servicemen's League Clubs. These are social clubs where one of the attractions is the poker machines, or slot machines as we call them. It soon became obvious that those who got rich got there before we did.

It was another 700 miles to Sydney. If we had wanted to go directly from San Francisco, we could have flown in 18 hours. Our trip, counting stopovers, would take 70 days. Had we flown, this chapter of this book would be a hell of a lot shorter. In the remaining 27 hours aboard the train we caught glimpses of Matahana, Euabalong West (we must have bypassed Euabalong East), Condobolin, Yarrabandi, Gamboola, Wallerawang and Katoomba. We passed through the Blue Mountains and saw scenery more familiar to Americans. We worked our way down through Valley Heights and Penrith and into the greater Sydney area. Only Parramatta and Strathfield remained before we finally pulled into Central Station. One journey had come to an end. Another was about to begin.

If timing is everything, mine couldn't have been worse. Since we'd made our decision to move, almost a year earlier, things in Australia had changed. The 1972 election brought the Labour Party into office for the first time in 25 years. The new Prime Minister was Gough Whitlam, whose campaign heralded the idea it was time to stop selling out Australia to the Americans and the British. It was an appealing concept, and had I been a native I might have bought it. There seemed to be the feeling the country needed a new spirit, one that sprung from Australian know-how and not something imported. That I had been deemed employable, and that under the previous administration my passage would be paid for, no longer seemed to matter. In fact, it became a liability. Not only was the Whitlam government encouraging the idea jobs should not go to outsiders, it was setting up the machinery to monitor hirings.

Despite my background in sports broadcasting, I hadn't gone down under to work on the air. I knew from the outset a foreign accent made such work unlikely. Besides, I knew little about their most popular sports. There were three kinds of rugby.

1. Rugby Union, which looked like a giant centipede trying to swim upstream.

2. Rugby League, which had among its positions one who was called the hooker. I deemed this worthy of further investigation.

3. Australian Rules Football, which is best understood by riding the New York subway at 5 o'clock.

There was also cricket. I reached a much too hasty decision about that sport. I deemed it one in which the contest seemed to go on forever, a feeling I retained until I began broadcasting baseball. Long before setting out on this odyssey, I'd discussed an idea with Ken Flower at NFL Films in New York. I knew Ken when he'd worked in San Francisco and, by reputation, as an outstanding basketball player at USC in the '50s. There were about 20,000 Americans living in Sydney at the time I decided to go. The plan was to fly in film of an NFL Game of the Week. I would find a suitable place to show it and charge admission. With that many Americans to draw from, there had to be enough to cover expenses and make a few dollars as well. It was clean. It was simple. It didn't work

About the time I was getting ready to put my plan into operation, I began to experience what for many Australians was a way of life. It was called labor chaos. In later years I would find it had spread to America, especially if one followed baseball and basketball. For me, in Sydney, it began with the air-traffic controllers. No international flights could land there during this dispute and had to be diverted elsewhere. It didn't take a genius to figure out that if I couldn't produce the films I had no product. I was going to have to find something else. I never did.

Carla and I found an apartment in an area called Darling Point. Our place had a wonderful view of Rushcutter's Bay, one of the many that branch off the harbour. There is no more beautiful setting in the world for a city than this one. The difference between Sydney and San Francisco is that in the former the city surrounds the water, while in the latter the water surrounds the city. The many bays and inlets branching off the harbour allow far more people to live close to the water and enjoy the gorgeous views. I've been fortunate to have seen many seaports, and to have lived in San Francisco. Over the years our travels have taken us to such places as Rio de Janiero, Hong Kong, Stockholm, Singapore, Cape Town, Vancouver and Copenhagen. All are spectacular, but none beats Sydney. Many in the world will discover this for themselves during the Olympic Games in 2000.

Before we set out on our adventure, the people we knew best in Australia were Tom Crow, his wife Cally, their children Jamie (now Jay) and Annabelle. Jamie was about 6 and already playing rugby on Saturdays. Annabelle was younger and the kind of little girl you looked at and said, "She's going to be a beauty when she gets older." We were right. Cally was a talented woman with a marvelous flair for decorating. The Crows had introduced us to several of their friends. The people we'd met on our previous visits were extremely cordial and remained so after we moved

To that group we now added the Lees. They invited us to their home. Sydney has a wonderful public transportation system, and being without a car we learned to make good use of it. Before long we were on a first-name basis with the regulars on the 369 bus and the train that took us across the Harbour Bridge to Killara.

The Lees lived in what was known as the northern suburbs — as distinguished from the eastern, western or southern suburbs. The northeastern suburbs were the United States. Julian and Judy had four children ranging in age from 11 to 3. Jonathan was the 3-year-old, and, based on similar interests, he and I became immediate friends. Debbie was 7 and learning quickly. One day she said to her parents, "I know what you're doing when you go in your room and close the door."

Being polite, but not necessarily wanting an answer, they asked, "What's that?"
Debbie responded, "You're eating chocolates."
Perhaps this was another lesson in the way life would be different in Australia.
Bruce and Mindy were 10 and 11 and had more than enough intelligence t share with kids who'd been shortchanged.
Despite what seemed like her attempts to downplay it, Judy Lee was a intelligent woman. It didn't take long to figure that out. Her knowledge of th

could not remain hidden behind the image of the harried housewife. Carla and I marveled at how she appeared to be going in 10 directions at once while producing a table and meal worthy of Martha Stewart. She seemed to get an adrenaline rush at times and spoke so quickly we didn't always understand what she was saying. Not that there's anything wrong with that. I made a living the same way. Judy has been a docent at Sydney University, and she and Julian are avid tennis players.

Julian was a pulmonary specialist with varied outside interests. We shared a mutual love of jazz, and he had more than a working knowledge of sports in the U.S. Although Carla and I had been many places, Julian and Judy had gone places we'd never heard of. The good doctor was a wine lover and belonged to an international food and wine organization. On Sunday afternoons he and I often drank wine and discussed books and authors. He knew more about all of those things than I, but at least I'd heard of F. Scott Fitzgerald. I'd seen him in the movie, "Going My Way," with Bing Crosby. I'm not as stupid as I look.

Julian was a kind and generous man, and if I needed anything I knew I only had to ask. We'd have never survived in Australia without the Lees. Over the years we've spent many wonderful times with them, both in Australia and the U.S.

My attempts to find work were not meeting with success. Efforts to break into the broadcasting field in any area (production, writing, etc.) were running into dead ends. I'd met many people, all of whom were pleasant and sympathetic but most of whom were unable to help. I was further frustrated by the continuing strikes. Every day, it seemed, some other union was walking out. These things weren't supposed to happen under a Labour government. I had the feeling I was the only one in the country who wanted to work. Despite all this, I was not having second thoughts. An adventure is defined as a dangerous undertaking or an exciting experience. Our move was taking on elements of both. Being in Sydney was still exciting. Trying to live without making any money could be dangerous. To make matters worse, the U.S. had devalued the dollar twice during the early '70s.

When I first traveled to that country in 1969, I received $1.33 for a U.S. dollar. By 1973 I was getting something like 67 cents. General Custer had better timing. We convinced ourselves to think only in terms of how much things cost in Australian currency. It sounded better that way. Food was not expensive, and our ‌nt was reasonable for such a desirable section of Sydney. We were almost ‌barrassed to answer when people asked where we lived. Residing in Darling ‌ was not going to convince anyone that you really needed a job. At times we felt wealthy just looking at the view from our apartment. We looked right down onto Rushcutter's Bay, the home of the Cruising Yacht Club of Australia. It's the starting point for the annual Sydney-to-Hobart, Tasmania, yacht race. We could see cruise ships, naval ships, freighters, vessels of all kinds as they made their way down the main channel of the world's most spectacular waterway.

Captain Cook would have loved our view. It's too bad he never got to see it. When the famed British sailor reached Australia in 1770, he dropped anchor at a place just down the coast. He named it Botany Bay for his botanist, Sir Joseph Banks. Before returning to England to report this would make a wonderful settlement, Cook continued his exploration. He sailed his ship, the Endeavour, up the east coast. It may have been foggy that day, or perhaps no one was paying attention, but somehow the Captain passed right by the entrance to a magnificent harbor. It was later discovered by the Greenwalds and, before that, Captain Arthur Phillip of the First Fleet, in 1788. On Cook's recommendation, Phillip landed his fleet of 11 ships at Botany Bay. It didn't take him long to conclude Cook must have been taking rum for breakfast. It might make a good place to dump convicts but you couldn't possibly live there. Nothing seemed to grow, and there was no drinking water. So Captain Phillip and his ships moved on, wondering perhaps if those natives in Hawaii who had Captain Cook for dinner might not have done England a good deed.

A few miles up the coast Phillip spotted what appeared to be a channel running, inland from the sea. In everyday language, he made a left turn and brought his ships into an area that would later become the heart of Sydney. Captain Arthur Phillip of the British Royal Navy stepped ashore and, cognizant of the historical aspects of the moment, uttered the words every Australian child would later learn by heart: "How the bloody hell did Cook miss this?" It was something like that.

Carla turned out to be more employable than I. With her background as a medical secretary, she found a job in an ophthalmologist's office. She worked four hours a day, or roughly equivalent to many others in the country, counting smoke breaks, tea breaks, coffee breaks and walking off the job for any other reason. I kept house. I'm not sure what that meant, but I was always there for her when she got home from the office. Although I wasn't working, I was beginning to adapt to other aspects of Australian life. I was spending time at the TAB. This was the Totalizator Agency Board, or off-track betting shop.

We knew some people who owned horses and invited us to the races. Horse racing in Australia transcends sport in a way that religion transcends a belief in the tooth fairy. There were four race tracks in Sydney alone, and that didn't count harness tracks. You could make a bet for as little as 25 cents at the TAB or 50 cents at the track. Bookmaking was legal at the track, and you could shop around for the best odds from the various bookies, who were lined up along a rail. You could walk into the track for nothing and, most likely, leave with the same thing. The big racing days seemed to be Wednesdays and Saturdays. I used to go the TAB, place my 25-cent bets, and come home and listen to the races. It was a full day's entertainment, and I never won or lost too much, especially the former. Carla was pleased I'd found something to occupy my time but probably wished it paid a little better.

By January 1974 Carla was pregnant. Apparently not all my time was spent at the TAB. We were thrilled, scared, and all the things couples experience at a time like that. One of us had occasional bouts of morning sickness, but I didn't let that slow me down. Carla continued to work, and I continued to be unemployed.

My letters to friends in the U.S. were beginning to take on a more bitter tone. The labour strife was especially galling to me. The transport workers walked out over the issue of paper towels vs. cloth towels in the employees' washroom. It was enough to make me want to wash my hands of the whole idea of living there.

Without public transportation, we were pretty well confined. It wasn't so bad that one union went out, it was all the others that struck in sympathy. Indeed, things were different in Australia. I had to keep reminding myself I hadn't moved down there because I wanted things to be the same. Somehow, though, this wasn't exactly what I'd had in mind. We had strikes in America, of course, but they usually occurred after negotiations broke down. In Australia, they struck first, then negotiated.

The Aussies were great at rolling with the punches. They were doing a much better job of taking things in stride than I was. Of course walking off the job was something they grew up with. It wasn't for them to adjust to me; it had to be the other way around. I was beginning to doubt I'd be able to do it.

Tom Crow announced to me one day that he and his family were moving to San Diego. He was going to start a golf club company. I wasn't in a position to lose many friends at this point, but knew I couldn't talk him out of it. It did make me wonder if a guy like Tom, well known and working, was moving to the United States, what was I doing in Australia? I was concerned for Tom and his family. It seemed to me there were enough golf club companies in America already without adding one, especially with a forbidding name like "Cobra." I didn't want to be the one to tell him he didn't have a chance.

We were living a fairly simple life. We took long walks around nearby Yarranabbe Park and watched eager students practicing at Duncan McClenahan's Boomerang School. Yes, there really was such a thing. The beauty of Sydney —

its parks, beaches and waterways — kept our spirits up. When Douglas MacArthur entered Tokyo at the end of the Pacific War, he said, "You can hate a government, but you can't hate a people." The Australians we'd met so far were terrific. It was Gough Whitlam and his government I didn't have much use for.

Our visits to the Lees' house continued. Often they'd come into the city as well, and we'd have dinner or go to a jazz performance.

One night we went to see the forerunners to the Three Tenors. They were the Three Guitarists, Herb Ellis, Joe Pass and Barney Kessel, appearing at the Town Hall Theater. Another night we went to see Dave Brubeck at the magnificent Opera House. Early in 1974 the official dedication of Sydney's most famous landmark took place. Queen Elizabeth came out from England. We didn't take it personally when she failed to call. We knew she was busy with all the events surrounding the opening. It was a momentous occasion. It should have been. It took 15 years to build the place, at a cost roughly equal to the monthly interest from Bill Gates' bank account.

As the months rolled by, Carla had far more to show for our experience than I. Her health was good, and we were getting more excited about the prospect of a child coming into our lives. I refused to let myself think I wouldn't be able to support it. Carla continued to work, and Doctors Pockley and Taylor were pleased with her efforts. Among other things, they knew she'd show up on time and wasn't about to go out on strike.

Among the many people we'd met through Tom Crow were H. Claire Higson and his wife Teddi. Mr. Higson was the Managing Director of Precision Golf Forging. His son John also worked for the company. The elder Higsons took a parental interest in us and contributed to our well-being with their kindness. They took us out to dinner on several occasions. Imagine how those two about-to-be-poor immigrants from America felt riding in their Bentley. More than once Carla and I looked at each other and wondered, "What are we doing here?" Teddi Higson looked upon Carla's pregnancy as if it was going to produce her own grandchild.

Carla was due in late September. It was late, all right. When it got to be 10 days late Dr. John Solomon decided to induce labor. The date was set, October 3, 1974. Without a car of our own, we'd lived in fear Carla would begin experiencing contractions at 3 in the morning. It appeared we wouldn't have to worry about it now. On the evening of October 2, the two of us went out for our last meal as a "single" couple. The next day we called a taxi and made the cross-town trip to King George V Hospital.

The delivery didn't go quite as smoothly as planned. The doctors detect some internal respiratory problems and decided on a Cesarean section. I had been in the anteroom with Carla, looking official in my mask and gown. Evidently I wasn't official enough. Dr. Solomon escorted me outside to a waiting room and said they'd be getting Carla ready. I had no idea how the procedure worked. I expected they'd call me back inside when it was time to deliver.

The next thing I knew, Dr. Solomon came out and said, "Congratulations. You have a boy called Douglas." I responded the same way any composed father-to-be would. I burst into tears. Moments later I was shown the baby. I won't go into detail about how adorable he was because Douglas might read this, and he'd never forgive me. You know how kids are.

Carla, meanwhile, was hurting. Surgery is not meant to be enjoyable, even if a baby is the result. She was lapsing in and out of sleep. It was better, at least, that she didn't know how much pain she had. I was standing beside her bed and telling her about the baby. The nurses tried to make her comfortable, but it wasn't easy. It wasn't until the next day that Carla got to see her child. Waiting that long didn't make her happy, but sleep and lowering the pain came first.

Julian and Judy Lee were out of the country and would return a few days later. Teddi Higson (now Grandma Teddi to us) came to the hospital on D-Day plus one, and several thereafter. She comforted us tremendously. Carla was allowed to remain in the hospital for 10 days. Australian health care was wonderful and affordable.

We were euphoric about the addition to our family. We recalled all those nights we'd lie awake thinking about names. Carla liked the name Kellie for a girl, though it would be a few years before we got to use it. Picking a name for a son wasn't as simple. The mom-to-be didn't share my enthusiasm for "Oscar Robertson Greenwald" and, while she liked the name Douglas, she wasn't buying MacArthur as a middle name. Eventually we settled on Douglas Aaron. The "Douglas" was obvious, while "Aaron" was for Hank Aaron, whom I'd always admired and who got his 3,000th hit on the day we were married. This way our son had two names he could live with, even if he never had any interest in the men themselves.

While Carla was far from her family in the U.S., both Grandma Teddi and Judy Lee gave her plenty of support when she got home from the hospital. Of course I was around as well, but mothering instincts were foreign to me. I was helping every way I could. I always loved little kids and never imagined having one of my own. It wasn't until I read the instruction manual that I even knew how. At age 9, I was somewhere between an old father and a young grandfather. I guess I viewed our baby from both perspectives. I helped with the diapers ("nappies," as they're called in Australia), and I really loved getting up in the middle of the night with him. I'll concede Carla was better equipped to feed him

After Douglas was born it was suggested I apply for unemployment compensation. I don't recall if that was the exact term, but it seemed like welfare to me. When I went for the interview, the clerk said, "I see on your application you arrived here in August."

When I pointed out to her it was August of the previous year, she exclaimed, "Where have you been all this time?" I explained I'd come to Australia to work, not to collect public assistance. This concept seemed as foreign to her as I was. My request was approved, and we began receiving weekly checks in the mail — as long as the postal workers weren't on strike. There were no Saturday deliveries.

It was becoming obvious to me that my dream of being able to sustain myself in that part of the world wasn't working out. I'd hoped to settle in Sydney, that most beautiful of cities. I loved the Australians, and I loved that far-off part of the world. The romance of the South Seas had captured me, and I dreamed of being able to explore the many islands close to our new home. While the realization it wasn't going to happen saddened me, I was also satisfied. At least I had chased my dream. There's no shame in failing. The shame is in not going after it. I knew I wasn't going to be one who sat around wondering what might have been. I knew something else — I wasn't through dreaming.

Many thoughts ran through my head as we made the decision to leave. Obviously the change in governments, and with it the change in attitude about hiring foreigners, made it nearly impossible to succeed. The work stoppages were hard to adjust to, and the acceptance of them even more difficult. In 1974 I felt, generally speaking, the attitude in Australia was to strive for the average. Certainly there were exceptions, as evidenced in professional fields, but labor unions didn't seem interested in having anyone do anything well.

It was a joke, at the time, how poorly made Australian cars were. It helped explain why so many foreign-made autos were sold there. The unions feared the popularity of the imports would cost their members' jobs. Instead of trying to make better cars, ones Australians might be proud to own, the unions had a better idea. They'd just refuse to unload the ships bringing in cars from other countries.

Perhaps these were simply cultural differences I didn't grasp. Australia seemed to be fighting for some kind of an identity of its own. It was a western nation in an Asian sphere of influence. World War II had shown how vulnerable the country was in terms of defending itself. With so few people (even today there are only 18 million) and such a large landmass, it made an inviting target for the over-crowded lands so close by. The country's natural resources were looked upon with envy, as well.

Australia had many talented athletes, actors, writers, singers and other per-formers. Yet it seemed the attitude was you never really proved yourself in those fields unless you made it big in another country. Many times I tried to sort out my own anguish versus objectivity. I didn't always like the answer. In the final analysis I had to admit it wasn't up to them to adjust to me, it was the other way around.

As difficult as the job situation was, there was something else. We were always taught in America to strive to be the best at whatever we did. The key word in that philosophy is "strive," not "best." Not everyone can be the best, but every-one can make the effort. Did I really want to raise a child in an atmosphere where striving for the average seemed to be the goal? Of course parents play major roles in shaping attitudes, but I didn't want my child to be ridiculed by his contempo-raries for trying to do the best he could.

Australia has changed in many ways in the almost 25 years since our little fam-ily left. The influx of Asians following the Vietnam War has helped demonstrate the value of a work ethic. Immigrants from southern Europe following the Second World War brought that same penchant for hard work and long hours in their family-run businesses.

They were, however, a minority. Perhaps the biggest change in Australia occurred, oddly enough, off Newport, Rhode Island, in 1983. It was there that the Aussies defeated the U.S. in the America's Cup yacht races and became the first challenging nation in nearly 100 years of competition to bring the cup home to a foreign land. The feeling of pride that swept over that country was enormous.

To most Americans, if an event doesn't involve baseball, football, basketball or the Olympics you might as well forget about it. Some might recognize the America's Cup as a tennis competition, or perhaps soccer. People in this country really don't get worked up about yacht racing.

To the Australians it was another story. The major cities in that country are all coastal. The sea plays a much larger part in life down under than here. While one can't say that most people there have yachts, a high percentage do spend time on the water.

But the significance of that victory in 1983 goes far beyond a series of yacht races. It was a victory by their country over the United States on a world stage. The coverage of those races was seen in many nations. It seemed to establish a tremendous amount of self-worth among the population. When I visited there the following year, evidence of local pride was everywhere. People wore shirts that read: "Proud to be an Aussie." Signs proclaimed: "Australia! Home of the America's Cup Champions."

You couldn't go many places without being aware this nation was feeling good about itself. It made me feel good, as well. It was time for them to get over an inferiority complex based on geography. If an event such as the America's Cup helped turn things around, so be it. I've been back twice since and plan to be there for the 2000 Olympics, too. Each time I go back I'm struck with a certain irony. I do things now I wasn't able to do when I lived there. In those days things were so near and yet so far away. In 1990 Carla and I went to Tonga and marveled at the beauty of the northern island of Vava'u. This was the South Seas I'd so often thought about.

We explored the South Island of New Zealand with its spectacular scenery. From there we went to Sydney for the wedding of Julian and Judy's oldest son, Bruce. Life was good, and I guess I had really been an Aussie after all. I couldn't have done any of the things I was now able to do in Australia until I'd proved myself in the United States.

12
TRIBUTES

Willie Mac

I was not among the more than 500,000 who now claim to have been at Seals Stadium in San Francisco that July day in 1959 when Willie McCovey made his major league debut.

The two boasts I hear most often in San Francisco are: "I've been going to 49er games since the days of Y.A. Tittle and Hugh McElhenny at Kezar Stadium," and "I was at Seals Stadium the day McCovey broke in and went 4-for-4 against Robin Roberts." The fact that some of those who make such claims weren't born at either time doesn't seem to enter into it. Not wishing to be a spoilsport, I just nod and try my best to look envious, even though I was among those who watched the 49ers at Kezar. I loved being able to park downtown on a Sunday morning and take the streetcar right to the stadium.

As for McCovey's career, while I wasn't there at the beginning, I can say I was there on another July afternoon 21 years later when it came to an end. To have played in four decades is an achievement. To have played as well as McCovey did gets a man elected to the Baseball Hall of Fame.

Witnessing a player's final appearance when you know it's his final appearance can be emotional. For a broadcaster, describing the moment becomes a test, especially when it involves a player of McCovey's stature.

It had been determined that Willie Mac's last game would be on Sunday, July 6, 1980, at Dodger Stadium. It was the Sunday before the All-Star Game, which would be played there. How appropriate that a man who had been such a key figure in the Dodgers-Giants rivalry should make his final appearance in L.A.

In the year and a half I had been broadcasting Giants games, Willie and I had spoken frequently on airplane trips. He told me that when he was a kid, his favorite was the great Ted Williams. He talked about getting to know Williams and the conversations they'd had about hitting. I recalled how fortunate I was to have called McCovey's final home run off Scott Sanderson in the fourth inning of a game at Montreal. It was number 521 of his career, tying Williams and forever linking the two on the all-time home run list. Few things in baseball have been more fitting.

Earlier in the week of McCovey's departure, fans at Candlestick Park had said farewell to him during a game against the Cincinnati Reds. He responded with a base hit off Joe Price and received a huge ovation. As emotional as this was, I had prepared for it. After all, these were the home-town fans, and he was their favorite. Los Angeles was another story.

As that Sunday unfolded, it seemed as if there would be no story at all. Giants manager Dave Bristol, not the world's most warm-hearted individual, chose to start Rich Murray at first base. In fact, McCovey had not started the last two games. As the game wore on, it began to appear as if Bristol was not going to use McCovey at all.

The game was tied 3-3 going to the top of the eighth. With one out, Jack Clark drew a walk from Dodger starter Jerry Reuss, who in his previous outing had thrown a no-hitter against the Giants. Rich Murray followed with a single to right, sending Clark to third. That was enough for Dodger manager Tommy Lasorda, who summoned Rick Sutcliffe from the bullpen

All eyes turned toward the Giants' dugout as the unmistakable figure of Willie McCovey started up the steps for the final time. There were more than 46,000 at Dodger Stadium that day, and row by row, section by section, they stood as one and cheered in tribute to this old warrior who had performed so gallantly against their team over the years.

Alone in the visitors' radio booth, I could feel a tear beginning its journey down my cheek. Sometimes even those of us who talk for a living have a difficult time finding words. This was one of those times.

McCovey wasted no time attending to matters at hand. With the go-ahead run at third, he ripped one to deep center field. Rudy Law caught it, but it was deep enough to score the run that put the Giants in front, and they went on to win. McCovey's sacrifice fly marked his 1,555th and final run batted in, on nal at-bat of his 22 seasons in the major leagues. What a way to go out.

Gentleman's Gentleman

ow many people have you known in your life? How many of them are without their flaws? Of how many can it be said, "I've never heard a bad word about him?"

I knew one: My former broadcasting partner Lindsey Nelson.

Even in Lindsey's days in World War II, no one could find a German or Japanese soldier with anything bad to say about him. The Japanese yelled, "To hell with Babe Ruth!" But they never spoke ill of Lindsey. As Casey Stengel used to say, "You could look it up."

What kind of man was this, who walked the earth from 1919-1995 with such an unsullied reputation? No one could do greater justice to the word "gentleman" than Lindsey. More remarkable, he chose to enter a profession not all that gentlemanly. The world of television networks and sports broadcasting is often highly competitive. . . a nicer way of saying cutthroat. Petty jealousies and big egos are often the order of the day. Lindsey Nelson walked through those minefields and never came close to danger.

He arrived in San Francisco in 1979 with a reputation established over many years of having broadcast Notre Dame football, the NFL, the Cotton Bowl and New York Mets baseball games. After 17 seasons with the Mets, he'd come west to broadcast Giants games. Joining him on these broadcasts was me. For one of us it was the break of a lifetime.

We spent three years together broadcasting Giants baseball. He taught me not to let the team's wins and losses affect my broadcasting, that if I got caught up in the way the Giants were playing, I was going to sound the way they were playing. Having broadcast the Mets from the time they came into the National League, Lindsey knew whereof he spoke. With the storytelling ability men from the South seem to possess, and blessed with manager Casey Stengel, about whom there was an endless supply of material, Lindsey was revered as a Mets broadcaster long before they won the 1969 World Series.

What I treasured most about the three years we were together had little to do with baseball or broadcasting. Lindsey and I had something in common that went beyond both. Each of us had a daughter with Down syndrome. When we met in 1979, his daughter Sharon was in her 30s. My daughter Kellie was not yet 1. Down syndrome was a new and frightening experience for me and Carla. The hours we spent with Lindsey that first spring training in Phoenix brightened our outlook considerably. The nights at dinner he spent answering our questions and allaying our fears enabled us to face the future with an enthusiasm and confidence we hadn't felt before.

While he helped make our lives better, life for Lindsey was not all that easy. His wife had died several years earlier, and he would travel to visit Sharon at a group home in Middletown, New York, every chance he got. He also had a younger daughter, Nancy, who was getting married later in 1979. He had a lot to deal with at age 60, but he never complained and was determined to make those around him feel better.

Naturally we talked sports, but it was the other topics that fascinated me while we sat together at dinner or on airplanes. He was at Normandy in World War II, not on D-Day but "as long after as I could possibly make it." If Ernest Hemingway liberated the bar at the Ritz Hotel in Paris, Lindsey Nelson served with the occupation forces at the nearby Scribe. He must have done a good job; it's still standing.

He loved Paris. When CBS sent him on assignments out of the country, he made sure he returned home via the City of Light. Lindsey was a romantic, and he and the French capital were made for each other. When Carla and I made plans to visit Paris in 1983, he said, "How I envy those who go there for the first time. I won't recommend or suggest things. Just go and discover places for yourselves, and they'll always be yours."

Lindsey left the Giants following the 1981 season and went home to Knoxville, where he taught a sports broadcasting course at the University of Tennessee. He still worked an occasional sports event, but had essentially retired.

Each year it seemed his two old ballclubs, the Giants and Mets, would play each other in May. Bob Murphy, one of Lindsey's partners in New York, and I would call him on or near his birthday, May 25. We delighted in hearing his voice again and catching up on events in his life. In later years he contracted Parkinson's Disease, and it kept him at home most of the time.

In May of 1995, the Giants and Mets played each other home and home within 10 days. Murphy and I tried calling Lindsey from both New York and San Francisco. There was no answer. Several days later we learned he had died in a hospital in Atlanta, not far from where his daughter Nancy lived.

By the conduct of his daily life, Lindsey taught me how to be a gentleman. I never completely got the hang of it, but that wasn't his fault. Whenever someone says, "Count your blessings," I count my three years with Lindsey Nelson.

The Polo Grounds

It's no longer there,
That place where history was made,
Where people cheered
And sat in the shade.

It's gone for good
And much more beside.
In its place stand apartments
With heroes' ghosts inside.
Within its walls of darkest green
So many wondrous sights were seen.
The victories and the defeats
Witnessed from the many seats
By those who loved the place.

It's gone.
And with it all traces
Of where Matty pitched
And Willie ran the bases.

It's gone,
The place where Hubbell showed his stuff
From that mound
Beneath old Coogan's Bluff.

No longer stands that place
Where John McGraw spit fire,
Where he glared and screamed
At more than one umpire.
Ten pennants stood
As tribute to his mettle.

McGraw,
Who had so many scores to settle.
Where did it go,
That place with so much grass
Graced by those
With so much style and class?

That stage on which
The home team sought to bury
Those who dared
To take on Ott and Terry.

Memories of years gone by recall
When Bobby Thomson hit that ball.
Those seconds that were so intense
Until it cleared the left field fence.

It's gone
That place we'd sit and gaze
That spoke to us
Of better days.

No more we hear
Those glorious sounds
From the place they called
The Polo Grounds.

It Might As Well Be Spring

Willie Mays is like Paris. You think everything that could possibly be written about him already has, yet you want more. Will we ever get our fill of either subject? Not likely.

It makes more sense, I suspect, to focus on Mr. Mays. It's likely Paris will be around another few hundred years, while Mays, like the rest of us, will check out long before. In most places I travel, checkout time is usually noon. But I don't need to know which day.

In linking Willie Mays with the French capital, I think first of spring. The romantic notion of April in Paris, despite all the rain, is embedded in so many of us. Le printemps — the symbol of renewal, hope, optimism.

To a baseball fan, the sight of Willie Mays, no matter the season, says springtime. What else can one associate with his youthful smile and boundless enthusiasm? April in Paris, Mays in October — it's still spring. A whole generation has grown up without ever seeing Mays play baseball. Even in his late 60s, Mays represents their best hope.

In the springtime of my life, I was a broadcaster in Syracuse, New York. In those days there was a football game played in August known as the Chicago Tribune All-Star game, which matched the top college draftees against the defending NFL champions. It was the first pro football exhibition played each season.

In 1963, I was en route to Chicago to cover the game and, in particular, ex-Syracuse stars John Mackey and Walt Sweeney. It struck me that one of the two Chicago baseball teams must be playing at home. Only rarely does such a perceptive thought arise in me.

It turned out the Cubs were playing host to the San Francisco Giants. To many of us, when you thought of the Giants you thought first of Willie Mays. Though I'd seen Mays play many times at New York's Polo Grounds from 1951-57, I'd never met or spoken to him. This was felt by many to be a far greater loss for me than for him.

The question became how to go about arranging an interview. If I had known then what I know now, I'd never have done what I did. With the nerve only the young and ignorant possess, I picked up the telephone and called Mays at the Edgewater Beach Hotel. It was amazing that he answered and agreed to talk with me before the game the following day at Wrigley Field. Despite my overnight fears he wouldn't remember, Mays greeted me the next afternoon by asking, "What're you doing covering a football game in the middle of summer? It's baseball season."

I muttered something like, "Why wait 'til it gets cold?"

He squealed. We talked. The calendar said mid-August, but he put spring in my life and in my step as I left Wrigley Field that afternoon and went off to Soldier Field to cover football.

As I got older, I learned that life wasn't that simple, a lesson reinforced each day. But whenever I see Willie Mays, the years and the season peel away until all that's left is springtime.

Will any team Tony Fossas hasn't pitched for please stand up?

13
EXTRA INNINGS

Many things have changed in my life from the time I was a kid in Detroit, most of them for the better. Advancements in science, medicine and technology have combined to improve our lives, though not everyone cares to admit it. Other things have changed as well, including baseball. I wish I could say the game has benefitted.

Today, people have a way of labeling those who feel things were done better years ago. The term they use is "dinosaurs," and any thoughts these folks might have are dismissed out of hand. Perhaps those who affix that label should come up with something different. Dinosaurs seem to be more popular than ever.

When I decided to leave the Giants, I cited travel as the reason. There's no question this was a major factor. There were others, however, which dealt with the state of the game itself.

Everything crystallized for me the day the owners fired Commissioner Fay Vincent in 1992. This sent a signal there were dark days ahead, though I didn't know how dark they would turn out to be. When you rid yourself of a man who had the interests of all of baseball at heart, and substitute a fellow owner, you're sending a clear message: "Forget the players, forget the fans, forget everyone else. We want someone whose sole interest is us." Hello, Bud Selig.

With the disposal of Vincent, there was no one who could unilaterally step in and get in the way of a labor dispute. The owners were itching for a showdown with the players in their upcoming negotiation. The lords of baseball had painted themselves into a corner. They'd lavished so much money on player salaries, they had to do something about it.

The problem was they knew they had no one to blame but themselves. But if there's one thing owners don't accept, it's blame. They don't have to, they're owners. Many of them have made fortunes in other businesses. They've never had a problem showing their employees who's the boss. Now they own baseball teams, and their uniformed employees make more than they do and have a union that can tell the employer to go to hell.

Since the bidding war for ballplayers began, with the introduction of free agency in the 1970s, the owners haven't been very successful at keeping salaries in line. It's been said that collusion is one of the most difficult things to prove. Baseball owners have been found guilty twice in the matter of player salaries. Nice going.

If there's one thing owners have learned about each other over the years, it's that they can't trust each other. The same guy who cries salaries are too high turns around the next day and signs a free agent for $12 million a year.

I asked an owner, "Why can't you do what the rest of the country does? Establish a budget and try your best to stick to it."

He replied, "Because if I set my budget at $40 million, the next guy might set his at 45 or 50."

In other words, owners don't feel they can compete if they don't spend as much as the next guy. Unfortunately for the owners, there are too many "next guys." Heading into the 1994 showdown with the players, the owners knew what they had to do. They weren't about to exercise restraint on spending money, so the only thing left was to get the players to exercise restraint on accepting it.

Put another way, "You must save us from spending so much money on you." Thus, was born the salary cap. The owners thought it would be a wonderful idea if the players agreed to help those who couldn't help themselves by agreeing to limitations on their spending habits. They weren't fooling anyone. They knew the imposition of a salary cap in a new contract proposal would never be accepted and would lead to their objective in the first place — a strike.

It was obvious that while owners change over the course of years, owner mentality never does. "We'll break that damn union yet," seems to be a motto etched in stone wherever these men congregate. Who in his right mind expects a players' association or union to agree to keep owners from spending so much money on them?

So these men, with this incurable spending habit, succeeded in forcing a strike. Forget the fact that baseball was in the midst of one of its greatest seasons. The owners got themselves a strike and by God they were going to show everybody who was boss. The fans? Who the hell are they? They'll come back in time. They always do.

The strike began on August 12, 1994. Both sides were now in a propaganda war. At this point it became evident the only group dumber than the owners were the players. Now, I don't have an abiding love for either side. In this case, however, I sided with the players. Who among us, as employees, wouldn't accept as much money as an employer would be willing to give? Why, then, should we as employees reach out to someone who says, "You have to save us from ourselves"?

In a dispute as clear cut as this one should have been, public opinion was running 2-1 in favor of the owners. How, you say, could such a thing happen, especially when the owners' side was presented on TV each night by Bud Selig and Richard Ravitch? The answer was simple. The players were represented each night by Donald Fehr and Gene Orza. It was incredible to me that in the public relations-conscious era we live in, those two sourpusses were the best the players could come up with to represent them on TV. Looking at Gene Orza was almost enough to make me side with the owners.

Wake up, guys. In the next dispute, which may be closer than anyone would like to think, you'd better give some thought to whom you let in front of the cameras. When you run second in public opinion to Selig and Ravitch, and your cause is the right one, you've got a big problem. Fehr and Orza may be great negotiators and fighters. If that's the case, lock them in the room with the owners next time and don't expose them to the public. Find some good looking, articulate spokesman who can sell your cause.

Something was wrong when the fans were left to think the players were striking for more money. There's a difference between that and having to accept less because the owners couldn't help themselves. What greater example did anyone need than Jerry Reinsdorf? The White Sox owner was the acknowledged leader of the hard-nosed wing of the party. While the battle was in progress, he went out and signed Albert Belle for $11 million a year. This undermined the owners' position and helped bring an end to the strike.

There was one other factor that helped: replacement players. Major leaguers were indignant that others would agree to come in and play while they were on strike. It didn't matter that some were realizing a forlorn ambition by attaining their 15 innings of "fame." Instead of castigating these big league wannabes, the major leaguers should have embraced them for making the owners look ridiculous.

Having to broadcast those games and attempting to take replacement players seriously was something I wouldn't wish on anyone.

While I won't say replacement baseball brought owners to their senses, it did help bring them to their knees. The absurdity of passing those players off as the real thing, with gatherings of 2,000 or fewer watching them, injected a harsh dose of reality. But despite all of this, there was nothing more repugnant to me than the sight of Bud Selig in 1994 announcing the cancellation of the remainder of the season, including the playoffs and the World Series. What two world wars couldn't do, a baseball civil war managed to accomplish. Selig's announcement left me with an empty feeling and made me embarrassed to be associated with the game. I knew I wasn't going to stay around much longer.

The 1998 season focused attention where it should be: on the exploits of the players. Even those who would not call themselves dedicated fans suddenly knew who Mark McGwire and Sammy Sosa were. Though not everyone associated with baseball would agree, the players are the game. The last time I recall anyone paying to see an owner was when my dad took me to my first game in 1943.

The Detroit Tigers were playing the Philadelphia Athletics, and Connie Mack, who owned the team, was also the manager. He wore a business suit and a straw hat and positioned the outfielders by motioning with his rolled up scorecard. He was the only one associated with the '43 Athletics worth paying to see. Connie Mack knew better than anyone that the players make the game

When he had great players, he won. When he sold them off, he had money but no one who could pitch or hit. In 1998 there were plenty of players in the major leagues who fit both categories. What a treat it was, not only for the fans but for those of us who'd worked in the game, to see those wonderful American League shortstops Alex Rodriguez, Nomar Garciaparra, Derek Jeter and Omar Vizquel. I was astounded at the ease with which McGwire and Sosa flew past 60 home runs en route to record-breaking totals. Just wait until the pressure gets to those guys, so many of us said.

Pressure, indeed! What about the year Mo Vaughn had? To some, he may have seemed lost in the shuffle, but think about his season. His team's front office left little doubt they didn't want him, and he went out and hit .337 with 115 runs batted in and 40 home runs in the final year of his contract. Roger Clemens won his fifth Cy Young Award. Even Cy himself never won that many. The list goes on: Tom Glavine, Kevin Brown, Randy Johnson, David Cone, Kerry Wood. Most impressive of all were the New York Yankees. In the proud tradition of their Bronx ancestors, the '98 edition dominated the game like no team in recent history. It was a wonderful year to be a baseball fan.

It's easy to single out the great players and a phenomenal team and suggest they're reflective of today's players. Of course they're not. They represent a handful of those one sees every day on big league diamonds. There is no doubt today's players are better athletes than their predecessors. They're bigger, stronger, faster, and they jump higher than players of my youth, but they don't play baseball as well. They can't. The system works against it.

If players of today have all these physical attributes, why can't baseball produce a starting pitcher who can go more than six innings? For some reason, those in high places have decreed these well conditioned, modern athletes must be placed on pitch counts and never allowed to develop the arm strength that might enable them to throw a complete game.

Major league teams fear that these young men, to whom large sums have been paid, might develop arm trouble. "Horrors," these executives cry. "We'd have to pay these kids if they get hurt." Get with it, fellas. Take a look at the disabled lists and see how many of those pitchers you pampered in the minor leagues are out for 15, 30 or 60 days.

Now we're told that teams only need starting pitchers to go six innings because there are specialists to finish the job. There's the seventh-inning pitcher, the eighth-inning pitcher and the closer. Why develop a starting pitcher to go the distance when you have these men to fill the late inning roles? Get serious. Only two or three teams have pitchers who fit those descriptions. The others are using guys who are now with their 12th clubs. Will any team that Tony Fossas hasn't pitched for please stand up? The last several years I was broadcasting I'd never seen such a mess as I did with pitching. I saw far too many who looked like they'd rather walk a batter than risk letting him hit the ball. History shows one of the best ways to get a batter out is to get him to hit the ball to somebody with a glove on.

Nowadays if a manager doesn't make six pitching changes a game, he isn't doing his job. So many of these changes are simply knee-jerk reactions to the sight of a left-hand-ed or right-handed batter. This is known in baseball terms as "covering your ass." If the manager doesn't bring in the left-hander, he'll be forced to explain his decision after the game.

The popular defense for all this is known as playing the percentages. Horse excre-ment! Percentages only mean something when the guy you bring in is better than the guy he's facing. I've seen too many games where that good old left-hander, who hasn't got anybody out in three weeks, is brought in just because the guy at the plate hits from the left side. Even the feats of the McGwires and Sosas can't hide that.

Many baseball people I've talked with acknowledge that too many players reach the major leagues long before they're ready. Again, it's not the players' fault, it's the system. A player is drafted. He's given a large bonus to sign. His agent insists that the player be brought to the major leagues in a year or two at the most. This, not because he's ready to play, but so he can start collecting major league service time and speed up his eligi-bility for arbitration. The owners, who give in on almost everything else, surrender on this one as well. Is it any wonder so many players appear lost concerning fundamen-tal aspects of the game?

Take outfield play. How many times have you seen outfielders dive for balls they had no chance to catch? Maybe they think it will look good on the highlights that night. Maybe they feel they can fool the fans into thinking they're hustling. Instead of giving the hitter what he's earned (a single), the outfielder costs his team an extra base, putting the hitter in scoring position at second. How many times have you seen an outfielder go all the way to the fence for a ball he can't possibly reach, instead of playing the carom and holding the batter to a single or a double? The ball bounces back over the fielder's head and rolls back toward the infield. By the time the ball is finally picked up, the batter is on third. Being a better athlete, in terms of strength, size, speed and jumping ability, doesn't confer better judgment on the player. Former New York Yankee outfielder Tommy Heinrich once said, "Catching the ball is a pleasure. Knowing what to do with it is a business." While it's true the speed of today's outfielders and the size of their gloves allow them to catch balls their ancestors couldn't, knowing what to do with it is often a problem. Throwing to the wrong base, or overthrowing a relay or cutoff man, has become so commonplace as to have gained acceptance. Managers are reduced to shrugging their shoulders as if to say, "What can you do about it? I have to use this guy. It's in his contract."

Because the system is so messed up, teams are often forced to keep their best instructors as coaches at the major league level. This is done to provide on-the-job training to players who belong in the minor leagues. Baseball's best instructors should be paid decent salaries and employed at the lowest minor league levels. The time to instruct players is when they're most receptive to instruction. When a young player comes into rookie ball or Class A, he's still at the point where he's familiar with the expression, "Yes sir."

All too often, major league teams take people to whom they can pay the smallest amount of money and make them minor league instructors. Some may be good, but I can assure you the best instructors are in the major leagues trying to make up for lost time. The system is wrong, and it's not likely to change. If my way of thinking makes me a dinosaur, then baseball is a glacier and I'll race against it any day.

Other things were discouraging to watch toward the end of my days as an everyday broadcaster. I suppose the problem comes from having cared too much about a game you loved and respected from the time you were a kid. I accept the fact that things change. I didn't complain that I made more money late in my career than I did at the beginning.

Change doesn't have to mean deterioration. There was a time in baseball when the last thing a batter wanted was to take a called third strike. Now it seems he'd rather be called out on strikes than swing and miss. If he strikes out swinging, he can't blame it on anyone else. If he's called out on strikes, he can always give the umpire a dirty look and make the crowd think he got a bad call. Perhaps that's overly cynical, but don't bet there isn't something to it.

One of the things that concerned me during my career was the possibility of being remembered as a bitter old man. I was finding more and more things I disliked about the game, and they were beginning to outnumber the things I liked. I enjoyed being on the air and telling baseball stories. I enjoyed the byplay with Kuip, Kruk and Ted. I didn't like the way the game was being played.

I abhorred the fact that on the rare occasion a pitcher went a strong eight innings, a manager felt he had to bring in a closer because management was paying him big bucks. Too many games have been lost for that very reason. It bothered me to read about pitchers complaining they didn't know what their roles were when their roles were to get hitters out.

I'm not talking about starting one time and relieving the next. I'm talking about pitching in the sixth inning one time and the eighth inning the next. How tough can that be? Baseball would have you believe this is an age of specialization. What we're really living with is an age of finding a spot for someone where he can do the least amount of damage.

It's possible these things matter only to me. To a fan seeking an autograph, it's not important if the player knows what a cutoff man is. A fan may not know, or care, that certain players are in the big leagues only because they were out of options, and that better players are being kept in the minor leagues because they could still be farmed out.

These things have gone on for years, and are of little interest to most fans. There was a time when people who knew baseball said, "Just because you put a major league uniform on a guy doesn't make him a major leaguer." That used to be true.

One of the most abominable practices in sports today is the selling of seat licenses. Owners who get communities to pay for new ballparks and then stick fans with seat license fees ought to be strung up by their resin bags. How much longer before they start selling seat licenses for the restrooms? If taxpayers agree to meet the civic challenge of the cost of a new ballpark, they've already done the club owner a favor. If the owner finances the park himself or through corporate funding, he's doing the community a favor. I wasn't happy when the Giants decided to sell seat licenses, but I understood the need. Every time I drive by the construction site and see the new ballpark going up, I'm astounded such a thing was begun in my lifetime. Peter Magowan may have his detractors, but he'll have a lot fewer when the new ballpark is completed. Magowan isn't using taxpayer funds. Try raising $250 million if your name isn't Al Gore. As distasteful as seat licenses are, the Giants have more of a right to them than most other franchises.

No matter who pays for new ballparks today, the fact they're being built is one of the best things to happen in baseball. Slowly but surely, the mistakes of the '60s and '70s are being erased as the grand old game moves out of glorified bomb craters and into proper facilities.

No matter what I may feel about other aspects of baseball, the new parks are wonderful, and fans will be getting the comforts and amenities they deserve. My hope is that baseball will take stock of who can afford to come to games and make sure the true fans aren't squeezed out. Why are there doubts gnawing at my insides?

The next big baseball war will involve umpires. I'm not talking about salaries here, but something that speaks to the question of integrity. Why is it that whenever you mention that word, it raises the cry, "How dare you question our integrity?" Why not? What is more important? Because baseball has lacked leadership far too long, the situation with umpires has gotten out of control. The relationship between players and umps deteriorates more every season.

Major league umpires have become untouchable. You can't get rid of them, and you can't discipline them in any meaningful way. If a player is disciplined for actions involving an umpire, it's announced to the world. When was the last time you were informed of an umpire's being fined or suspended for his conduct?

Let's address the question of integrity. Is there integrity when an umpire deliberately follows a player who is walking away after an argument and tries to bait him into saying something so he can throw him out of the game? Where's the integrity when three umpires know the fourth has missed a call and won't say anything because they don't want to "show him up"? Where's the integrity when an umpire misses a play and refuses to ask for help? Where's the integrity when an umpire decides to "stick it" to some player who has the nerve to question a call? How many people around the game of baseball, besides umpires, would doubt that happens? Where's the integrity when umpires put themselves above the rule book and announce they'll decide what the strike zone should be?

I'm not talking about bad judgment with regard to balls and strikes. That speaks for itself. I'm talking about the arrogance that allows umpires to adopt the attitude they're all-powerful and rule book be damned. I'll try not to get too far into the area of judgment calls, although it seems more than a little curious that a pitch a foot outside can be called a strike while a pitch an inch above the waist is called a ball. The point is, the questions of integrity raised here are not ones I alone should be raising.

They should be raised by league presidents and the commissioner. What else do they have to do that's more important? For that matter, why do we even need league presidents? Oh, I forgot. Someone has to announce the fines and suspensions of players and managers while cowering at the thought of announcing discipline against an umpire — if any is ever taken. When were umpires granted infallibility status, and how did I miss that?

As one-sided as the relationship between players and umpires has become, what happens on those occasions when umpires have gone out on strike? Major league umpires apparently believe they're the only ones who can umpire at that level, yet they make mistakes every day just like everybody else. When replacement umpires are brought in during strikes, the first time a player gets a bad call he cries, "We've got to get the regular umpires back."

No matter that the regular umps may make the same call, or even throw the player out for giving him a dirty look. With the opportunity of a lifetime to expose an umpire to the word "humility," the players panic at one or two calls. Ballplayers who do that would seem to forfeit any right to complain when the big boys come marching home with more arrogance than before.

It's so discouraging year after year to hear baseball people say, "We have to do something," and do nothing. Baseball's black eye has gotten so bad it's now blind to the problem. How come baseball can deal with Pete Rose, but won't raise the question of integrity when it comes to umpires? Do you think for a moment that an umpire can't affect the outcome of a game by "sticking it" to a player on a ball or strike call at a crucial moment? Do you think an umpire can't affect the outcome of a game by arbitrarily throwing a player out?

Of course he can. Naturally, umpires will deny such things occur. Do you expect them to admit it? Next time you hear an umpire say he threw out a player because "he showed me up," ask yourself this question: To whom?

Umpires often throw players and managers out of games because they're afraid they'll look bad in the eyes of their fellow umpires. They're afraid not only of what the other guys on their crew will think, but of what their brethren watching the highlights on TV that night will think. They're officiating not in the best interests of the game but in the best interests of their image. I've had people tell me umpires have had TV games taped for them in their clubhouse so they can hear what announcers said about them afterward.

Years ago Lindsey Nelson and I received an intimidating phone call from an umpire before a Giants game. He didn't like what friends told him we may, or may not, have said the night before. I'd mention his name except I really believe he's matured a lot since then and may even be embarrassed he ever did that. Nobody's perfect — not players, managers, umpires, or even broadcasters. Imperfections are one thing. Arrogance and the question of integrity are something else.

Over the years I've sat around with baseball people and listened to a lot of great stories. I can think of few things I've enjoyed more than these sessions. However, there's one thing I never quite grasped. What made a pitcher so tough just because he drilled a batter in the ribs, or the shoulder, or the head because he didn't like the way he stood at the plate? What was I missing?

Time after time I heard stories from teammates and opponents of Bob Gibson and Don Drysdale about how tough they were. These two guys are Hall of Famers and their records speak for themselves. The admiration expressed for them never dealt with wins and losses, but with batters hit or knocked down. I don't doubt that either could hold his own in a fight. What I don't understand is how deliberately throwing at a hitter and jeopardizing his career makes one so tough.

I may have needed help getting out of college, but it seems to me you can be a hell of a lot tougher if you're the guy holding the ball. I could find a lot of reasons to glorify the deeds of great pitchers, but "stickin' it in his ear" isn't one of them. Nobody says a hitter has a right to claim both sides of the plate. I understand a pitcher's need to stake his claim to half of it, as well. A hitter has to know there's a price to be paid for trying to take advantage. Guys like Frank Robinson and Don Baylor understood this and were willing to pay for it. That part is fair. But as long as I've watched baseball I never understood why so many pitchers blame everyone but themselves when things go wrong.

A batter hits a home run, and the next time up he gets hit by a pitch or knocked down. A batter hits a home run, and the next batter gets hit or knocked down. It doesn't happen every time, but it happens often enough to take coincidence out of the equation. Whose fault is it the pitcher hung one over the plate, or threw a fast ball right down the middle?

The explanation for all this is: "That's the way the game is played. The pitcher has to show he's a man." Excuse me?. I thought wearing a cup had something to do with that. If the cup is empty, that's another story. If swinging a round bat at a round ball and hitting it squarely is the hardest thing in sports, then give the hitter some credit. The standard for what constitutes a great batting average suggests who holds the advantage in most pitcher-batter match-ups. How about the pitcher who knocks a hitter down because "he took too big a swing"? Did you ever notice it's usually a little guy at the plate? The pitcher's logic: "A little guy shouldn't be swinging that hard."

Maybe there are logical answers to all these questions. I haven't heard any yet.

Baseball can be a beautiful game. You don't have to be a Hall of Famer to be graceful. Watching Darren Lewis go after a fly ball is a sight to cherish. Few second basemen were smoother than Manny Trillo. The swing of Dave Justice or Will Clark will be remembered by all who saw them. What could be prettier than an outfielder's throw to a relay man and on to the plate as the converging lines of runner and ball bear down on the catcher?

What a shame baseball is so insecure about itself. The day when you could go out to the ballpark on a lazy summer afternoon, relax and watch the game is gone.

Geniuses upstairs have decided you must be "entertained" every second you're in your seat. They say you want to hear ear-splitting music before and after every pitch and that anyone who objects just isn't with it. They're afraid if they don't "entertain" you every second, you might go somewhere else.

I'm not suggesting only the game itself should be presented, and nothing else. But as long as the word "moderation" is still listed in the dictionary, someone connected with baseball ought to read the definition. To run baseball highlights and unusual plays on the giant screen in the outfield is entertainment. To run dot racing and to tell people when to cheer is simply the further dumbing down of America. What is it about baseball executives that makes them believe every fan is deaf?

I used to hear such incessant noise come out of the PA system at Shea Stadium, the airplanes taking off from LaGuardia became music to my ears.

Baseball people will tell you this is what fans want. Of course they do, if you ask them whether they'd enjoy hearing music at the ballpark. If you ask them if they'd enjoy hearing it between every pitch and at decibels designed to blow up the Empire State Building, you might get another answer. This is how pollsters get any result a client is willing to pay for. For years the Giants have had problems drawing crowds at Candlestick Park. But do those dogs chasing Frisbees really make folks want to come back?

I am not unmindful of the more fortunate aspects of a lifetime of following baseball. I saw many wonderful players and moments, as a child and as a broadcaster. To have witnessed the great players of the last six decades is enough riches for anyone. If I had seen no one other than Willie Mays, it would have been enough. It was important to write this chapter to give vent to legitimate concerns and pent-up feelings, born of a deep caring for the game.

I wanted to get out while I still had good memories. I wasn't sure I'd be able to say that much longer. Now that I don't have to be around baseball every day, I might even get to like it again. Many times, I wanted to say something like that on the air, but I wasn't Harry Caray. I wasn't larger than life. I couldn't get away with it, as much as I was tempted. I always believed if things were bothering me that much, it was time to move on. Maybe that's one reason why people write books.

INDEX

144, 145, *181*
Greenwald, Kellie, 10, *69*, 117, 119, 123-147, *181, 184*, 246, 253
Greenwald, Ray, 13, 205
Grieve, Bob, 41
Gross, Jerry, 174
Grove, Lefty, 14
Guerin, Richie, 166, 170
Guley, Marc, 32

H
Haar, Gil, 167
Haas, Walter, 90
Hagan, Cliff, 153, 166
Hagan, Walter, 41
Hale, Bruce, 174, 194
Haller, Tom, 64, 73
Halsey, Admiral William F., 215
Hamilton, Milo, 15
Hammond, Col. Lyman, 216-218, 220
Hammond, Sarah Ann, 217
Hancock, Eddie, 167
Handler, Marty, 30, 33, 40, 41, 46
Hannum, Alex, 54, 151, 153, 154, 155, 159, 160, 161, 162, 164, 165, 168, 170, 171, 172, 173, 174, 186-190, 192, 196
Hanson, Vic, 220
Harrelson, Woody, 83
Harris, Merv, 195
Harrison, Les, 150, 152
Harwell, Ernie, 14

Haviland, Jim, 79, 80, 88
Havlicek, John, 159, 172
Hayes, Charlie, 100
Hayes, Von, 100
Hearn, Chick, 15
Heilmann,Harry, 13, 14, 206
Heinrich, Tommy, 264
Heinsohn, Tommy, 15, 153
Hemingway, Ernest, 41, 254
Henderson, Dave, 107
Henderson, Ricky, 88
Herold, Joe, 168, 169
Hesburgh, Father Theodore, 48
Hetzel, Fred, 170, 172
Heumann, Sandy, 155, 156, 163
Hightower, Wayne, 165
Higson, H. Claire, 245
Higson, John, 245
Higson, Teddi, 245, 246
Hill, Marc, 128
Hirohito, Emperor, 211
Hodges, Russ, 14
Hoffman, Jerry, 32, 43, 66
Hogan, Ben, 186
Hogan, Ed, 45
Holland, Al, 73, 74
Holzman, Red, 150, 153
Hornung, Paul, 49
Horton, Willie, 51
Hottelett, Richard C., 221
Howell, Bailey, 173
Hrabosky, Al, 115
Hubbell, Carl, 255

Hume, Ellen, 230
Hunsburger, Ruth, 229, 230, 232
Hunsburger, Warren, 229, 230, 232, 233
Hutton, Tommy, 80, 81, 82, 83, 84, 85, 88, 89, 90, 115, 137, 138, *178*
Hyman, Merv, 41

I
Irish, Ned, 152, 166
Isaacs, Stan, 17, 85
Izenberg, Jerry, 41

J
Jackson, Luke, 172
Jackson, Reggie, 22
Jacobson, Steve, 85
Jeltz, Steve, 100
Jeter, Derek, 262
Johnson, Dr. Alan, 125, 127
Johnson, Arnie, 150
Johnson, Earvin "Magic," 159
Johnson, Gus, 159
Johnson, President Lyndon, 78, 163
Johnson, Randy, 262
Johnson, Walter, 14
Jones, Bobby, 41
Jones, K.C., 117, 119
Jones, Lee, 117, 119
Jones, Sam, 172
Jones, Wali, 172
Jordan, Michael, 158, 159
Jupiter, Harry, 175